MICHAEL P. DEMARIA

FREEDOM

Navigating the Middle Path between Order and Chaos

Copyright © 2021 by Michael P. DeMaria

All rights reserved. No part of this publication may be reproduced, stored or transmitted in any form or by any means, electronic, mechanical, photocopying, recording, scanning, or otherwise without written permission from the publisher. It is illegal to copy this book, post it to a website, or distribute it by any other means without permission.

Michael P. DeMaria asserts the moral right to be identified as the author of this work.

Michael P. DeMaria has no responsibility for the persistence or accuracy of URLs for external or third-party Internet Websites referred to in this publication and does not guarantee that any content on such Websites is, or will remain, accurate or appropriate.

Designations used by companies to distinguish their products are often claimed as trademarks. All brand names and product names used in this book and on its cover are trade names, service marks, trademarks and registered trademarks of their respective owners. The publishers and the book are not associated with any product or vendor mentioned in this book. None of the companies referenced within the book have endorsed the book.

The author does not intend to use this book to provide professional advice or mental health services to the reader. The concepts and suggestions described in this book should not be used as a substitute for consulting your medical or mental health provider. Matters of mental and physical health require monitoring via appropriate medical and psychiatric health providers. The reader should not delay seeking medical or mental health treatment because of something you have read in this book. The author of this work is not liable or responsible for any advice, treatment, diagnosis, loss, or damage resulting from the methods, information, suggestions, or teachings contained herein.

First edition

ISBN: 978-1-7379504-0-0

*This book was professionally typeset on Reedsy.
Find out more at reedsy.com*

Contents

About the Author   v

I   Freedom

1 The Beginning   3
2 The Causes of Suffering   12
3 A Brief History of Free Will   18
4 The Phenomenon of Polarization   26
5 Degrees of Freedom   34
6 Order and Chaos: Dynamic Shifts   60

II   Freedom through Acceptance

7 Acceptance and Change   85
8 Finding Non-Self   98
9 Meditation and Mindfulness   109
10 Enter the Human Shadow   120
11 Nothing Good or Bad   132
12 Methods of Acceptance   144

III   Freedom through Change

13 Vision   159
14 Planning and Preparation   164

15	Self-Discipline	172
16	Problem-Solving	187
17	Persistence	193
18	Methods of Change	205

IV Freedom through Understanding

19	Generating Self-Awareness	219
20	Methods of Self-Understanding	239
21	The Middle Path between Acceptance and Change	255

Acknowledgements 266
Notes 270

About the Author

Michael DeMaria is a Licensed Clinical Social Worker from Staten Island, New York. He is employed at an inpatient psychiatric hospital where he works in tandem with an interdisciplinary team to stabilize, treat, and discharge individuals with severe and persistent mental illness. Michael holds a bachelor's degree in social work and a master's degree in social work. Additionally, he is a black belt in karate and a Zen practitioner with over a decade of experience with Zen meditation.

I

Freedom

Freud believed that suffering stems from the unconscious, starting in childhood; the existentialist sees suffering as arising from a lack of meaning and purpose. To Buddhists, life is suffering caused by attachment. To those who feel at the mercy of circumstance, a lack of freedom is the cause of their suffering.

1

The Beginning

The early years of my childhood were, for the most part, riddled with intense emotional pain and crippling fear. I experienced emotional, physical, and psychological abuse perpetrated mainly by schoolteachers and their punitive religious doctrines. As if fearing I would spend eternity in hell for telling a lie or missing church on Sunday wasn't bad enough, the unrelenting bullying in high school only made things worse.

I assumed at that time that this was normal; I had no idea about the effects it would have on me as I entered adulthood. As I got older, my intellectual capacity grew faster than my emotional maturity. Thinking I was too smart for society, I quickly became a defiant rule-breaker with little respect for authority. Then, in my early teens, I was hit by a car, breaking several bones and requiring a visit to the emergency room. The trauma caused me to have frequent panic attacks, and I developed a fear of intersections. From then on, I would suffer from anxiety, depression, and derealization periodically, and I had no idea how to manage it. My first romantic relationship ended horribly due to my emotional instability, leaving me feeling shattered and alone.

It was a very challenging time for me, and I began smoking cigarettes and drinking alcohol heavily. My life continued to get worse, eventually leading to a point where I felt depressed and directionless. I spent much of my late teens and early twenties in and out of detention, suspension, and expulsion, followed by run-ins with the law and hospital visits. Some of my doctors and therapists eventually refused to see me because I wasn't making progress. Finally, my closest friends (understandably) began to distance themselves from me.

I got the message from my peers and elders that I would always be this way. People told me that I could not succeed in life and that I would never amount to anything. After being abandoned by my friends, my drinking binges increased. My unresolved issues plagued me, and most of my endeavors ended in disaster. I became unable to take responsibility for my actions and saw myself as a victim. I knew I wanted to better myself, but I didn't know where to start. Although, in school, I learned quite a bit about solving for X and the detailed anatomy of a frog, mental health-related life skills were simply not taught, at least not in my day.

I eventually managed to pull my life together into what I can only refer to as functioning chaos. I was able to hold down a job working as an emergency medical technician (EMT), and I had a girlfriend and some acquaintances for a short while. At this point, however, I was barely making enough money to survive. I had no direction or purpose, and I didn't know if I could continue living like that forever.

While stationed in my ambulance, outside a local hospital on a hot summer afternoon, I felt motivated to get out and walk, not entirely sure why or where I was going. I took my two-way radio. If an emergency call came through, I wouldn't be far away. It was a scorching hot day, so I wandered into the air-conditioned hospital where the cool air would give me a reprieve. As I walked through the halls, I saw a sign for the multi-faith chapel and felt drawn to it. I entered this room of spiritual refuge, hoping that I could somehow receive a spiritual awakening. I wasn't much of a believer, but I had nothing to lose.

On the chapel altar, I saw about five different holy books. I thought to myself that maybe the answer was in one of those books and began to silently deliberate over which to choose.

One of the holy books was the Dhammapada, a Buddhist sacred scripture. Buddhism was typically portrayed as a religion of peace and was becoming more mainstream around that time, which made me curious. I opened the Dhammapada and read the first two lines: "Our life is shaped by our mind; we become what we think."

I was astonished. Here was this 2,000-year-old book with a similar message to what contemporary psychology was beginning to validate. If my mind is the source of my suffering, I thought, I must learn how to control it.

I began to meditate daily. Learning to meditate helped me believe in the power of my mind and my will. Though I was smoking two packs a day, with my newfound self-confidence I threw away my cigarettes and never looked back. I also began excitedly experimenting with other challenges I'd told myself I couldn't do in the past, like martial arts, hiking, and backpacking.

Then, one day, while stationed in my ambulance outside of a college in New Jersey, I began to reflect on my life. Up to this point, I was training in martial arts and meditating daily. Though life was noticeably improving, I couldn't help feeling like something was missing. I glanced over at my partner and thought about his life: he was about thirty years older than me and had worked as an EMT for twenty years. He would always complain about how he didn't make enough money to support his family and had to work very long hours to make ends meet. My instructors always taught me that becoming an EMT is just a stepping stone, the first of many upward career advancements. Yet, here I was, with no plan to speak of, looking at my potential future in the driver's seat. I didn't want that for my life. I wanted more, but I had no idea how to get it.

I began to feel trapped, and I was frightened at the prospect of ending up like my partner. I gazed out of the ambulance window and watched as the college students went to and from their classes and dorms. They seemed to be brimming with the light of potential and possibility. I thought about the promising futures they would have that I would not, unless I made a change. However, I knew the only reason I didn't continue with college or further my education was because of fear and self-doubt.

Suddenly, I realized that if the skills I developed through meditation had helped me see past my fears, overcome addiction, and strengthen my mind and body, they could also help me ignore self-doubt. I became determined to go back to college. I would no longer let fear determine my reality.

My philosophical inclination, coupled with my desire to help others, led me to pursue a master's degree and work in mental health. After I graduated, I was employed at a psychiatric hospital, where I now work in tandem with an interdisciplinary team to stabilize, treat, and discharge individuals with severe and persistent mental illness. After years of studying the mind and, in a professional context, seeing people's mental health problems affect their behavior, I eventually began to wonder: are we free to determine our own fate?

I started to think about the ingredients that create a life of disfunction. Why do some people, like me and those I treat, experience emotional challenges in the aftermath of adversity, while others under similar or near-exact conditions don't? Why do some fail where others triumph? I became curious as to why some of us repeat the same mistakes without ever learning from them, such as in the case of criminal behavior, conduct disorders, and addiction. Throughout my studies, I saw that many clinicians, philosophers, and other thinkers took a deterministic view of human behavior (i.e., psychic determinism) and believed that the answers to those questions had to do with circumstances wholly outside our control (i.e., genetics, upbringing, etc.) I later learned the neuroscience and psychology of impulse disinhibition and poor judgment and realized that we all struggle with our impulses in different ways. This understanding helped me let go of my troublesome past. However, it also dramatically influenced how I think and feel about the concept of free will. As we will see, what we believe about free will has significant implications for how we live our lives.

I found myself in a puzzling position. While determinism made sense, it did not account for the situations where I witnessed empowerment, personal change, and the exertion of will and control over one's life circumstances. Moreover, in light of my journey out of despair, I knew that, if I believed, as many do, that free will is an illusion, I would not have recovered. Ultimately, I felt it was a false dilemma and that determinism and free will were not opposed. I knew deeply that change was possible for anyone, and I wanted to explain that to those yearning for it. But, to see *how* we can change, we must first *believe* that we can: we must know that, regardless of what the mainstream opinion suggests, change *IS* possible.

The Importance of Free Will and Autonomy

There is something remarkable and undeniable about human nature; we yearn to be free and exercise our will. The erection of a 125-ton monument in the New York City harbor symbolizing freedom is evidence enough of this fact. Still, you only need to think about times you've felt the agony of the absence of choice to realize this universal truth. In my life and work, I have noticed that the *feeling* of free will has more bearing on our well-being than whether we are confined in a literal sense. That is, you can feel psychologically confined when you are physically free, and you can feel psychologically free when physically confined. In the former case, for example, it's easy to see that you don't need to be bound by shackles to feel paralyzed by a tough decision that can profoundly affect your life, or, for instance, constrained by an employer with an authoritarian style of leadership. In the latter case, there are many stories of people who have found meaning, purpose, and psychological freedom while imprisoned or in an otherwise restrictive situation or setting. What's more, our beliefs regarding free will have significant implications for our lives as individuals and as a society; it also affects how we behave.

Typically, debates regarding free will have centered around moral responsibility and questions of faith. However, the issue of free will extends further than the supposed impracticality of philosophical quandaries. Moreover, the mainstream ethos of rational thought reveals a gradual emergence of the belief that free will doesn't exist.[1] Many people believe in a sort of "behavioral fatalism" and do not think that people can self-direct their fate. Especially in my line of work, I've observed people dismiss the notion of helping others recover from mental illness. They subscribe to the idea that no one ever really changes; that "a tiger can't change its stripes."

Even Freud believed that, like the physical world, human behavior is deterministic. He thought that our actions are outside of our conscious control; that we are essentially slaves to unconscious processes.[2] Formally, this is known as the freedom versus determinism dilemma, and it has been hotly debated for thousands of years – a topic to be explored later in the book.

In my frustration, brought about by constantly hearing people I admired and respected say that free will was an illusion, I began to explore the concept of freedom more deeply. I refused to believe it was a fantasy as it was the one thing that felt more real to me than anything else. I started to realize that the architecture of human free will is far more nuanced than most people think and is exponentially more relevant to our lives than we realize.

Nothing seems more certain than the fact of our free will, and indeed, *there is no feeling more familiar than the loss of it*. For most of us, freedom is a visceral certitude, the absence of which is overtly noticeable and which I believe lies at the core of human suffering. Thus, I've written this book in an attempt to change the prevailing zeitgeist: the denial of free will.

Part One discusses the historical and contemporary philosophy of free will, order and chaos, the phenomenon of polarization, and the middle path. Through research and clinical and personal experience, I illustrate the importance of free will (which I define as autonomy) and explain its underpinnings. I discuss some of the everyday habits that cause us to lose our freedom and show how to achieve more of it in our lives. I explain how "order" and "chaos" take innumerable forms that we tend to polarize, often at the expense of our inner freedom. I describe how they unfold in the personal struggles of the modern age, and I attempt to make sense of the confusing messages we sometimes hear from our society's gatekeepers. Using my experience as a student under spiritual teachers, clinicians, and even my patients, I examine the issues which arise when we go too far in either direction on the spectrum of order and chaos.

Parts Two, Three, and Four analyze the concepts of acceptance, change, and understanding through the lens of current science, psychology, and spiritual practices. I discuss how they relate to the notions of free will, autonomy, and self-determination. The last chapters of Parts Two, Three, and Four include a methods section. The methods section provides tools and techniques for achieving greater freedom through acceptance and change and understanding how to traverse the middle way between them. The methods I list have been extracted from ancient and contemporary wisdom and include techniques that I've observed benefit people in clinical settings.

THE BEGINNING

* * *

When I reflect on my life, it seems almost impossible to believe that I could have come this far, given where I started. In the beginning, the relentless suffering I experienced kept me locked into a negative cycle. I wasn't ever able to learn from my mistakes, and the painful consequences of my behavior reinforced my negative outlook. Eventually, however, I began to use the pain to motivate myself to improve my life. Over time, I transformed into someone unrecognizable to those who knew me, especially those who doubted me. Now, working in the service of people who deal with such great suffering allows me to give back and pass on what I've learned. Indeed, I believe that we *do* have free will. Perhaps a tiger can't change its stripes but a person *can.*

2

The Causes of Suffering

"Life, liberty and the pursuit of happiness"
 The United States Declaration of Independence[3]

When I was young, I had great difficulty controlling my impulses, and I often found myself in jeopardy for misconduct in school. In the '90s, when I was growing up, the mental health profession had a name for this behavioral phenomenon: attention deficit disorder (ADD). The psychologists diagnosed me, and just about every other child who displayed unruly behavior, with ADD, as was the trend since at least the 1970s. As I transitioned into my teens, the repercussions of my impulsive behaviors started to become more severe than being sent to the principal's office. My peers and authority figures constantly told me that I needed to "make better choices" and "behave," as if it were that simple. I *wanted* to behave, but I just couldn't.

The emotional pain of failing to live up to my parents' and teachers' expectations only magnified my anguish, further reducing my capacity for self-control and thus trapping me in a vicious cycle. I began to feel helpless.

Unfortunately, this is often the position we take toward those we see struggling with addiction, dieting, and other aspects of will and self-control. Assuming that our friends, loved ones, and acquaintances can change deeply-rooted addictions or problematic behaviors after only hearing utterances of disapproval is invalidating and disempowering. Indeed, while forethought comes naturally to some, it can't be instilled in others simply by urging them to think before they act. Moreover, very rarely do these negative utterances lead to any lasting change. If it were that easy, addictions like alcoholism and cigarette smoking would have ended long ago; addicts would have quit the moment they began seeing anti-smoking and anti-alcohol ads.

I'm not trying to reduce life's complexities and our adversities to whether we feel free or not, or whether we have the capacity for self-control. Nor is it my aim to offer a banal solution of "freedom" as a cure-all. However, increasingly I couldn't deny what I began to perceive as one of the more common obstacles that lie at the root of a person's suffering. In my profession, I often hear the laments and frustrations of those I treat and have gradually noticed a common theme emerge: the sense of feeling "trapped" or "powerless" seems to underlie much of their pain. Their perception of feeling unfree is sometimes further exacerbated by the uncertainty of their length of stay. The duration of inpatient hospitalization is not like a jail sentence but rather depends on factors such as the rate of their psychiatric stabilization and the procurement of supportive housing when they are homeless.

But it's not just psychiatric patients for whom this is a problem; the feeling of being trapped or powerless, literally or figuratively, is the foundation on which much of our misery rests. Whether you are feeling trapped in a job you hate, in a body you don't feel proud of, or in an abusive relationship you cannot escape, feeling like you aren't free can lead to numerous mental, emotional, and physical ailments. This has been well documented in the literature.

I often hear the personal stories of individuals who grapple with issues that, on the surface, seem like problems of ineffective coping. However, they really result from a feeling of a lack of control over their lives.

John was a thirty-year-old former investment banker who attempted suicide after being released from federal prison. During our sessions, he would often talk about how he felt his new situation was inescapable. After being released, he had no job, no money, and no support. Of course, many factors led to his depressive state. However, his words reflected the sentiment of feeling no control over his life. He didn't see a "way out" and was, in essence, still imprisoned by a perceived lack of options and mobility. Thus, suicide seemed to him a form of control; the last act of self-direction aimed at escaping his wall-less inner prison.

When we lose our sense of agency, our sense of self and ultimately our sense of well-being are lost as well. In studies on suicide survivors, many of their stories convey powerful messages of feeling a loss of control over their lives, like there is no way out.[4] Unfortunately, for some people who feel hopeless, suicide seems, at least to them, to be a final act of self-determination, enabling them to escape from the harsh constraints of their world. Sadly, this comes at the expense of losing everything, and leaving behind grieving friends and family members. At any rate, if powerlessness or involuntary coercion is one of the primary causes of despondence, what then is the effect of freedom on well-being and behavior?

Not a Mere Phrase

"'Self-determination' is not a mere phrase; it's an imperative principle of action."
President Woodrow Wilson[5]

The freedom to self-determine is not just a fancy phrase; it's a necessity. It is the feeling of being intrinsically autonomous: that what you do matters. Research has shown that feeling a personal sense of autonomy and self-determination significantly impacts well-being and life satisfaction[6] and improves health outcomes.[7] Moreover, a meta-analysis of well-being, burnout, and anxiety across sixty-three societies found that the number one contributing element of well-being was autonomy, even more so than wealth. According to the study, having wealth is a state of having material things; having autonomy and freedom is a state of ever-accessible liberation.[8]

Moreover, in academic settings, autonomy has been associated with greater interest in coursework by college students, lower anxiety levels, and improved academic performance.[9] Self-determination is a significant part of clinical social work practice as well. It's considered an ethical responsibility for social workers in the mental health field and in other settings to allow clients to self-determine their treatment[10] – that is, to work collaboratively with clients to find solutions to their issues. In social work, freedom and self-determination are considered necessary for growth.[11]

Furthermore, freedom plays a significant role in the development of traumatic stress disorders. For example, individuals who experience a highly stressful event in which they have no control over their circumstances, like a natural disaster, terrorist attack, or rape, are more likely to become traumatized if they were utterly helpless in the situation. In contrast, individuals who retain some sense of control or exert their will somehow (i.e., help save another, run to safety, or subdue the attacker) are less likely to become traumatized by the event.[12] Those who felt trapped and powerless to change their circumstances are at greater risk of developing mental illness than those who actively seek to derive a sense of purpose and to free themselves from the coercion thrust upon them.

All of these things – doubt in free will, believing that you aren't responsible for your actions, and feeling no control over your life – are not just harmful to your mental state, but may also be detrimental to society. For example, in 2008, researchers conducted an experiment designed to examine the effects of belief in free will on behavior. A group of undergraduates reviewed a text intended to discourage belief in free will; a second group read a neutral passage. The researchers found that encouraging disbelief in freedom increased cheating on an assignment in which they could allow a defective computer program to show them answers to test questions they were expected to solve unaided. The less someone believed in free will, the more they cheated. Moreover, their second experiment found that group members discouraged from believing in free will had cheated by rewarding themselves with more money than they deserved on a performance task, whereas participants who were influenced to believe in free will did not.

The researchers concluded that there might be significant moral implications of belief in free will and that disbelief in free will could lead to people feeling less concerned about the consequences of their actions.[13] *Why?* It may be that an individual has less regard for their behavior if they believe they have no choice. Subsequent studies have also shown that disbelief in free will is associated with diminished pro-social behavior and increased aggressive behavior.[14] Moreover, it shows the critical implications of what we encourage people to believe; it matters how much people *feel* they are in control of their lives. Hopefully, by now, I have impressed upon you the significance and importance of freedom. In the quest to find freedom, it's crucial that we first embark on a brief review of the history of free will.

3

A Brief History of Free Will

Most people take the fact of their free will for granted without ever giving it more than a second thought. Indeed, it might seem like the most obvious certainty to you that to even question it sounds nonsensical. Yet, the battle for your freedom is age-old and has been raging on since the beginnings of philosophical discourse. The question: are we free to make choices that impact the world around us, or are we helpless observers to events as they unfold, unable to intervene?

Throughout history, conjecture on the topic of human free will has taken place from the vantage point of many fields of human inquiry. Free will presents a conceptual conundrum that originated with the ancient Greek philosophers. However, the birth of Newtonian mechanics in the seventeenth century and Einsteinian relativity in the twentieth century demonstrated the predictive power of mathematics, and showed how we could determine future effects with a degree of accuracy by knowing initial causes. Furthermore, studies in neuroscience conducted in the 1980s showed that choices are (seemingly) made unconsciously, without any input from the conscious mind.[15] Things were beginning to look bleak for free will.

Indeed, aside from merely being a thought-provoking and intellectually stimulating topic, the reason it seems to have permeated the bookshelves and occupied the minds of philosophers and scientists is (among others) because of its moral and psychological implications. For example, take the notion of fate; the theory that human beings have predetermined futures. This concept suggests our lives are in some senses scripted from start to finish and that we are helplessly watching them play out without any control over what happens. We are like audience members in a movie theater; we can watch the movie, but we cannot control or change events. Furthering the analogy, if we are subject to fate, our futures can only unfold in *one* way. From the fatalist point of view, we are perpetually strapped into the rollercoaster of life and there is no getting off; you'll be pulled around and launched upside-down whether you want to be or not.

In modern times, the notion of fate seems to have taken a back seat to the concept of determinism, which instead suggests that antecedent (preceding) conditions cause future behaviors. That is to say that none of the things we do are within our control but are all results of past events, extending back in time long before we were born. As with fate, the idea of free will is precluded by determinism. If every behavior is the result of a prior event (e.g., a thought, action, or circumstance), then according to determinism, it was not freely made.

Indeterminism, the notion that events are not caused and only appear to be, was proposed as a solution to the free will debate. However, that too fails to provide a coherent account of free will. A world with uncaused events would mean that everything occurs haphazardly, which hardly aligns with our day-to-day perception of life, in which causes always precede their effects. It depicts a world in which control is entirely absent – even the control we might assert ourselves by utilizing our free will would be illusory as events would transpire without rhyme or reason. Many other theories have attempted to find resolutions to the issue of free will, but none so far have been satisfactory. Since determinism has become the dominant position of many scientists and philosophers, I will briefly describe its history.

Determinism and Laplace's Demon

Albert Einstein famously said, "God doesn't play dice." By this he meant that the physical laws which govern the universe are not random and that causes always come before their effects. However, he was not the first to posit the deterministic nature of the universe. Pierre Simon Laplace, a French scholar in the 1800s, wrote a treatise entitled: "A Philosophical Essay on Probabilities." In his work, he illustrated the scientific notion of determinism, known today as Laplace's demon.

In essence, Laplace's demon is the notion that, if we knew the forces and positions of every particle in the universe from its very beginning at the big bang, we could conceivably forecast every event up until the universe's end, assuming it has one. A super-intellect of this sort would conceivably be able to know the future as entirely as the past; all it would require is data from the universe's initial conditions, that is, the very first push of the proverbial domino.

Einstein and others postulated that since physical matter follows deterministic laws, and humans are comprised of physical matter, then with precise enough physics, human behavior could be predicted as accurately as the direction of a billiard ball. Thus, if all of our actions are pre-determined, there can be no place for free will.

The forebears of contemporary psychology seemed to have been following the trends of twentieth-century science, causing them to view human behavior in the same manner. This was probably due, in part, to their attempts to establish psychology as a legitimate science, and distance themselves from being seen only as philosophers. Thus, psychoanalysis and behaviorism arose.

Sigmund Freud, the father of psychoanalysis, created the term "psychic determinism,"[16] which expressed the fact that mental events are subject to the laws of causality and we do not possess free will. Moreover, B.F. Skinner, one of the pioneers of behaviorism, saw free will as an illusion and believed that all human behavior was a consequence of interactions between reward and punishment.

Eventually, in the 1980s, neuroscience began to weigh in on the free will debate as well. A series of now-famous experiments conducted by Benjamin Libet showed, *almost* irrefutably, that humans make decisions without any input from their conscious thoughts or awareness. His investigations revealed that our decisions and subsequent actions occur unconsciously, and we only become aware of our decisions after they have occurred.[17] While this appeared to be yet another fatal blow to the concept of free will, the case hasn't been entirely closed.

The Libet Experiments: Ending the Debate?

Benjamin Libet was one of the pioneers of neuroscience, studying human consciousness at the University of California in San Francisco. In the 1980s, he conducted an experiment to investigate free will and volition using an electroencephalogram (EEG) to measure neuronal activity in the motor cortex. In this experiment, participants were asked to flex a muscle whenever they wanted to. They were instructed to watch a clock and record the time interval at which they believed they consciously decided to flex their muscle. The experiment found that the brain generates motor potential corresponding to the chosen movement, in this case a muscle flex, before the participants reported awareness of their decision to flex. About 0.2 seconds elapsed between the participants' conscious will to act and the subsequent action, but the buildup of electrical activity was generated roughly 0.5 seconds before their muscle contraction, meaning that the brain exhibited signs of being ready to produce physical motion approximately 0.3 seconds before participants became consciously aware of having decided to move.[18,19]

Many philosophers and neuroscientists have interpreted this as a total defeat of the notion of free will. If our unconscious mind makes the decision and only informs us of it afterwards, we aren't free to choose our actions.[20] Free will, they believe, is an illusion that our brains invented in retrospect to give us the feeling of having made a conscious choice.[21]

However, Libet himself did not use his findings to conclude that free will was an illusion. Instead, while he maintained that, based on his experiments, our conscious systems don't necessarily initiate actions, he concluded that the conscious mind might inhibit or "veto" urges and their subsequent behaviors. Since participants became aware of their desire to move about 0.2 seconds before acting, he reasoned that this is a period in which the potential action can be inhibited, sometimes called "free won't." Thus, even though we don't consciously initiate behaviors, our conscious mind monitors automatic processes and essentially *chooses* what to allow; this seems to indicate a degree of free choice (i.e., free will).[22] Moreover, some philosophers have noted that the subjective self-reporting of time (so important in analyzing the findings in these experiments) is an unreliable indicator of objective time.[23]

How often do we notice incongruence between our subjective perception of time and its actual, objective passage? Sometimes, when I am doing something particularly engaging, hours can pass by, but it will feel like minutes for me. In fact, psychologists have a name for this. They are called "flow" states, a term initially introduced by Hungarian-American psychologist Mihaly Csikszentmihalyi. Flow describes a state of skillful engrossment in a challenging and often fun activity. This is a state that I think is familiar to most of us. It is an experience which the reader may more easily recall by reference to the conventional phrase: "Being in the zone." In the flow state, time seems to evaporate as we become wholly immersed.[24] It is the quality of having an "optimal experience," often reported by artists, musicians, and athletes. Some of them have described it as a feeling of deep concentration or being "jacked-in" during the performance. However, it can occur in a broad range of contexts.[25] As a musician myself, I can attest to this phenomenon of "flow." During my drumming career, I would regularly tap into this stream-of-consciousness-like mental state, often without trying. Many times, an hour of stage time would go by in a flash. Flow often includes these additional components of heightened concentration, a merging of behavior with awareness, and an altered sense of the passage of time. It also seems to increase feelings of autonomy and internal control.[26]

At any rate, the idea that decisions are made "unconsciously" doesn't preclude the free will of the decider. The supposedly "unconscious" parts of the brain may still have aspects of awareness. Indeed, famous psychoanalyst Wilfred Bion postulated that what we call "unconscious" is just unarticulated consciousness.[27] In that case, the generation of a motor-potential is just one form of consciousness and awareness of volitional urges is another. Both are, in fact, conscious experiences generated by a free decider. Whether conscious or unconscious, it's still the individual who decides, and I believe it's the very act of making a choice that contributes to much of what makes us "free."

***

The belief that there is no contradiction between free will and determinism is known as compatibilism; conversely, the view that it precludes free will is called incompatibilism. As with many theories, compatibilism can mean slightly different things to different thinkers. Those who hold the incompatibilist perspective, however, define free will as "the ability to have acted differently."[28] Incompatibilists regard free will as an "illusion" and contend that while we may *feel* free, we aren't. This is a considerably invalidating viewpoint for those of us who feel free at our core. As a compatibilist, I feel that there's a way we can glimpse free will through a pragmatic lens without sacrificing any scientific truths. Determinism is an essential concept in science. That is to say, we rely on the future to resemble the past so that we can effectively navigate our environments. Thus, how can free will be saved without having to dispense with these facts about the universe? The answer, I believe, partially resides in the notion of polarization and its remedy, as I'll now explain.

4

The Phenomenon of Polarization

There is a human tendency to divide things into two exclusive and often opposing categories. That is, we tend to take a position and wholly reject competing viewpoints. It's a habit that is referred to by a different name in every discipline. It's been called polarizing, splitting, dichotomous thinking, and black-and-white thinking. However, for the purposes at hand, it will mostly be referred to as polarization.

This propensity to see the world in either-or categories has been the source of as much contemplation as it has been a cause of consternation throughout human history. It's a thought process that comes naturally to us all and undoubtedly serves an essential function in our lives. It's a practical way of thinking that helps us organize and sort out our daily ventures. It's probably also what our hunter-gatherer ancestors relied on for their survival. A binary threat-detection system would have been advantageous because you may not have survived very long if you had to contemplate the gray area or philosophical implications of either fleeing from an angry tiger or fighting it.

But there is more to binary thinking than survival. It's an essential aspect of logical thinking, and much of our society hinges on a foundation of either-or categories. For example, computers rely on binary code (i.e., zeros and ones) to encode data and the notion that a person is either innocent or guilty of a crime is essential to the proper functioning of our justice system. Things are either broken or working, either righteous or immoral; the people we love are either alive or dead.

These are situations in which, for the most part, a middle ground would not be acceptable. Indeed, we want our family members to be alive and well, but we would also desire closure in the event of their passing. We would not accept being told by a doctor or coroner that they were neither alive nor dead but some bizarre mixture of both. When traveling, if I want to reach my destination, I have to make either right or left turns. If my map tells me to make a right turn, and I attempt to take both a right and a left, or find a middle ground and go straight, I may never reach my destination.

Indeed, the polarization of concepts into neat and comprehendible categories serves a crucial function in many areas of human experience. At our core, we all believe that this cut-and-dry method is essential to the integrity of truth. Our world experience would appear very unstable without the assumption of binary choice to serve as the base for our principles and conventions. However, as philosophers have known for a long time, while it's useful and at times *indispensable* to see things in this way, the world is not as precise and finely delineated as it seems.

Since at least the fifth century, philosophers like Parmenides of Elea have argued about the true nature of reality. For example, Parmenides rejected the concept of dualism and believed (in a very Buddhist sense) that everything is "one." The ancient Greek philosopher, Zeno of Elea, wrote a book of paradoxes defending Parmenides' ideas and illustrating the notion of "infinite divisibility," the idea that reality can be dissected into smaller parts infinitely. Infinite divisibility is a concept often explored through the lens of many different subjects, including physics, geometry, philosophy, and mathematics.

We usually think of reality as consisting of dual elements: up and down, black and white, good and evil, and so on. However, infinite divisibility shows us that binary pairs can be characterized as existing on a continuum, with nearly no discernable line at which one can be said to be distinct from the other. For example, the temperatures of cold and hot exist on a spectrum. When measuring temperature, we never say that a thing is simply "cold" or "hot." Instead, we specify *how* cold or hot something is. But at what point does hot officially become cold? Reality isn't so cut and dried, even if it's more convenient for us to see it that way. The real world is far messier, and polarizing can create as many problems as it solves.

A False Dichotomy: The Problem with Polarization

But it's not just supposedly innocuous philosophical concepts for which polarization is a harmful act. You need only flip on any news program to witness polarized thinking and the destruction it can cause when not properly handled. Everywhere we turn, we see dichotomist thinking play itself out in individuals, groups, and in society at large; in sports, culture, music and elsewhere. Human beings are wedded to their split ideologies and polarized opinions. We often see polarization, too, in politics and religion, where people cling so tightly to their political ideologies and beliefs that they are willing to commit acts of violence against those with whom they disagree. I have witnessed polarization on both sides of the political spectrum, where both liberals and conservatives are wholly unable to see even the slightest kernel of truth in their rivals' arguments. In religion, we see the dichotomy of good versus evil anthropomorphized through depictions of God versus Satan.

The history books are replete with records of the many battles which have taken place between warring factions unable to find common ground. Polarization is still pervasive in our social circles and across cultures and nations, continuing to be a factor that divides us today. We create conflict for ourselves when we behave based on extremes, especially where middle ground is available, a fact that our Buddhist and Stoic ancestors knew quite well. Polarizing makes us unable to see middle-ground resolutions. Indeed, the world of ideas and concepts is full of gray areas; it's rife with contexts in which a combination or blend of ideas is superior to either one alone.

Polarizing can also be a hindrance to urgent matters in which concise appraisals require consideration of uncertainty. Earlier I mentioned some necessary dualities, ones that help us navigate our uncertain world, such as the boundary between life and death; however, the truth is that the boundary between life and non-life, or life and death, is not always binary. For example, in pregnancy, does life begin at conception, self-awareness, or somewhere along the way? If brain function is absent in someone who is comatose but the heart continues to beat, are they alive or dead? Indeed, if these were strictly binary events, there would likely be no ethical debate over abortion, and families might have less ambivalence over how to deal with a loved one in a coma or unresponsive state. In more extreme cases, we need only learn of the many horrors and atrocities that have befallen humanity under the regimes of Stalin and Hitler to see where thinking in extremes can eventually lead.

Dialectics: The Psychology of Polarization

The Buddhist teaching of finding the middle way between extremes (which will be discussed in greater detail later) is a practice that forms the basis for what is known in some disciplines as a "dialectic" or a "dialectical method." Dialectics, notably originating from the fifth-century Greek philosopher Socrates, is defined as a dialogue or discussion between individuals with opposing viewpoints who aim to use reason and logic to ascertain a resolution with which both can agree. We seem to have strayed from this dialectical approach, and instead, we insist on rigidly sticking to our guns regardless of whether it's productive or useful in the long-term.

How come we split so many aspects of our lives into competing factions? Though several theoretical positions discuss the tendency to polarize, they roughly converge on similar causes. Object relations theory, formulated in 1994 by Ronald Fairbairn, a psychiatrist, philosopher, and psychoanalyst, provides one possible answer to this question. Fairbairn studied the theories of Sigmund Freud in great depth, but his work was also heavily influenced by the dialectical philosophies developed by Aristotle, and later Hegel and Kant. They considered human nature's fundamental essence and purpose in aspiring toward integration and social cohesion.

Fairbairn considered the act of splitting (aka polarizing) to be a defense mechanism that starts during infancy, when the infant perceives they are separate from their mother. This mental separation is considered one of the first "splits" in the ego and is ubiquitous in all of humanity.

Splitting is also a feature of some personality disorders; it manifests as an inability to integrate the idealized aspects of early caregivers with the negative ones, causing a split of the ego and other conceptualizations.[29] Splitting may develop as a protective mechanism in the context of childhood abuse. Psychologists explain that an abused child is still entirely dependent upon their caretaker. Thus, the child, being inexorably constrained, is compelled to compartmentalize both the characteristics of and feelings towards their abuser (into *all good* vs. *all bad* categories). Moreover, polarizing helps ease the suffering they experience from uncertainty by providing a sense of security, albeit an illusory one.

It is difficult for the child to deal with the internal conflict arising from loving their abusive parent while simultaneously feeling frightened by them. The child may feel that in order to preserve good experiences and continue to get their needs met, they must bury negative thoughts and feelings.[30] Splitting helps manage the psychological dissonance resulting from experiencing conflicting feelings towards their caregiver.[31] However, this prevents them from integrating pleasant and painful experiences, which can cause significant issues in the future, such as a propensity towards idealization (seeing self or others as all good) and devaluation (seeing self or others as all bad).[32]

In clinical settings, I've observed many instances of idealization and devaluation. I've worked with patients who would perceive me as having an elevated status, with no faults or flaws whatsoever. In these cases, I was held by them in very high regard (idealized), but the instant I was, for example, unable to fulfill a particular request, they became extremely upset and viewed me as uncaring.

Social psychologists have studied the phenomenon of individual and group polarization for decades. Social comparison theory, widely regarded for its success in explaining group polarization, considers our innate hunger for social acceptance a contributing factor; that is, the individual will conform, ideologically, to the group's values in their attempts to be seen favorably. Some social psychologists have found that this polarization effect is augmented via a process called "group-induced attitude polarization." That is, the original proclivity of a group member toward any given opinion, belief, or value, will be intensified after a group deliberation or discussion. Typically, when an individual has a moderate inclination toward an ideal or ideology, the unifying capacity of group dialogue produces a greater corresponding polarization. It's as if the individual who fears rejection and desires approval magnifies their formerly suppressed views for acceptance; extreme polarization emerges once every member adopts this mode of thinking.[33]

The tendency to split or polarize concepts is as tempting as it's common. It doesn't surprise me then that incompatibilists have fallen into the same mental trap when contemplating the subject of free will. Since the early days of the free-will dilemma, very rarely have thinkers considered the possibility of a harmony existing between free will and determinism, except in a small minority of compatibilist thinkers. This age-old dichotomy has long been seen as irreconcilable between freedom on one side and nonfreedom on the other, instead of being recognized as two sides of the same coin. Contrary to this polarized view, I believe our capacity for free will and free action exists on a continuum, or rather a sliding scale. The question then becomes not *if* we are free but rather *how* free we are, and how we can learn to increase our freedom.

5

Degrees of Freedom

This book's central theme is the idea that free will exists, but more specifically, that free will and determinism aren't enemies – and, more importantly, that free will can be developed and improved. We may be nearer or farther away from freedom on the proverbial "spectrum." I do believe that having too much freedom can be as problematic as having none at all. However, since many of our life struggles have far more to do with our lack of freedom than our abundance of freedom, my mission is to show how we can gain more of it.

Most mainstream definitions of free will explain it as the ability to act per our desires. However, while this is undoubtedly part of what gives us free will, it's not the whole story. To fully understand the role freedom plays in our lives, it's essential to distinguish between the diverse types of freedom that sit along the continuum. As far as I can tell, there are at least three notions of free will.

Three Degrees of Free Will

At the most basic level, we can define free will as *freedom from constraint,* commonly referred to as "negative freedom,"[34] most notably by philosopher David Hume, who saw free will as relating to anyone not in prison or bound by shackles.[35] There are further subcategories within negative freedom. At a fundamental level, a free person is situationally unconstrained, not imprisoned or physically paralyzed, and can move freely if they so desire. In this conception, outside imprisonment and shackles, our will is ours, whereas if we are working in a labor camp, for example, our will belongs to someone other than ourselves. We are forced to fulfill the will of another. With regards to the case of bodily paralysis, if it's complete then, at that point, our freedom rests almost entirely in our ability to think our thoughts and nothing more. I believe the feeling of being trapped in a social or interpersonal situation produces similar psychological and physiological effects to that of forced imprisonment, social isolation, and general coercion.

I will call the second type of freedom second-order volition, a conception of freedom derived by philosopher Harry Frankfurt. This is the sort of freedom cultivated and strengthened by willpower. It's the ability to act according to your higher-order desires and to inhibit your primal urges. Being unable to exert inhibition over your primitive drives places you at the mercy of your unconscious autonomic system. With this type of freedom, you can inhibit your unruly impulses and delay gratification, which greatly improves your ability to make rational choices.

However, this is only the second degree of free will because being capable of making rational choices doesn't necessarily mean you *feel* in control of your destiny. For example, thwarting an urge to punch your oppressive boss might not make you feel any less trapped by the thought that you may have to endure this treatment until your retirement. Thus, our last stop on the free will continuum is third-degree freedom, as I'll explain.

Finally, I consider "autonomy" the highest level of freedom. It is closely linked to the concepts of autonomy and self-determination as defined by fields like social work and self-determination theory. This is the type of freedom in which one may possess freedom of the will and freedom of action. Those who have autonomy live life with intentionality. Someone autonomous may have an internal sense that they control their destiny and are responsible for the outcomes of their lives, even if they are imprisoned or otherwise in captivity. Autonomy deals with what you can control here and now, regardless of the immutable nature of the past. It's about self-determining the kind of future you desire and relating with others in a way that helps them achieve theirs. Free will, as seen in these conceptions, is thus both a psychological state as well as a physical behavior.

Autonomy, as it is currently understood, usually describes the feeling of pursuing something of genuine interest versus being compelled to pursue a goal for reasons that don't necessarily align with your higher motivations. For example, someone who attends college because they are interested in a particular subject behaves autonomously as opposed to someone who goes because their family has pressured them. Similarly, someone who takes a job out of genuine passion has a higher degree of autonomy than someone who takes a job solely for financial gain but has no interest in the work. However, although I consider it the highest form of free will, being autonomous in this way does not necessarily mean you have the capacity for impulse inhibition or delay of gratification (i.e., second-degree free will). Thus, the highest form of free will/autonomy encompasses both; that is, freedom is both a psychological and a behavioral state. And it is obtaining this level of independence that we are most concerned about. Next I will explain the importance of all three kinds of freedom.

First Degree: Negative Free Will and the Feeling of Freedom

Not being imprisoned is a simplistic form of freedom that many don't need to read a book about to understand or achieve. What's more, though we may be free in a *"negative"*[36] sense (i.e., free *from* captivity), this self-evident truth alone does nothing to advance our well-being. Still, it's worth briefly discussing because, in terms of our cognitive-emotional state, we don't need to be in prison to feel imprisoned. Conversely, we can feel free even when wholly physically constrained. Thus, "freedom" can be accessed in a broad range of contexts where little to no objective freedom exists. Moreover, understanding negative free will and the "feeling" of freedom will serve as a strong foundation for the forthcoming sections.

Perhaps no situation is more quintessentially depictive of having no freedom than being enslaved, imprisoned, or otherwise held captive. Research overwhelmingly shows that restriction of freedom has harmful consequences. For example, a large, observational, cross-sectional study in 2015 evaluated the various factors regarding violence, exploitation, and unsafe working conditions in survivors of trafficking from Cambodia, Thailand, and Vietnam. They found that trafficked individuals subjected to harsh living conditions, threats, and severe violence were more likely to experience mental health issues. However, importantly, they found that trafficked individuals *whose freedom was severely restricted* were roughly *twice as likely* to experience post-traumatic stress disorder (PTSD), anxiety, and depression as those who were trafficked but didn't have their freedom restricted.[37]

Moreover, research on the impact of criminal imprisonment on physical and psychological functioning conducted in the '70s and '80s has shown that freedom deprivation in solitary confinement results in profound emotional and psychological disruptions.[38] In the majority of cases, those symptoms subsided after being freed from segregation and confinement.[39] Furthermore, the amount of control that inmates perceive they have over their circumstances is a primary determinant of the psychological effect. Someone voluntarily isolated will experience less severe consequences than someone involuntarily confined.[40] Research shows that the uncertainty of an inmate's release from solitary confinement also contributes to adjustment problems for some prisoners[41] (a fact that aligns with my clinical observations regarding the emotional impact of uncertainty). This engenders a feeling of helplessness – a similar experience to reports of solitary confinement in prisoners of war.[42] Uncertainty inhibits the forward momentum of our lives and limits autonomous functioning by stripping away our sense of control.

Second Degree: Freedom as Second-Order Volition

"Between stimulus and response, there is a space. In that space is our power to choose our response. In our response lies our growth and our freedom."
Viktor Frankl, *Man's Search for Meaning*[43]

To understand second-degree freedom, it's necessary to discuss philosophy and neuroscience. Philosopher Harry Frankfurt presents his logical conception of free will as acting according to our higher-order goals and desires. Frankfurt outlines several constituents of free will and uses them to determine a coherent definition. To begin with, he identifies a *"first-order desire"* (i.e., lower-order) as a general desire or urge (i.e., to eat junk food). He identifies the *"first-order will"* as acting on this first-order desire. Next, he classifies a *"second-order desire"* (i.e., higher-order) as a desire to inhibit a first-order desire in favor of a better choice (i.e., to eat healthy food). He then defines a *"second-order volition"* as acting on our *second-order desire* instead of our *first-order desire*. Frankfurt's dissection effectively demonstrates that the classical compatibilist notion of unconstrained action is just one aspect of freedom but that a greater level of freedom, and arguably one that matters more, requires that a person's actions be in alignment with their higher-order desires.[44]

Try to think of a time in which you were uncontrollably angry. Maybe you said something to someone you wish you hadn't, or perhaps you reacted in panic to a situation that everyone around you seemed unfazed by. We have *all* done things that, in hindsight, we wish we hadn't. And, certainly, we have all felt that we were not in control of our behaviors at that time. Indeed, we can consider this to be a situation in which we *couldn't* have acted differently. As we think back to this experience, we did not *feel* free, nor can we identify the behavior as aligned with our higher motivations – that is, our second-order desires. In those moments, we can be said to have acted *without* free will. And, rather than being forced by an *external* source, we were instead coerced by an *internal* force that we could not override. Had we been able to, we would have acted according to our higher vision, that we can now only access in hindsight, often with guilt and regret.

In psychology, the process whereby we act without thinking is called *impulsivity*,[45] a form of emotional reactivity, and it's an example of acting on a first-order desire. We can all think of times we yelled or fought during a dispute instead of addressing the situation calmly, times we *reacted* instead of *responded*. Impulsive actions often carry with them undesirable social consequences and sometimes lead to dangerous behaviors. To understand this occurrence, it's necessary to understand some basic (and simplified) neuroscience.

During human evolution, the brain underwent many changes. The limbic system, made up of the hippocampi and amygdala, is thought to have developed about 250 million years ago,[46] about 150 million years before we developed the newest part of the brain, the neocortex.[47] The limbic system deals with more complex functions, including emotional, sexual, and fighting behaviors (e.g., first-order desires/will.) A part of the neocortex called the prefrontal cortex (PFC), which resides in front of the cerebral lobe, is responsible for higher-order executive functioning, like planning, decision-making, and inhibitory control (e.g., second-order desire/volition). The prefrontal cortex is also the part of the brain which puts the "brakes" on risky or socially inappropriate behaviors. The function of the amygdala is to modulate emotional responses and activate a cascade of stress hormones from the adrenal glands in the event of an immediately threatening situation, prompting what is known as a "fight-or-flight response."

During the fight-or-flight response, various body systems, like the cardiovascular system, begin to increase energy production to prepare you to fight or flee a dangerous situation.[48] In addition to this, the amygdala sends out an array of neurochemicals that inhibit the action of the prefrontal cortex (executive functioning like decision-making, etc.) and activate the sympathetic nervous system, triggering a release of the stress hormone cortisol which raises our blood pressure and suppresses our immune system. The body does all of this to prevent you from critically evaluating a situation that requires an automatic response. If, hypothetically, we tended to plan and strategize during a threatening situation that required immediate action, it's unlikely that humans would have survived through the hunter-gatherer era.

Though we no longer live in a world plagued with the same kinds of dangers, our brains have evolved to override rational thinking in highly stressful situations. It's thought that the reason for failures of will or self-control have to do with the limbic system's ability to override the prefrontal cortex during emotionally challenging situations; this is why stress can often reduce our capacity for self-discipline and inhibitory control, increase impulsivity, and cause a failure of willpower. Stress pushes us to pursue immediate rather than delayed gratification.

For example, during impulsive and violent behaviors like physical aggression, there is often a hyper-sensitivity of the amygdala[49] and a failure of the PFC to inhibit reactions activated by anger-provoking situations.[50] In his book, *Emotional Intelligence: Why It Can Matter More Than IQ*, Daniel Goleman calls this "amygdala hijacking" because, in some senses, the amygdala is taking control of the driver's seat when it shouldn't (although it takes control at times when it should, too).[51] When second-order volitions are necessary, the amygdala hijacks your control system, making you a slave to your unconscious rather than conscious processes.

Now, emotional reactivity in and of itself is not the problem because there are instances when acting on lower-order processes is necessary and potentially life-saving. However, modern society doesn't contain the dangers of the jungle, but our brains continue to act as though it does. There was undoubtedly a time when it would have been appropriate to allow your automatic, reactive brain to take over if, say, you had to protect your family against a hungry wild animal or fend off a rival tribe. Nowadays, though, such behavior is the reason why some individuals find themselves in legal trouble, or worse, morgues. In today's society, acting on impulse at the wrong time or in the wrong situations can have costly and dire consequences. People in these situations almost always wish that they *could* have behaved otherwise, that is, according to the higher vision of themselves that they can now only access in hindsight.

Our fight-or-flight response is a necessary physiological process. However, it needs to be tamed to help us make decisions in our best interests. In modern society, the PFC functions are much more useful for our survival, whereas failures of impulse control can have social consequences. Some people have genetic predispositions toward impulsivity, whereas some have a natural ability to quiet any emotional arousal and utilize their higher-order executive function.[52] However, whether genetically predisposed or not, there is evidence that we have more control over these brain functions, and ultimately our behaviors and decisions, than we might think.

"Veto power," which we talked about when discussing the Libet experiments, is precisely what occurs when someone chooses *not* to act on an impulse. Recall that Libet found the participants in his study were able to cancel a behavior consciously. In a sense, this can be considered another kind of *negative* free will. That is the *freedom from* acting in a certain way, rather than *freedom to* initiate an action. Some free will proponents consider this to be an unsatisfactory kind of free will. What is the quality of my freedom if I only have the ability *not* to act, rather than initiate action?

However, when viewed in the proper context, I find this "veto power" reasonably sufficient from a psychosocial, rather than a strictly philosophical, perspective. Let us imagine your mind presenting possible courses of action in a particular situation. You must choose between a first- or second-order desire. By consciously deciding to veto (cancel) the first-order desire, you will have, in essence, freely allowed or "chosen" to act on the second-order desire. This choice to act may not be as obvious from the outside, but it has still occurred. As mentioned earlier, your unconscious reactions reveal their usefulness primarily in situations in which you must defend yourself or "think on your feet." However, they aren't helpful in situations that require patience and forethought.

Free will is afforded to us by our ability to consider likely eventualities and make wiser decisions based on them. When we project these potential future states, we can carve out a path to travel toward our desired goal. Making a "mental forecast" in this way is not the same as claiming that our minds have supernatural predictive abilities but rather that imagined states prepare us for real-life situations, and in this way, help us to achieve our higher vision. Thus, it becomes paramount to consider how we can increase our ability to *respond* rather than *react* to situations that provoke us but are otherwise not life-threatening.

Third Degree: Freedom as Autonomy and Self-Determination

"Freedom of will is the ability to do gladly that which I must do."
Carl Jung[53]

In clinical psychology, autonomy is defined as a state of independence or self-determination.[54] The term "autonomy" originates from the Greek word autos, meaning "self," and nomos, meaning "rule" or "law." It's a concept that has come to be known as living your life independently and according to your own values.[55]

Aristotle was probably the first philosopher to explain the concept of autonomy, which was a primary element of his codification of eudaimonia, a term that is discussed in the next chapter. He defined autonomy as behaviors generated by intentionality – that is, acting according to higher-order values and convictions. Other philosophers have developed similar conceptions of free will as "autonomy," including Immanuel Kant and Friedrich Nietzsche. Since then, psychologists like Abraham Maslow and Carl Rogers, who sought to move away from the reductionistic trends of behaviorism, began viewing human behavior through a growth-oriented lens.[56] In contemporary times, the concepts of autonomy and self-determination are explored within frameworks like self-determination theory,[57] social work, and other humanistic professions.

In the 1970s, psychologists Edward Deci and Richard Ryan, who developed self-determination theory, conducted experiments that offered an alternative perspective from the behaviorists. These experiments showed that, rather than acting as a reinforcement, external rewards such as valued material items or money could, under some conditions, generate the opposite effect and *reduce* rather than *increase* a person's motivation to complete a particular assignment or goal.[58] In the experiments, subjects paid to complete puzzles were less motivated to attempt to solve them than when they had the option of doing them of their own free will. Those who had the choice of solving the puzzles at their discretion also desired more complex challenges. This was termed the "undermining effect" because when individuals are paid or otherwise externally encouraged to perform tasks they already enjoy doing, it undermines their reason for doing them from the outset. This occurrence was observed across a wide range of subsequent experiments using varied activities, showing that not all of our behavior is determined by external conditions.

According to Deci and Ryan, autonomy is the ability to self-regulate rather than be compelled by internal or external elements – that is, your behavior is in alignment with your sense of self.[59] Their self-determination theory presents a tripartite framework that includes autonomy, competence, and relatedness, although they consider autonomy the "master" need. They posit that lacking autonomy causes people to become more depressed and anxious and have an overall lower quality of life.[60] Similarly, when behavior is motivated by non-autonomous causes, well-being is negatively affected. Thus, theorists within the self-determination paradigm consider that our ability to exert free will is realized through each transitory and intentional decision we make.[61] So, to have autonomy, the third degree of freedom, we must have the cognitive ability to decide and the physical ability to execute the decision. Indeed, I consider autonomy to be similar to, if not synonymous with, free will.

The Psychology of Autonomy: Motivation, Locus of Control, and Causality

When it comes to psychology, there is no concept of greater relevance to autonomy and self-determination than the notion of "locus of control," at least as far as scientific research is concerned. According to social learning theory, locus of control (LOC) is the degree to which people believe they have control over their thoughts, behaviors, actions, and life events. The concept of LOC was developed in 1954 by psychologist Julian B. Rotter. According to Rotter's theory, individuals tend to either have an internal LOC or an external LOC. Those with an internal LOC are described as having the inner belief that they have control over their lives, whereas those who are externally oriented tend to believe that their lives are primarily determined by factors beyond their control, such as chance, luck, or fate.[62]

According to this theory, people with a high internal LOC attribute their successes to their actions and believe they can self-direct and self-determine their fate. Additionally, they are likely to take accountability for their actions and accept responsibility for outcomes resulting from their choices, whether positive or negative. In contrast, people with a high external LOC often don't take accountability for failures and blame their shortcomings on external forces; furthermore, they tend to attribute their successes to factors beyond their control, such as luck or happenstance.[63]

Social psychologist Bernard Weiner, one of the pioneers of attribution theory, considered Rotter's conception of LOC incomplete. He believed that having a *locus of causality* is a more accurate descriptor of autonomy. He observed that internal forces may cause our behavior, but that behavior still might not be within that person's control. In the example of impulsive aggression examined earlier, you would not feel autonomous even if the cause of your behavior originated from internal processes. Thus, perhaps autonomy relates less to whether internal or external factors coerced someone, but rather whether someone can view themselves as having exerted the effort required for the outcome. In this sense, autonomy is described as having an internal locus of causality, meaning that controllable factors like voluntary intention and volition can be attributed to the outcome of any given result rather than uncontrollable internal or external factors.[64]

From this perspective, the autonomous person is self-regulated and integrated, an individual whose perceived locus of causality is largely internal.[65,66] Indeed, research has shown that people can feel forced and constrained by environmental circumstances just as much as by themselves.[67] At any rate, to avoid confusion, we can assume that *locus of control* and *locus of causality* have some overlap, at least as far as experimental research is concerned. So, broadly speaking, this points toward the fact that cultivating an internal sense of intentional self-directedness is essentially synonymous with autonomy, ergo: it represents *free will*. Thus, free will is a dynamic psychological and behavioral *process* rather than a *possession*.

Accordingly, this form of freedom seems almost indispensable, especially if it can be acquired and developed. Research has shown that people with an internal LOC have fewer psychological disorders than those with an external LOC, who feel at the mercy of their circumstances.[68] Furthermore, research shows that, regarding physical illnesses, people who have an internal LOC have an enhanced ability to psychologically adapt to their disability or disease in comparison to their external counterparts.[69] Those with an internal LOC are also more likely to be proactive and take concrete actions toward changing occupations.[70] The literature on LOC unambiguously reveals that having an inner sense of intentionality is correlated with improvements in many domains of life and functioning. Though factors such as genetics and upbringing can influence a person's LOC, it is possible to change this over time. Those with an external LOC can gradually shift their perspective from seeing themselves as a prisoner to perceiving themselves as autonomous, self-determining agents. Interestingly, some research has found evidence for what is called a *"bi-local expectancy,"* meaning someone who can find a middle ground, integrating an internal and external sense of control and thus generating a balanced sense of well-being.[71] This means that those who can skillfully navigate between an internal and external LOC have been found to have superior adaptation abilities and coping skills than those with a solely internal or external disposition,[72] a finding which aligns perfectly with the chapters to come.

At any rate, perceptions of intentional self-origination of action are fundamental to autonomy. Also, as mentioned above and explored in more detail in later chapters, it can also be enhanced through conscious effort. Not only can autonomy be intentionally strengthened, but it has been found to increase with age; as we get older, we tend to feel a greater sense of self-ownership.[73]

Learning and Unlearning Helplessness

Psychologist Martin Seligman performed a series of studies on animals in which one group was administered electric shocks that they were able to escape. A second group was administered shocks that they were unable to escape. The animals that *could* escape seemed to experience no ill effects or stress reactions later on. However, the animals that could not escape exhibited what Seligman called "learned helplessness." The animals in the latter category eventually became indifferent to repeated shocks, even when they were in positions in which escape was possible; they had learned they had no control and no ability to exert their will to avoid a stressful or painful situation.[74] Seligman believed that learned helplessness, defined as the perceived absence of control over our unchangeable circumstances, could result in depression.

Later, neuroscientific studies found that rather than helplessness being learned, it's the default reaction to prolonged, inescapable pain or unpleasantness. That is to say, we are in some ways designed to give up when all hope is lost. However, regardless of which way the helplessness is embedded, these studies state that it's possible to unlearn it and instead learn control. Studies have shown that it's possible to improve our ability to override this inhibitory process and gain greater control via the medial prefrontal cortex, which we know is involved in executive self-control functions.[75]

Furthermore, LOC plays a crucial role in the outcomes of situations in which individuals are in an inescapable, aversive situation, like trauma or other chronic stressors. In a study in which participants were placed in an inescapable, unpleasant circumstance, the participants with an external LOC were significantly more helpless than those with an internal LOC.[76] In another experiment, participants were assigned to perform mental tasks while an aversive noise was being made. The results showed that participants who could turn off the distracting noise did so rarely but performed significantly better than the participants who could not escape the noise. One way to interpret this is that being aware that they had the option to escape the noise was enough to be less fazed or troubled by it.[77]

Depression is not the only illness associated with learned helplessness. Those who have attitudes of helplessness or hopelessness are much more responsive to stress than those who don't.[78] The research supports the idea that the subjective sense of having no control over our life can result in physical ailments such as heart disease and a weakened immune system, and is linked with antisocial behaviors, poor problem-solving abilities, and work dissatisfaction.[79]

Autonomy and Self-Determination in Social Work: Empowering Individual Freedom

The social work profession's ethical and philosophical foundation is grounded in autonomy and self-determination. According to the values outlined in the National Association of Social Work's *Code of Ethics*, self-determination is a basic human right. It's an ethical principle that underlies much of what we do regarding interactions with our clients. The dictates of self-determination from a social work perspective require that our clients be given choices. To the extent that we can *help* them, it's not so much via telling them what to do but by assisting them to achieve their own self-determined goals.[80] There are, of course, limits to self-determination as it relies on the individual being able to understand their options.

In psychiatric hospitalization, the basic assumption is that individuals will be hospitalized until they are considered psychiatrically capable of making decisions. The social work profession operates under the general assumption that individuals want to make decisions in their own best interests. From a clinical standpoint, providing access to resources and information allows individuals to make decisions aligned with their values. It's understood that, typically, people only incur problems when they are, in some way, uninformed about the multiplicity of options available to them.

Intrapersonal Heteronomy: A Prison of the Mind

In a book that heavily influenced the way I see the world, *Man's Search for Meaning*, Viktor Frankl recounts the horrors of imprisonment in Auschwitz during the Holocaust. He tells stories of the many who perished and the few who survived. Indeed, he provides an account of the abhorrent and impermissible conditions to which the prisoners were subjected – victims who were eradicated at random, through absolutely no fault of their own. Through this heinous and dreadful experience, he somehow found a beacon of hope which he chose to share with the world, and thankfully so.

During his time in Auschwitz, an infectious disease called typhus spread through the labor camps, claiming the lives of many inmates. He began to notice a difference between those who succumbed to typhus and those who recovered. He explained that those who gave up hope, who psychologically withdrew from the will to live and could no longer mentally endure their conditions, were more often than not the ones who perished from their infections.

However, those who could derive a sense of purpose, even in the most hopeless moments, usually recovered. Frankl spoke of how he derived a sense of purpose by helping other prisoners and writing his future manuscript on scraps of paper and cloth, with the hopes of one day being freed and sharing his message with the world. It's hard to see how anyone in those conditions could retain any semblance of faith or optimism, but he and others like him did. And when the cavalry finally came to free the remaining prisoners of Auschwitz, he had survived to not only tell the tale but turn his horrific ordeal into a story of hope that has inspired millions of people, including many mental health professionals such as myself. Frankl showed that, although he was physically imprisoned, consciously choosing to live with intention helped liberate him from suffering a worse fate.[81]

As an inpatient therapist, I have noticed many conceptual

parallels between their experience and Frankl's accounts of the interaction of freedom and imprisonment on inmates. Frankl reported that one of the most challenging experiences he and others had to endure in Auschwitz was the uncertainty of their release. Not what you'd expect, perhaps. Indeed, the same is true for many patients I've worked with over the years; the indefinite length of their stay is notably hard to bear. They find that it's tough to get through each day and week without a concrete release date. As I said earlier, it's impossible to predict when a patient's mental illness will stabilize and thus giving a release date beyond a general approximation would likely be inaccurate and dishonest.

One day I had been interviewing a patient who had come to my hospital from a local prison. When he told me that he would have rather been sent back to prison, I was baffled. It wasn't the first time I had heard a patient say that, but I could not understand that concept; why would anyone prefer prison over a hospital? When I asked what he meant, he made it clear to me: "When you're in prison, you have a set date of release. You can count down the days, and you know when you are getting out. Even if it's far away in time, you feel that you can look forward to something: you know exactly when you're going home. It's not like that here [nor in most psychiatric inpatient settings] and that is a tough thing to deal with: the uncertainty, the lack of freedom."

What this patient touched on was very profound – namely, that not knowing your fate, not having something to look forward to, and not having the freedom to do so was more soul-crushing than physical imprisonment. I found that when I empower my patients by giving them a detailed, step-by-step process whereby specific criteria must be met for them to be discharged, and they are kept in the know throughout their time, it alleviated much of their anxiety and subsequent suffering.

Because I Choose To: Empowerment and Self-Determination

At the end of *The Matrix Trilogy*, we see Neo, an ultra-powerful man with abilities beyond any human being, square off against the evil Agent Smith, a perhaps equally powerful but non-human opponent. Initially designed to keep order in the Matrix, Agent Smith is a rogue computer-program-turned-virus that began infecting the entire Matrix. Unlike Neo, Agent Smith can see into the future, and knows everything that will happen before it occurs; this makes him a formidable opponent to the nigh-omnipotent Neo, since he will know every move that Neo will make before he makes it. Neo is, therefore, in a position in which continuing to fight Agent Smith is a futile endeavor; Smith already knows what's going to happen.

After a long and roughly even battle, Smith appears to have defeated Neo. After Neo crashes into the ground and crawls back up to his feet, Smith becomes visibly confused and frustrated; he doesn't understand why Neo continues to fight when it's clear he will not win. Neo's response to Smith is, "Because I choose to." I never really understood the significance of that last line in the movie. Only when I truly began to understand the significance and power of choice did it finally sink in. To see how I realized this, we need to rewind to when the seed of understanding was first planted.

When I was in my second year of college, a series of stressful life events prompted me to see a therapist in the school's counseling center. During one of my sessions, I asked my therapist for advice on a particular issue. He replied with several possible actions, without telling me which one he thought was the "right" choice. He did this fairly often, and one day I had a particularly pressing problem to which I needed a concrete answer. Once again, he stated, "I can't tell you what you should do, but..." Perplexed and frustrated, I cut him off before he could finish and asked, "Why can't you just tell me what I *should* do rather than what I *could* do?"

He replied, "What makes my opinion superior to yours? My job is not to tell you how to live your life, it's to help you understand that you have options. Ultimately, when you make your own decisions, you become empowered to self-determine your own future."

At the time, I was unsatisfied with that answer. I didn't trust my own judgment because I felt that was what got me into the position where I needed to go to therapy in the first place. However, a year or two later I learned about the notion of self-determination and empowerment. The philosophy of self-determination is one in which psychotherapy is not necessarily a directive process. It's a process whereby the therapist works in alliance with the client toward empowering them by strengthening their innate ability to make their own choices. I once again found myself confused. I reasoned that if I went to a mechanic for a problem with my car and they responded by handing me some tools and asking me how I'd like to fix the car my way, I'd think there was a severe problem. However, after I began working as a therapist myself, I began to see the effect of the power of choice on improving outcomes for my clients.

Below are some clinical observations which solidified my belief that self-determination and empowerment increase a person's internal LOC:

1. **Providing options:** The simple act of giving someone a choice can be compelling. My patients often report feeling safer and more in control when they are given options. People are often surprised when their therapist asks them how they'd like to work together toward treatment. When therapists provide clients and patients with person-centered treatment options and allow them to elect which method they'd prefer, it strengthens their natural autonomy and makes them more willing to engage in a collaborative therapeutic relationship. Ultimately, it's an effective way of helping to increase someone's autonomy and self-determination.
2. **Empowering transparency:** Aspiring therapists are taught that the therapeutic alliance is perhaps the most critical aspect of therapy. Studies have shown that a patient's relationship with their therapist is a greater predictor of a positive outcome than the technique or type of therapy used (i.e., psychoanalytic, cognitive behavioral therapy (CBT), Gestalt, etc.) When a person can trust someone and have their trust validated, they become empowered to explore the world. The therapist acts as a stabilizing foundation on which a person can safely (re)construct their life. Many theorists believe that early relationships with our parents strongly determine our relationships later on in life. If those early relationships are largely negative or tumultuous, a person might have impaired psychosocial functioning

as they get older. Thus, it's no wonder that the therapeutic relationship is so important. It can, in some ways, be a corrective experience. Therapists have a challenging job that often relies on the competent and prompt work of other individuals and agencies in a big churning wheel. Even a minor snag in this process can be enough to delay or even prevent successful treatment and discharge. Therapists usually have multiple patients on their caseload, so this problem becomes magnified as they must navigate between diverse and complex social, political, administrative, personal, and clinical aspects of delivering patient care. This is a process that is often invisible to our patients. However, an institutionalized patient who desperately wishes to have their freedom back is in a very vulnerable place, and thus transparency should be included as part of their treatment.

Sometimes, when I see a patient attempt to ask their therapist for the details of their discharge plan, I observe the therapist tell the patient, "I don't know." Very often, this is true; as mentioned earlier, there's no set discharge date because it's impossible to predict when someone's symptoms will improve. However, never knowing when they will be discharged has been described as worse than prison and knowledge of their release date helps to ground them. Knowing this made me realize that I needed to prioritize transparency.

I have noticed that transparency is a calming element for many patients. That is, we may not know exactly when someone will be released, but we can certainly inform them of all of the steps that are either required or are currently being taken toward that goal.

This has the effect of doing two crucial things. One, it puts the onus on the patient to take accountability for their treatment and understand they play a significant role in their progress. Second, it quells the anxiety caused by uncertainty by revealing the concrete steps toward their goal.

I have seen this method work well in establishing trust and a strong therapeutic alliance and observed its effect on their anxieties. Here we see that enhancing someone's internal sense of control creates positive outcomes.

The therapy process is not always like processes in other professions with clear solutions to complex and multivariate problems. Indeed, going back to the scenario of the mechanic, it might be a wild idea to ask someone to fix their own car, but when it comes to empowering people, which is the job of a therapist, it's not preposterous to encourage them to learn how to fix their own metaphorical cars. The more independent a person becomes, the less reliant they are on other people. It should be noted that there are certainly times when a therapist can and should offer direction to a client, as is the case with CBT and other action-based strategies geared toward the management of complex mental and emotional problems.

After years of working with others, empowering them, and seeing the effect that incremental steps toward self-determination had on people with severe mental illness, I understood why my therapist would not tell me what to do. He was aiming to help me take accountability for my problems; I just couldn't see it at the time. I robbed myself of my own power by relying on other "more qualified" people to solve my problems and framing my issues as a result of external circumstances. I saw myself as a victim of opposing, uncontrollable forces that caused terrible things to happen to me.

By helping to strengthen my internal compass, my therapist was helping me realize that I could be the author of my own destiny. I realized that if I had the power to destroy my life, I also had the power to fix it. For Neo, freedom was contained in making a choice, whether that choice was pre-determined or a result of determinate processes. Smith couldn't understand why Neo persisted despite an inexorable fate, but it was Neo's final and profound act of freedom, of which he took complete and unequivocal ownership.

6

Order and Chaos: Dynamic Shifts

When I began meditating at a local meditation center, I met a man named Dr. Kenneth Byalin. A Zen master, retired social worker, and president of a local charter school, he embodied almost everything I wanted to become. He became one of my many mentors and helped me further my meditation practice. Sometimes, at the end of my meditation group session, Dr. Byalin would give what is known as a dharma talk. Similar to what is known in the West as a sermon, a dharma talk is part of the Buddhist tradition and originates from rituals whereby the Buddha would talk with his disciples. Dr. Byalin would talk about various subjects, and at times, I had no idea how they connected to the deeper philosophy of Zen or Buddhism.

For example, one day, early on in my Zen training, I came to meditation class after having had a rough day but hoping to experience profound insights. After a forty-minute meditation session, the bell rang. We made ourselves comfortable and prepared for the dharma talk. My legs were sore and half asleep from sitting still in a cross-legged position.

Eagerly awaiting my enlightenment for the day, Dr. Byalin began his address. He started to talk in-depth about the fundamentals of posture while sitting in Zazen (Japanese for sitting meditation). He spoke of how having the correct posture mitigates the risk of soreness and the numbing of extremities, which is common during long meditation sessions. He explained that it's necessary to sit upright, stay still, and remain centered. He advised against getting too relaxed while sitting because it can cause us to become slanted or unbalanced; if you lean too far on one side, inevitably you must change to another, more comfortable side, but eventually, even the new, more comfortable side would get sore too, and you'd have to shift your posture once again. He said that finding the correct balance would protect against this constant shifting back and forth. I assumed that this was just a warm-up for the "real" talk, but the class ended and we all went home.

I left feeling somewhat robbed of the spiritual insight I had been seeking. I didn't understand why Dr. Byalin talked about posture and rarely about the ideology, tenets, or conceptual wisdom of Zen. Having been an avid reader and somewhat erudite, I wanted to absorb knowledge from all those I thought possessed it. With Dr. Byalin's mostly practical descriptions of the "how-to" of Zen practice, I was often left wanting. I was interested in how the Buddha became who he was and the different mental strategies he used to attain enlightenment. I eagerly waited for the answers to these life questions through his dharma talks but always left without them – or so I thought.

After some years, it finally dawned on me that this talk of posture, as well as many of his other seemingly unphilosophical discussions, was a metaphor for life. It's often the case that whenever we finally feel like we have become comfortable in our lives, we cannot stay there forever. Eventually, we must shift to a new position; otherwise, we will find ourselves in pain or become numb, just like my legs at the end of the class. The metaphor was that disharmony within our life, most often brought about by our clinging to one side of things, is the locus of human suffering, and that attaining the closest semblance of balance possible is the path to freedom and liberation.

Ultimately, I realized that our freedom to change rests within our conscious control and often involves our own perceptions and choices. I learned that the deep understanding of ourselves that we generate through spiritual practices like Zen help us to achieve inner harmony. It's not just Zen, though, that enables us to traverse this path; there are many ways to navigate the middle road. In the coming chapters, I will discuss the methods that I've come to understand as conducive to self-insight, acceptance, and growth. But it's also important that I discuss the conceptual foundation onto which this perspective of self-liberation can safely and securely rest. This involves a discussion of the fundamental foundation or "substructure" of reality, at least in an abstract sense. This substructure is what some have called[82] and which I will refer to as order and chaos. This concept, I think, elucidates and connects much collective wisdom from past and present systems of thought. Indeed, as we will see, a reoccurring theme throughout history has been that of a bifurcation between these two elements, as I will now explain.

Order and Chaos: The Myriad Forms of Symbolic Representation

As previously mentioned, polarizing helps us make sense of our world. It's part of how we bond and find singleness of purpose in deeply-held beliefs. In the past, our need to belong to one group or another probably served as an evolutionary advantage. That is, if you were kicked out of your tribe for failing to commit to your group's values or beliefs, you might not have survived on your own for very long. Thus, it's plausible that we evolved to suspend our rationality in favor of "choosing a side"; being "right" doesn't matter very much if you can't keep yourself alive. Splitting can be a useful habit, and at times, a necessary one. Still, it would be good to understand how it relates to freedom.

To begin to understand this rather abstract prequel to the forthcoming chapters, it helps to start at the most fundamental level. With minimal mental effort, we can understand terms such as light, good, happy, positive, prosperity, warmth, and pleasure as overlaying the bedrock of "order." At the same time, it can be said that concepts atop the foundation of "chaos" are expressions like dark, evil, sad, negative, cold, suffering, and pain. Order and chaos appear in almost every story portraying a struggle between a protagonist and an antagonist. Though we see it in all of our movies, comic books, and novels, modern-day authors aren't the first people to explore this concept. Our ancestors grasped these elements of reality long before the written word existed, often expressed through symbols.

In the book, *Twelve Rules for Life: An Antidote to Chaos*, and in his biblical series regarding symbolic representation in

Genesis 1, Dr. Jordan Peterson describes order and chaos as symbolically exemplified through religions and systems of thought like Christianity and Daoism. He explains that the creation stories necessarily parallel human interactions with the world. For example, it seems apparent that humans create order out of disorder, an idea expressed in Genesis 1 of the Bible, when God created the universe from the void.[83]

Once recognized, it becomes impossible to unsee the interplay between order and chaos in its various forms and expressions throughout history. Indeed, I understand that one of the early conceptions of the inseparable duality of order and chaos can be traced back to Daoism (aka Taoism). A philosophical and religious tradition of Chinese origin from the second century BCE, Daoism represents this inseparable duality in the form of the "Taijitu," also known as the yin-yang symbol.

In Chinese philosophy, the yin is characterized as the negative, passive, chaotic force and the yang the positive, active, orderly force. The dark region represents the force of chaos, and the light region represents the force of order. This symbol depicts the two forces as equal and shows that nestled within either element exists its opposite. Thus, these two seemingly opposing forces are forever intertwined rather than irreconcilable opposites that must annihilate each other. Harmony is achieved in perpetually seeking to balance these forces within oneself and one's environment. It's only when this natural state becomes unbalanced and either force attempts to overwhelm the other that disharmony occurs.[84] The yin-yang perfectly and symmetrically illustrates the idea that to go too far in the direction of light is to ensure an emergence, at some point, of darkness, and vice versa. Thus we must see the consequences of polarizing these fundamental forces. This will be followed by a discussion of the middle path between order and chaos and its implications for freedom. Next, I examine the polarization of order and chaos.

The Polarization of Order and Chaos: Good vs. Evil

Another common theme relating to order and chaos is the perpetual battle between good and evil, wherein evil or darkness should be eradicated to create never-ending peace, yet another splitting of inseparable forces. The striving for good and abolishing of evil is a story as old as time. Similar sentiments are echoed throughout Judeo-Christian texts. We also see the battle between good and evil depicted in the form of angels and demons. Namely, an angel on one shoulder and a devil on the other, both of whom are often shown in television and movies as constantly competing for the individual's attention and attempting to influence their judgment. This idea is so engrained in our subconscious that we presume it to be an incontrovertible truism that the only life worth living is the "good" life and that we must be afraid of anything which is "bad." While this is certainly a prescription for a wholesome life, it should not be taken without one caveat. While we can strive for the positive and avoid the negative, the negative will never disappear.

In psychoanalysis, Freud distinguishes between the "chaos" of the id – which he defined as the locus of passion, instinctual drives, and the desire for immediate gratification – and the "order" of the superego, which deals with the delaying of gratification as well as inhibitory and moral aspects of the human psyche. Indeed, as we discussed earlier, neuroscience shows us that the brain has areas that map to this concept, like the prefrontal cortex, which integrates order into our lives by allowing us to reason through our problems and conduct higher-order operations. In contrast, structures like the amygdala are sometimes involved in behaviors that create disorder in our lives, like aggression and disinhibition.

For the sake of simplicity, and to remain consistent with the major themes of this book, we will dispense with the terms which tend to carry pejorative connotations like "morality" and "virtue." Instead, we will refer to behaviors that increase our autonomy as "ordered behaviors," which stem from our "ordered selves," and we'll refer to actions that decrease our autonomy as "chaotic behaviors," originating from our "chaotic selves." This will aid in laying the groundwork for what follows.

The Middle Path between Order and Chaos

"Moderation in all things is the best policy."
   Plautus (c. 250–184 B.C.)[85]

As previously discussed, order and chaos have been consistent themes since antiquity, and so too have the concepts of moderation, balance, and the middle path.[86] Indeed, the Greek philosopher Socrates, thirteenth-century Christian priest St Thomas Aquinas, and Chinese philosopher Confucius, all taught their adherents about the middle path or middle way (sometimes referred to as "the golden mean"). But what exactly does it mean?

While this concept conceivably existed since the dawn of

humankind, in the West it's believed to have originated from the sixth-century philosopher Aristotle. He described this "golden mean" as the desirable middle between two extremes, one of excess and the other of deficiency. In the East, the philosophy, psychology, and spirituality of the "middle way" or "middle path" can be traced back to Siddhartha Gautama (who later became the Buddha), who also lived around the sixth century BC in India. The Buddha also explained the middle way as the path between deficiency and overabundance; his teachings involved following an "eightfold path" whereby one attempts to balance their thoughts, desires, words, and behaviors through contemplative practices. Therefore, the middle path is essentially the dialectical resolution to polar extremes. It shows us how to understand the various concepts we have discussed in this book and apply them to reduce our suffering and increase our personal freedom.

I will now discuss Aristotle and the Buddha, considered the primary contributors to the middle way as a philosophy and psychology, ethical system, and spiritual practice. I'll start first in the East with Buddhism, a spiritual belief system predicated on the notion that, fundamentally, life consists of suffering and that the solution to this suffering is to follow the middle way. The teachings of Siddhartha Gautama are documented in a holy scripture called the Pali Canon. Whether you believe that the events described in the Pali Canon are real or not doesn't matter as much as the value of the concept represented by the Buddha's life and story. And, although the Buddha mentions the middle way in the preceding excerpt, it's through the Buddha's *example* that we come to know the middle way, rather than through detailed explanations like those found in Aristotle's *Nicomachean Ethics*.

It's believed that Gautama was born of royalty, a prince raised in present-day Nepal. His father, King Suddhodana of the Shakya clan, was heavily protective of him, and he was prevented from seeing human weaknesses like aging, disease, and death. He was so sheltered that when the young prince asked his father if he could go on a ride in his chariot through the city, his father put out an order that all sick, poor, or old people be prohibited from coming into contact with the chariot.

However, his father's controlling nature would prove unsustainable. One older person had not been accounted for and he crossed paths with Gautama, to the young prince's surprise. After taking more trips and seeing more illness and death, he became disillusioned. He left the safety and comfort of the kingdom and began to live a life of impoverishment and asceticism, thereby devoting his life to meditative practices. He had gone from one extreme to the next, splitting himself between the heights of privilege and the depths of destitution.

Eventually, having lived for years in poverty and indigence, he became gaunt and emaciated from lack of nourishment and realized that this, too, was not the way toward liberation. Some accounts describe the moment of his enlightenment, which came when he vowed to sit under what is known as the "Bodhi tree" in meditative silence. He declared that he would not leave until he had transcended pain and suffering. During this time, he was tempted by Mara, the god of desire, who tried to break his will and concentration, but when all attempts proved unsuccessful, Mara gave up. After that, Gautama continued to meditate, beholding numerous visions of godlike entities and ultimately emerging from his meditative state having achieved "enlightenment."

As previously mentioned, the Buddha's notion of the middle path is essentially a dialectic between indulgence and abstinence; and the resolution to this dialectic is balance instead of polarization.[87] Applied to real life, it means that pursuing only hedonic pleasures will eventually lead to problems like crime, drug addiction, and destitution. On the other hand, pursuing only puritanical discipline and delaying gratification will inexorably lead to issues like burnout and depression. The Buddha knew that, if left unchecked, either extreme would result in the stripping of one's freedom at best and illness, injury, or oblivion at worst. While non-duality is the fundamental philosophy of the Eastern Buddhist tradition, the value of this particular theoretical orientation is contained more so in practice than in principle; to truly understand non-duality, we must live it. Aristotle, too, taught that the middle path between extremes of abundance and deprivation was the way out of suffering and toward personal liberation; he believed that freedom of the "will" was a matter of reasoned choice and determination.[88] He posits, however, that the concept of the middle path will not always be interpreted positively or welcomed and tolerated by others.

So, although we see in Buddhist teachings the idea of striving to eliminate negativity and cultivate positivity, Buddhist literature advocates seeking balance within one's life. This concept is taught alongside the idea that the negative parts of life will exist whether we seek to eliminate them or not. Well-being, in the Buddhist sense, is not necessarily the same as pleasure and euphoria, as the teachings warn against holding on too tightly to pleasant feelings. In this view, suffering is not synonymous with pain; a life of too much pleasure can be harmful, while a life of too much pain is not worth living.

Rather, well-being is a state of balancing pleasure with pain, achieving contentment and equanimity. True suffering arises when there is unbalance and disharmony.

However, we all desire goodness, pleasure, and happiness, and surely it feels good to be "good"? Still, the Buddha taught that even positive feelings don't last forever and, at times, will evaporate into a never-ending cycle of death and rebirth, of change. So, again, the "right" path is focused on seeking to strike a balance between the positive and negative forces of reality rather than seeking to eliminate unpleasantness altogether and experience only bliss.

Buddhism represents this idea through the use of the lotus flower. The lotus grows in muddy water, yet this very environment gives birth to the flower and represents rising above adversity to achieve spiritual enlightenment.[89] Suffering is seen as a natural part of the human experience, so striving for what is "right" will always be a perpetual but worthwhile struggle. Pain, discomfort, and misfortune are seen as necessary for growth. A world devoid of pain and suffering would render pleasure and happiness non-existent. In the following, I discuss how the notion of "happiness" has been polarized.

Order and Chaos: Eudaimonia, Hedonia, and the Polarization of Happiness

"Blessed are those who mourn."
(Matthew 5:4)[90]

Typically, when we read books, listen to lectures, or watch videos on the subject of well-being, we hear the buzzword "happiness" thrown around. However, this term is as convoluted as it is popular. The prescription of "happiness" as a life goal has as many proponents as it has detractors. Although philosophies concerning "how to live" have existed for centuries, the study of human happiness formally originated in the early- to mid-1900s and is often associated with positive psychology, which places much emphasis on "feelings" and theorized that the creation of pleasant feeling states is what constitutes a happy life.[91]

Nowadays, bookstores and library shelves are lined with publications concerning psychology, philosophy, self-help, and spirituality. Innumerable books and papers have been written by authors ranging from spiritual gurus to life coaches to psychotherapists, all to teach people how to live a "happy" life. Within these diverse texts, we observe a plentitude of differing opinions on what the ultimate purpose of humanity is or ought to be.

The psychotherapist and psychiatrist can help us ease or eliminate depression. But simply *not being depressed* is not the same as being "happy." After all, innumerable people aren't clinically depressed but aren't "happy" with their lives. Moreover, gurus, mentors, and life coaches promote and encourage growth and personal development methods like challenging yourself, stepping outside your comfort zone, and facing your fears. But if happiness is contingent upon occasional suffering (of the kind experienced while overcoming a fear or making yourself uncomfortable), how can perpetual bliss be a practical goal?

Eastern spiritual teachers assert that we must disconnect from desire, which is seen as the root of suffering and which must be eliminated to attain enlightenment. But, again, we run into a conundrum: this suggests that living in perfect balance is to live in neutrality, but being disconnected from our feelings (which are not neutral) is what often leads to depression in the first place.

Moreover, the boundaries regarding living a "happy life" and living a "moral life," for example, aren't always obvious. Indeed, we can, of course, commit immoral acts that are nonetheless pleasurable.

We all seem to know what happiness feels like – we usually don't have any trouble recalling moments of joy or extended periods of life satisfaction – yet we cannot quite pin down an exact definition. When we reflect on our lives, pain in some form or another has always been part of the picture. Indeed, existentialist philosophers Søren Kierkegaard[92] and Friedrich Nietzsche maintained that it's impossible to achieve a state of happiness or well-being unless the counterpart of pain and suffering tags along intermittently.[93] We know that pain certainly doesn't make anyone happy (save masochists), so how can well-being be found if pain cannot be eliminated?

Perhaps happiness is having lived a life in which you experienced more states of pleasure than states of pain? In thinking about this, it's perhaps useful to recall the many celebrities who have more money than can ever be spent in a lifetime. Their lives are far removed from pain, filled to the brim with the pleasures of a wealthy life. Yet, many of them fall into depression, commit suicide, or succumb to substance abuse, to the bewilderment of the poor and middle classes who dream of fame and fortune. In our world of sophisticated scientific rigor, which has been built upon the sturdy foundation of thousands of years of philosophical thought, we are still left with countless definitions of what it means to have a "good life."

Thus it's necessary to explore how these various insights contained within the compendium of collective existential wisdom can map on to our experiences. As a field of human inquiry, happiness and well-being have deep historical roots that date back to ancient Greece in the forms of "eudaimonia" and "hedonia." The term "eudaimonia" originated with Aristotle and translates to "flourishing" or "excellence." The eudaimonic approach defines well-being as consisting of autonomy (freedom), meaning, and self-realization.[94] Conversely, the Greek word "hedonia," which can be translated to "pleasure," is considered a competing view of happiness and is most often attributed to the philosopher Aristippus, a student of Socrates. A hedonic life can be defined as the pursuit of pleasurable feeling states and experiences and deliverance from painful states.[95]

Aristotle's vision of eudaimonia has influenced many philosophers like Zeno of Citium (the founder of Stoicism), Marcus Aurelius, and nineteenth-century philosophers John Stuart Mill and Friedrich Nietzsche. It has also influenced contemporary psychologies, especially ones which promote self-discovery and personal growth like humanistic psychologists[96] and self-determination theorists.[97] Moreover, many spiritual practices from our ancient Hindu and Buddhist ancestors share similarities with the Western notion of eudaimonia. These days, however, there is at least some recognition among both eudaimonic and hedonic orientations that pursuing only pleasurable feelings and trying to extinguish negative ones is not necessarily a recipe for well-being. Indeed, they understand that at least some pain is required to "reset" our capacity for pleasure.[98] Certainly, this is a key concept to help us understand how to reconcile *pain* with notions of *well-being*. It seems we cannot avoid invoking a middle way between these two aspects of human experience.

The polarization of "happiness" is, I think, at the root of much of the suffering we experience. That is, if our standard for happiness or well-being is a state of perpetual bliss, the only thing we will find is perpetual disappointment as we chase this impossible ideal. Indeed, it's questionable if happiness, in the form of "pleasure," is a realistic goal, as there seems to be no evidence in scientific literature for the existence of a state of eternal euphoria.

On the other hand, I can hardly conceive of a definition of well-being that consists solely of challenge and struggle. It seems necessary for positive feelings to be part of the equation, at least at some point in a person's life. Many thinkers have sought to reconcile the balance between pleasure and pain. For example, well-being researchers have suggested that a ratio of anywhere between 3:1 and 13:1 of positive feeling states to negative feeling states is the range in which psychological flourishing is optimal. At higher levels, the value of positive feelings is diminished without introducing negative states to restore balance.[99] To me, this suggests that balance, defined as choosing the middle way between extremes, is an integral part of autonomy and, ultimately, well-being.

So, we must balance the order of eudaimonia with the chaos of the hedonic. It's not the case that giving in to momentary pleasures will *always* cause harm later on; rather, it's that problems arise in cases where this attitude becomes the primary mode of living and decision-making. And, in fact, some research has shown that, as far as well-being is concerned, people who are oriented toward integrating eudaimonic and hedonic lifestyles achieved superior scores on happiness measures than those who were adherent to either one alone.[100] But how can we find a middle way in practice without showing preferential treatment toward either the eudaimonic or hedonic lifestyle?

On one end of the spectrum is the view that a highly-ordered life is the recipe for well-being, and on the other, the view that a chaotic life of wanton accumulation of pleasure and avoidance of pain is the answer. Thus, in seeking to understand how balance creates freedom and true well-being, we can start by viewing eudaimonia through the lens of order and hedonia through the lens of chaos. Perfectly balancing order and chaos would lead to neutrality. Thus, one must either achieve this balance with a preference toward order or toward chaos. I posit that attempting to achieve this balance with an inclination toward order will lead to a life of inner freedom and autonomy, whereas attempting to live a balanced life with a preference toward chaos leads to turmoil, as I'll explain next.

Descent into Chaos: Hedonic Adaptation

It's undeniable that there is a natural balance of things in the universe; this is exemplified in almost everything we do, especially regarding pleasure and pain. We all seem to know that too much of a good thing can turn into a bad thing. No matter how gratifying an experience or activity is, nature forces us to realize this balance, as it will eventually lose its pleasurable effects. For example, anyone who has ever binged on a delicious snack can attest to the fact that, eventually, even the sweetest tastes can, without losing any of their inherent qualities, become nauseating. Try as we might to cling to pleasurable experiences, they all eventually fade, an aspect of human experience that psychologists refer to as "hedonic adaptation."[101]

At first glance, and without further inspection, the concept that things should *be* good all the time and that people should *feel* good all the time is attractive. But, when explored further, we find that, without any contrast, the "good" would actually lose its "goodness." For example, studies have shown that roughly six months to a year after winning a considerable sum of money, people return to their baseline levels of happiness.[102] For better or worse, we have a natural tendency to become desensitized to any thrill or indulgence, regardless of how much we may enjoy it. Given enough time, any positive state you experience will eventually lose its intensity.[103] Indeed, hedonic adaptation all but ensures that the endless accumulation of positive or pleasurable feelings cannot provide a lifetime of satisfaction.[104] We continually run into this problem, but some of us pretend it doesn't exist for most of our lives.

Moreover, as mentioned earlier, some methods for achieving a hedonically *happy* life might not be the same as those for achieving a *moral* life. The hedonic approach lays the groundwork for a world in which many pleasure-seekers are willing to trample over one another to fulfill their own desires. There are endless examples of how hedonic pleasure can pave the way toward committing acts that put oneself or others in harm's way. Some studies have elucidated the extent to which we appear wired to perpetually pursue pleasurable experiences, often at the expense of our relationships, livelihoods, and dignity. The hedonic approach, cultivating pleasurable experiences to generate a life of well-being, only creates more chaos and suffering.

Research conducted more than fifty years ago by psychologists James Olds and Peter Milner from McGill University, grants us insight into the nature of pleasure and pain. In these experiments, rats had their brains implanted with electrodes in regions hypothesized to be the pleasure centers. When the brain regions were stimulated, the rats would experience euphoria. The rats were given the capability to self-administer the stimulation and feel pleasure by pressing a lever placed in their vicinity. The researchers found that the rats would press the lever continuously, up to approximately 2,000 times in an hour, to the point of physical collapse.

What's more, the rats would even cross a metal grid that would administer painful electric shocks just so that they could reach the lever and stimulate their brains. Researchers found that the rats took four times more painful electric shocks to reach the lever than they did for food when hungry.[105] I can think of several human habits that mirror these experiments. Consider how these studies parallel our willingness to experience pain if it also means experiencing pleasure, most notably in the case of drug and alcohol addiction. It seems that the intellectual part of us knows that it's futile to attempt to experience joy permanently, but another, more primitive part of us doesn't care.

So far, we have seen that the hedonic lifestyle leads to chaos. Moreover, attempts to balance it by adding occasional periods of pain to reset our capacity for pleasure also lead to chaos. Thus, freedom cannot be found through a middle path that leans toward chaos. Therefore, the remainder of this book will focus on achieving freedom through navigating a middle path that leans toward order.

Entropy: Order to Chaos

"The truth will set you free."
  John 8:31-32[106]

I believe that, fundamentally, we wish to behave in the best interests of both ourselves and our loved ones. The most effective ways of interacting with the world aren't always clear to us. That is sometimes a consequence of only being told the "what" and "how" but rarely the "why" of particular moral virtues. Moreover, though moral virtues are traditionally considered divinely authored and universal, they are nevertheless useful regardless of your particular religion or lack thereof. At any rate, I believe that the reason the eudaimonic perspective as a method of achieving well-being has a lot of overlap with what we normally consider "moral" and "virtuous" – and indeed why it was originally rooted in virtue ethics – has to do with the notion of entropy.

ORDER AND CHAOS: DYNAMIC SHIFTS

In his book, *A Brief History of Time*, Stephen Hawking spoke in depth about three different "arrows of time" – that is, the thermodynamic, psychological, and cosmological arrows of time. The thermodynamic arrow of time describes how any orderly or organized state will become more disordered as time passes, a phenomenon also known as entropy.[107] Each arrow of time, according to Hawking, is intertwined with the thermodynamic arrow of time.

The concept of entropy, the second law of thermodynamics, states that the natural, default state of a closed system is inclined toward increasing disorder; this means it will always take more energy to be ordered, whereas it takes almost no energy to be disordered. For instance, it's harder to build a house than to demolish it, more difficult to climb a snowy mountain than to ski down it, and more challenging to save money than to squander it; because of entropy, it will always require less effort to take the easy route than the more difficult "road less traveled." However, through this interplay between order and disorder, we can see an interesting theme emerge. Behaviors historically considered virtuous usually involved some delay of gratification; some type of ordered action against the backdrop of disorder. In contrast, sinful behaviors were typically those which involved immediate gratification, and that aligns with an environment of chaos.

Importantly, it's not only because it requires much effort to introduce order to a chaotic system that an action is considered virtuous, or because it requires no effort to add disorder to order that a behavior is considered sinful. It is also because, typically, the ordered behaviors would lead to long-term payoffs. The chaotic ones lead to, well, more chaos. Though it will always be *easier* to live in disorder, chaos is always accompanied by *suffering*. Thus, ordered actions are virtuous because, while they don't guarantee a life free from pain, they ensure a life free from suffering.

Negentropy: Chaos to Order

As previously discussed, entropy, the second law of thermodynamics, tells us that all closed systems in the universe will tend toward disorder if left alone. Physicists like Hawking even believed in a kind of psychological entropy.[108] This is a somewhat pessimistic view of human psychological and social behavior which predicts that our minds and interactions will become more disordered as time goes on. However, humanistic psychology and related fields have a more optimistic view in which people are seen as "negentropic." Humankind's fundamental purpose, if nothing else, is to create order out of chaos.

Within the dialectical perspective of organismic philosophy, life is characterized as a perpetual struggle between order and chaos, challenge and achievement, and problems and their solutions. A person who feels capable of controlling their lives and generating order out of disorder will feel free, whereas an individual who feels unable to exert control over their world and is at the mercy of chaos will likely feel unfree.[109] We humans are order-creating beings who exist against the backdrop of a chaotic universe. In some ways, the meaning of our lives is contained in this process. Without an entropic universe, we would be unable to engage with challenges sufficient to bring about our own growth. The interplay between order and chaos is the story of humanity; our very nature is to be autonomous, self-determining creatures that maintain harmony by virtue of our existence and our commitment to continued growth.

Order and Chaos: Acceptance and Change

It's now abundantly clear that "happiness," when analyzed in-depth, is a troubling term. In expressing the pursuit of positive feelings, it fails to describe any truly desirable state of being. By the best approximation, happiness, as it's colloquially understood, says more about how a person feels than it does about how they live their lives. I felt that it was essential not to make this yet another book about happiness, to be buried among the densely-populated psychology and self-help bookshelves. The "how-to" of happiness has been written about ad nauseum, and I have very little to contribute.

I am not shortchanging myself in saying this. It is because I believe freedom to be something else entirely. Autonomy is much more than a fleeting, affective state; it's an ever-present and deeply personal state that we can learn to align with and which is elucidated through multiple modes of wisdom. Freedom is a state of liberation from the entrapments of life in its myriad forms. As far as feelings are concerned, freedom requires the successful balance and utilization of pain just as much as pleasure. Achieving harmony with oneself and the world is not just a new-age phrase; it's a necessity for liberation. I will now share a basic framework that I find useful in helping me position the concepts within the purview of my own life. I believe that within the dense stockpile of prescriptions for a fulfilled life there appears a vaguely discernable common theme. Also, while conjecturing about these conceptual dilemmas can be intellectually stimulating to some, I think what matters most is how we can apply these philosophies to our lives.

As I see it, acceptance and change are the equivalents of order and chaos in regard to human thoughts and behavior. By peering through the lens of acceptance and change, we can see how both can be used as tools to build greater autonomy. While I tend to place change in the category of order and acceptance in chaos, it's not important to assign a specific designation of order or chaos to either one. It's the dialectical interplay between them and resistance of the urge to split them which matters most. I believe this dialectic manifests itself as the decisions we make on a daily basis between choosing when to *accept* our circumstances or when to *change* them. It should be noted that these decisions aren't always entirely clear. I will begin by explaining the concept and methods of acceptance.

II

Freedom through Acceptance

Acceptance is a way of thinking and living that helps us make peace with what cannot be changed; this includes acceptance of oneself and of one's circumstances. Resistance of the immutable is the true adversary of acceptance.

7

Acceptance and Change

In my personal and professional life, I've noticed a form of polarization that seems to be occurring within the contemporary ethos of personal development ethics and in both public and private cultural spheres. There appears to be an increasing divide in our society, a split between ideologies that ought to remain connected – namely, the concepts of acceptance and change. As I've mentioned previously, the tendency to split ideas into two extremes is a natural one, a feature of human thought since the earliest days of discourse. So, it's not at all surprising to see this divide occurring in present-day society. However, this polarization continues to split our perceptions and prevents us from achieving autonomy without realizing it.

We have access to a seemingly endless amount of knowledge from innumerable regions of the world and throughout almost every period extending as far back as the very beginnings of oral and written communication. Books, news articles, academic journals, and resources of all kinds can be retrieved at the push of a button. With the availability of near-infinite information, it's natural for interpretations to vary among distinct groups and individuals; this, I believe, is a phenomenon occurring within present-day self-improvement culture and clinical settings. Thus, I became motivated to bridge this gap between conceptions by drawing on my experience as a Zen practitioner, martial artist, and clinical social worker. As I see it, acceptance and change, the *psychosocial* analogs of order and chaos, are inseparable and must be balanced to achieve harmony and increase autonomy. Some of us live by the philosophy that we can only accept *the way it is* and surrender to fate, whereas others believe in pursuing constant change and growth and maintain that rest is for the weak. However, acceptance and change are not opposing teams; we are not obligated to pick one side and exclude the other. Rather, they are tools we can utilize according to the circumstances. In other words, there are times life presents us with problems that are best dealt with through acceptance, whereas pursuing change may be a more viable option at other times. Choosing, for example, to accept an issue that you can change will create needless suffering.

Similarly, attempting to change an unchangeable circumstance will also create inner turmoil. Often, we unwittingly polarize acceptance and change. Polarizing *acceptance* leads to surrendering to life's challenges and never venturing beyond the comfort zone. At the same time, polarizing *change* can lead to perfectionism, toxic productivity, and the like. It is essential to understand them in their proper context and balance the two; that is, rather than pursue either extreme, instead seek the middle way. This is not a new idea; as I've mentioned before, many religions, philosophies, and mental health practices have taught me to find a middle way between extremes, the details of which I will elaborate on in the coming chapters. However, to learn how to traverse the middle path between acceptance and change and integrate them into our lives, we must first understand them in their proper context, starting with the concept of *acceptance* and its associated misperceptions.

Misperceptions of Acceptance

There is no shortage of ads, songs, idioms, books, videos, and slogans that endorse self-acceptance or its many analogs: self-love, self-compassion, and the like. However, it's seldom elaborated on, especially in a society which more readily promotes "hard work" and "persistence," endorsements which feel more like a call to toxic and unhealthy productivity. Though the concept of self-acceptance has morphed into a popular trend, it's not often accompanied by instructions on how it's achieved or even why it should be. For example, we hear people say, "If you can't change it, you just have to accept it," and we don't question this because it seems simple enough. However, to "just accept" something that cannot be changed offers us no clues about what that means in practice. A call to begrudgingly tolerate things we wish to change but can't is already a description of our current state. The only thing we *can* do in an unchangeable situation is quite literally to accept it. Thus, this expression in and of itself offers no solution to the pain associated with whatever it is that we must tolerate.

Moreover, while the internet has made communication easier and information more accessible, it has also brought with it the easier transmission of falsehoods. As a result, many conflicting messages are shared in the social media sphere regarding self-acceptance, and myths are perpetuated.[110] The widespread accessibility of social media offers us a keen insight into just what kinds of messages are permeating popular culture.

For example, a famous acronym meant to express a version of "carpe diem" or seize the day[111] began to circulate on the internet sometime around 2012: YOLO, which stands for "you only live once." This phrase was often attached to posts and hashtags on social networks like Twitter[112] which depicted individuals acting recklessly, spending money to excess, or behaving in ways that put them at risk. This was a way for anyone to absolve themselves of responsibility, while simultaneously claiming they were just being themselves or accepting how things are. However, it's not just the reckless who misconstrue the meaning of self-acceptance. Those unwilling to live with abandon and who favor the pursuit of personal growth often feel that unconditional self-acceptance will lead to passive resignation, relinquishment of responsibility, and promotion of a hedonistic lifestyle,[113] a turn-off for many who were seeking self-improvement.

Indeed I, too, was confused and repelled by what I thought was an advocation of self-apathy and indifference. It didn't appear to be a tremendous departure from how I had already been living my life before deciding to change. It seemed like a dangerous weapon aimed at annihilating my motivation and often stirred up conflicting feelings in me. Wasn't it precisely because I *refused* to accept and *refused* to admit defeat that I recovered? By thinking this way, however, I was stunting my own growth.

A nagging feeling persisted; a constant thought in the back of my mind was that my story was not one of acceptance but one of change. So, should we accept ourselves just how we are or work to change ourselves? While I was skeptical of this ideology, I knew that a host of experts from multiple disciplines and ancient teachings could not be wrong about the importance of acceptance. There had to be something that I was missing. I eventually learned the problem was with my interpretation of acceptance; my reading of it was just another polarization. As we will see, true acceptance is a powerful tool with nearly nothing in common with conventional perceptions prevalent in the media and social networks.

Self-Neglect and Indifference: The Antithesis of Acceptance

As I mentioned before, those opposed to the concept of self-acceptance seem to reject it because they believe it means self-pity, weakness, or resignation, as I once did. But acceptance, in this context, doesn't mean to quit or give up; it means simply understanding the reality of the situation. Those who behave with abandon are not practicing self-acceptance; they are practicing self-neglect.

In clinical settings, acceptance-based strategies have been of great benefit in the treatment of certain issues. For instance, in addiction treatment, acceptance is actually a recovery method. It does not encourage or engender indifference toward the addiction; instead, it does just the opposite. For example, acceptance and commitment therapy (ACT), which is an evidence-based therapy used to help people overcome addiction, suggests that rather than trying to control urges or desires to use, adopting an acceptance strategy is preferred.

ACT therapists don't promote surrender to addiction. Rather, instead of attempting to control thoughts and urges, clients are encouraged to non-judgmentally "notice" their cravings without trying to change them. It's a method that teaches a person to cultivate mindfulness of their feelings.[114] Through this method of acceptance, they learn not to overreact to or avoid emotionally provocative situations. The resulting state of congruent behavior is referred to as the "observational self": a combination of the "thinking self" and the "conceptual self." The process of mindfully accepting one's emotional states yields positive feelings for the individual, leading to a ripple effect of improved mood, increased psychological flexibility, and reduced desire to use.[115]

Indeed, genuine acceptance is a change in itself. To accept oneself, in some ways, means to know and commit to what you wish to improve in your life without needing to loathe yourself to get there. It means to bravely challenge and transform your world while calmly making peace with the immutable. To accept yourself is ultimately to love yourself unconditionally and use this self-love as the sturdy foundation on which you build and (re)create your life. To some, being kind and compassionate toward yourself may sound like an endorsement of self-centeredness and narcissism. However, this couldn't be further from the truth. A great deal of our pain stems from failing to achieve an unrealistic self-perfection. Being obsessed with achieving an idealized version of yourself will cause negative feelings when we inexorably fail to attain it. These negative feelings are often referred to as *cognitive dissonance*.[116] To practice self-compassion is to let go of this impossible, idyllic vision of yourself.

It's clear that I had erroneously interpreted acceptance as

a selfish surrender to the mutable; that is, as a failure to be "better." It's hard to avoid this perspective when many of the messages from the media and our social environment promulgate unrealistic standards as necessary in order to be a human being worthy of love and respect. They have laid the groundwork for acceptance to mean fitting into a mold rather than finding inner peace.

The goal of perfectionism permeates almost all modes of communication and entertainment. Social media, television, music, and movies all spread, in some form or another, propaganda that is antithetical to true acceptance. Consider the highlight reels we all post on social media; we desperately fear accidentally sharing an "ugly" photo or posting a status update that depicts us in anything but a positive light. Movie stars and models are digitally enhanced to look like no human being ever could. We constantly get the message that we aren't good enough if we are anything short of perfect. So, in reality, self-compassion is the opposite of self-centeredness and narcissism; it's the antidote to it.

Self-Acceptance Explained

"To be or not to be?"
   William Shakespeare[117]

Along the continuum of acceptance is the concept of being "yourself." Frequently, in modern society, when we hear the famous adage, "Just be yourself," it can come across to some as empowering and to others as confusing. The obfuscation arises when individuals who are being told to "better yourself" and to "be all you can be" are, within the confines of that very societal ethos, also being told to "be who you are." So, the question becomes, should I accept myself or work toward changing aspects of myself that I cannot accept? Indeed, understanding this is central to self-liberation, the type of freedom that I talked about in the first part of this book. So, what exactly does it mean to "be yourself"? And, why should you? True self-acceptance is when we can make peace with all of our traits and attributes. It includes body acceptance, self-protection from negative criticism, and believing in your capacities.[118]

Carl Rogers, an American psychologist considered to be one of the founders of humanistic psychology, noted many positive benefits of self-acceptance through his lengthy career in the practice of psychotherapy. He also detailed the psychological consequences when someone cannot accept themselves and chooses to be other than themselves. Through anecdotes from his therapy sessions, he observed that this was the most common despair. He found that true inner liberation came from the act of purposeful acceptance, that is, of being who and what you are. Through this self-acceptance process, facilitated by psychotherapy, the person who emerged became more open to experience, more trusting, and more varied in their assortment of feelings. When we can be true to ourselves, we can be liberated from the prison of being "other" than what we are. Thus, to be yourself is not just some cliché; changing who you are to conform to others' often unrealistic expectations, in my view, represents one of the ultimate psychological self-constraints.

Rogers saw that people became more accepting of themselves through the freedom of the therapeutic relationship, which consisted of non-judgmental attitudes on the therapist's part and a commitment to unconditional, positive regard for their client. When clients could be themselves in a safe setting, they also began to realize that they were a "process" rather than a "product." They would discover that, like the rest of the universe, they were not a fixed, static entity but rather a constantly changing and fluid process of "becoming." As they permitted themselves to be who they fundamentally were, they enjoyed the liberating feeling which came with it. Research has shown that people who conform their character traits to different roles are vulnerable to mental and physical disorders.[119] Moreover, those who, through whatever means, can cultivate self-acceptance tend to experience greater mood regulation, a decrease in depressive symptoms, and an increase in positive emotions and overall well-being.[120] As we will see, Rogers observed that this process of self-acceptance and being "what one truly is" does not occur through psychotherapy alone. Accepting yourself, your circumstances, your friends, and your family all require an act of mental effort. It requires you to cease resisting your feelings. Though we don't just resist our feelings, nor do we simply resist aspects of our experience that we don't like, we also resist our thoughts, which comes at a price.

"Ironic rebound" is a term coined by Harvard University psychology professor Daniel Wegner. It describes the process whereby attempting to suppress (i.e., resist) a thought is, paradoxically, what causes it to remain unsuppressed. Wegner postulated that attempts to suppress our thoughts caused them to linger near to or just outside of conscious awareness, thus creating the conditions for the suppressed thought to re-emerge into awareness effortlessly,[121] a process called "hyper-accessibility."[122] Wegner found this phenomenon to be generally consistent among participants, but it was more prominent for those who experienced excessive amounts of stress (aka cognitive load[123]). When people engage in thought suppression while their working memory is being taxed, thoughts increase rather than decrease.[124]

The ironic process is not isolated to thoughts regarding suppression of neutral or innocuous stimuli; it's also implicated in disorders such as depression, anxiety,[125] obsessive-compulsive disorder,[126] low self-efficacy, low self-esteem, drug addiction,[127] and post-traumatic stress disorder.[128] Ironic rebound is a major factor in unwanted thoughts and even behaviors. It can weaken our willpower and decrease the strength we have to exercise behavioral inhibition. The ironic process model can explain why we so often commit acts of self-sabotage; why we often find ourselves thinking about or doing the very things we vow not to do. We allow our fears to linger on the outskirts of our mental worlds, allowing them to pop in for a visit at the most inopportune times. However, if the very act of resistance causes so much of our consternation, it makes sense then that letting go of resistance and cultivating acceptance should reduce our suffering and give us a greater sense of control. The research has shown that reducing stress levels, letting go of control, and achieving non-judgmental awareness of the self are ways of attaining inner peace.[129] It's in the act of surrender that we find our freedom. These studies echo and validate what our ancestors have been telling us for thousands of years.[130]

All the methods of accepting ourselves are concerned with achieving inner harmony, not creating an inner rift. Ending unnecessary internal struggles doesn't mean giving up; it means ending the resistance toward ourselves. It's about self-integration, not self-division. Thus, we must take an in-depth look at what science and spirituality offer to help us get there. In the coming pages, I will discuss methods that help achieve acceptance, nonjudgmental awareness, and generate inner peace through acts of surrender. But first, a brief discussion of acceptance through the lens of some prominent theoretical perspectives.

Acceptance within the Psychological Paradigm

Within the contemporary paradigm of mental health and self-actualization exists several different interpretations and methods of acceptance. Many of these (but not all) have been adapted from Eastern spiritual practices like Buddhism. In dialectical behavior therapy (DBT), for example, Marsha Linehan uses the term "radical acceptance" (a feature of the mindfulness module of DBT) to denote ending resistance toward reality and completely accepting that which cannot be changed.[131] In DBT, the successful integration of the rational mind (the rational part of self) and emotional mind (the emotional side of self) is what generates the "wise mind," a concept with similarities to the "observational self" of ACT.[132]

We usually think that rationality is always favorable compared to emotionality and, in many instances, being rational can be enormously helpful. However, when we are exclusively rational, we become cut off from our feelings and may make decisions that don't benefit ourselves or our loved ones. By suppressing our emotions, we wouldn't experience sorrow, but we also wouldn't be able to experience joy (more about this later). Emotions are central to what gives life quality and flavor. However, when our feelings become unmanageable and hijack our behavioral steering wheel, this can cause us social and interpersonal problems. Thus, in DBT, equilibrium is found in the "wise mind," a grounded and responsive state wherein you can effectively manage your emotions and choose *wisely* how to respond (rather than react) to a situation.[133]

Linehan's dialectical approach captures the heart of balancing acceptance and change and utilizing the middle path. It's no surprise that this form of therapy has been of so much benefit to those struggling with borderline personality disorder (BPD), an illness characterized by having high emotional arousal and a more pronounced propensity toward "dichotomous thinking." DBT has been adapted to manage other mental illnesses but remains a primary therapy for those who struggle with self-harm, suicidality, and features of BPD, with remarkable success.

Along with DBT, acceptance is an essential component of psychotherapies such as mindfulness-based cognitive therapy; these are commonly referred to as the "third wave[134] of behavioral therapies."[135] Other theories that explore and encourage concepts relating to acceptance, besides Carl Rogers' personality theory, include Abraham Maslow's hierarchy of needs and Carl Jung's individuation process (some of which we will be exploring in later chapters). Positive psychologies, too, consider self-acceptance to be an important aspect of eudaimonic well-being. Humanistic and existential psychology proponents regard self-acceptance as critical to engaging with others openly and empathetically in our social environment and believe that authentic self-acceptance entails facing life with honesty.[136]

The most crucial point is that these theorists (and their

theoretical perspectives) all believe in and promote acceptance as a precursory, not a preclusive method for personal change and improvement.[137]

Lastly, while different psychologies, philosophies, and spiritual practices have been fruitful in helping to manage people's mental and emotional problems, they can benefit everyone. Indeed, psychology continues to shift further away from viewing human behavior through the lens of treating pathology[138] and closer toward a growth-oriented framework that is universally applicable. Unsurprisingly, many of the methods that are successful at treating mental illnesses are of equal or greater value in helping to create life satisfaction and greater happiness. Next, we will be exploring the quintessence of acceptance as taught by Eastern philosophies like Buddhism. The teachings of Buddhist meditation and mindfulness capture the heart of situational acceptance and self-acceptance and show us how to free ourselves from suffering. In the next section, we will see that perhaps the first step to self-acceptance is, ironically, relinquishing the self.

8

Finding Non-Self

"This is not mine, this I am not, this is not myself."
The Buddha[139]

There is perhaps no more important aspect of our experience than our sense of self or personal identity, which is often taken for granted. We go through life with a fundamental assumption that we are individual selves with unique identities that separate us from others. After all, if you did not have a self, you would not be reading this book; you would not have a need or urge to inquire about the nature of humanity. Everything you know, feel, and have ever experienced is possible because you have a conscious self. All of reality is fed and filtered through you. We hold our self-concept dear; it's who we are and who others think we are. Most of us consider the reality of the self to be the most obvious fact above everything else we can know. Most of us go through life without giving it a second thought.

Indeed, in popular culture, much emphasis is placed on "finding yourself" and "soul searching," playing on the idea that there is a hidden self underneath the masks that society forces us to wear. On social media and elsewhere, it's impossible not to come across a post or picture that is depictive of this self-searching. There is something of a collective human urge to inquire about yourself and explore our place within the universe, the world, and our family and social networks. This is especially true in times of existential crisis, when many people cling not only to the notion that they must "find" themselves but also the equally unanswerable conundrum of why we are here at all. But, is there *really* a self to find? As we will see, the answer is not as straightforward as we might think.

In the Hindu tradition, there is a concept known as anātman, the doctrine of non-self (and the subject of this chapter). The non-self/anātman concept is the idea that, just like matter and its underlying particles, there is no static, unchanging, permanent self. The Buddha, too, taught of the anātman, or absence of self. In this view, the more one tries to distinguish the self, the more questions are created, leading to no solid conception of self. This doctrine is admittedly vastly divergent from our collective understanding of who we are. That is, we are born and we are given a name by our parents which we come to learn and eventually respond to when called. Everything we do from the time we are born until the time we pass rests upon the notion of having a solid self, a lasting identity. So, it is understandable why this idea will seem foreign to those unfamiliar with Eastern thought. As we will see in the following, our self is much more elusive than we think.

The ancient Eastern religious philosophies show that you can experience the illusion of self through meditative practices that focus on increasing awareness of your inseparableness with the universe rather than intellectualizing this age-old concept. Though talked about often through the lens of Eastern philosophy, I think it can be helpful to understand the anātman through more than one lens. Doing so will lay a solid foundation on which spiritual and personal growth practices can firmly rest.

The Elusive Self

"What we call 'I' is just a swinging door which moves when we inhale and when we exhale."
Shunryu Suzuki[140]

I believe the social analog to the Buddha's teaching that we become what we think is encapsulated in a famous quote by Jim Rohn: "You're the average of the five people you spend the most time with."[141] This means that people often change their behavior to conform to different social settings and situations,[142] mostly without consciously realizing it. In truth, we aren't completely individual entities, but rather, we are partly comprised of a collection of psychosocial interactions; our identity is inextricably bound to our social environment. The famous saying, "no person's an island," seems to convey this point accurately. Though we would all like to think of ourselves as uninfluenced by social trends or conventions, in truth, we are all interconnected and interdependent.

Who and what we choose to surround ourselves with determines what kind of people we become. Your desires, interests, and tastes will, at one point or another, be influenced by your environment, a concept known as social influence.[143]

Sometimes you may even give in to temptation due to social pressure, regardless of whether you previously opposed a particular belief or practice. We often think that we know ourselves well and have solid identities, but who are we really if we can be shaped by our social groups without even realizing it?

Moreover, it's certainly the case that we tend to behave differently depending on context. I don't mean to say that we are all being artificial with ourselves and others; rather, it's meant in the most elementary and conventional sense. That is, at work you rightly assume the role of the professional. With your significant other, you presumably take the role of someone caring, loving, and dependable. Similarly, we often act differently with our friends than with our families, and so on. As such, we aren't immutable selves but rather ever-changing entities.

We take the self as a given; however, upon closer inspection, we can see that personal identity doesn't have a fixed location. For example, in his book, *Metaphysics*, philosopher Richard Taylor elucidates the nature of this problem. He starts by setting the foundation for which one can discern the absurdities which arise when we assume that our "selves" are identical with our physical bodies. For example, he states that, logically speaking, if X and Y are identical, then whatever is true of X must also be true of Y and vice versa. Moreover, if anything is true of X that is not also true of Y, they must be two different things. He then extrapolates this to the topic of the self and the body. Taylor points out that there are states that are true of the self that aren't true of the body. For example, it would be absurd to say that one's hand or foot is morally blameworthy or praiseworthy or that if one *desires* to be in another country, their finger or toe must also want to be in another country. In this way he shows that the *self* and the *body* cannot logically be the same thing. But, if the self and the body cannot be identical, where can we find the self?

Taylor also points out the problem of the persistence of self or identity over time. That is, throughout an entire lifetime, I will eventually pass from childhood to adulthood into old age, at which point I will bear no resemblance to that infant upon which my name was bestowed. Given this fact, what is it that connects adult "Michael" to infant "Michael?" Certainly, we behave and conduct ourselves in society in a way that assumes we are the same person from birth to old age. But, if not for the unanimous agreement of our friends and family, this could not be proven. Indeed, not only do we change in appearance, but we don't technically inhabit the same body from birth to old age.[144]

We might then be eager to use the brain and consciousness as the residence of a central "I." You might think the brain generates thoughts, memories, and all that you are, and that you would cease to *be* without it. But, when we go to sleep every night, our consciousness fades and, when we are in a dreamless sleep, we are totally "unconscious." Yet, we don't think that we cease to exist each night when we enter a dreamless sleep.

Furthermore, while the brain seems to be the seat of consciousness and the generator of all experience, neuroscientists believe there is no central brain region in which consciousness exists.[145] This is essentially the Zen Buddhist position on the concept of the "self" as well. Split-brain procedures are often referenced to elucidate the propensity for the brain to integrate information to generate consciousness. During split-brain procedures, the corpus callosum is dissected, which has been shown to ameliorate seizures in individuals with epilepsy. An interesting discovery was that when the brain is dissected at the level of the corpus callosum, two consciousnesses are subsequently generated rather than one, suggesting that there is no specific region of the brain that contains the "consciousness."[146] It seems that even if we attempt to find the self in the brain, we are still at a loss. Indeed, self-hood is an emergent phenomenon generated by the complex integration of innumerable individual and social elements. In the book, *The Way of Zen*, Alan Watts points out, "Thus Anatman might be expressed in the form, 'the true self is non-self' since any attempt to conceive the Self, believe in the Self, or seek of the Self, immediately thrusts it away."[147] Indeed, when we attempt to pin down the self, we ultimately realize that there is no self to be found.

Being and Becoming: The Gift of Non-Self

Throughout our lives, we have been certain that, if nothing else, we are at least our individual selves. However, as we look closer, we find that what appears to be a self on the surface vanishes. Upon learning of the absence of a persistent self, which we can call "I," we may begin to lament. It can be a destabilizing thought that there is no "I," no "me."

How can this be? We may ask, "I feel real. I see myself in the mirror, and when pinched, I feel pain; how can I not be real? If I am not real, then do I mean anything? Do I have a purpose? Does it even make sense for me to call myself 'I'?" Moreover, those more inclined to live their lives pragmatically may question the purpose of calling attention to the illusory self; indeed, they may think that the question of whether we have a central self has never mattered to human survival and conventional existence. And, finally, you may ask, what does the non-self have to do with acceptance?

Often, what gets lost in the translation of obscure ancient concepts like non-self is the nature of their applicability to our lives. You may think it matters little whether or not I can find a solid, immutable substrate onto which "I" can be attached. Indeed, we must still wake up for work every day, we are still obligated to care for our family, and we are still duty-bound to fulfill our responsibilities. However, as I will explain, the importance of this concept is revealed through its mind-shifting methods, which act as helpful guides for present-day humanity.

In some Eastern belief systems, it's thought that the cause of human suffering, ultimately, is clinging to desire. In a sense, the highest form of human enlightenment is liberation from desire, mainly through meditative practices. From this perspective, the Hindu-Buddhist concept of anātman was used to reduce or eliminate clinging to our sense of self because, eventually, we must all pass on from this life. Remember that holding onto something at your peril is a form of resistance, while letting go is a form of acceptance. The more we resist fundamental aspects of ourselves, the stronger their hold on us. And acts of acceptance like surrender help us alleviate our suffering. If you could experience non-self through your spiritual practice, that is, to "let go" of the self, then your existential fears could be diminished or extinguished altogether.

Our time here on earth is limited, a truth that we must all eventually learn to accept. Understanding anātman is one prescription for this problem, rooted in Eastern spirituality, and it aims to deal with the suffering that arises when we must eventually contend with our mortality. The Buddhist practices of meditation and recognizing the non-self are methods of acceptance because they help reduce the suffering encountered when we hold on too tightly to our egos, allowing for a more realistic perspective of our own importance.

In Buddhism, clinging to the self is the source of suffering, and letting go of the self is an avenue to well-being. The Buddhists believed that since the self is an illusion, letting go of the stress you experience from searching for a fixed self is the path to liberation.[148] Attachment is seen as the root of psychological anguish, including attachment to the notion of an individual self. It's seen as an emotional dependence no different from any other attachment or focus on worldly possessions. Attempting to locate the self in the body reveals nothing more than a collection of flesh and blood. Seeking it in the mind only unveils a compilation of transient thoughts. Looking for it in our memories is to cling to that which has already passed into the recesses of time.[149] The self is thus nothing more than an illusion; a convenient concept that is only helpful in referring to individuals, locating people within our social circles, and claiming ownership of ideas and possessions. Beyond that, it becomes a limitation that can hold us back from actualizing our true potential.

Moreover, the Buddhists consider the self to be a continuum of changing, inter-relational experiences. In this view, trying to locate the self is like attempting to find the true essence of a river somewhere in the perpetual movement of its flowing stream. Through this notion, you realize that you are inseparable from the world around you; that is, your identity changes with your environment, sometimes referred to as a "relational self."[150] However, alleviating existential anxiety and feeling "one with everything" is not the only thing we gain when realizing or "finding" the non-self. When we reframe this realization from "I don't exist" to "I am free to become," we realize that the possibilities are endless.

Once again, the purpose of non-self is not to coldly imply that we aren't meaningful, unique, and purposeful beings. Instead, it breaks down the fundamental assumption that the self is unchanging, static, and immutable. Challenging this assumption is important for two reasons. Firstly, it demonstrates that people can change; in fact, people are changing all the time. Secondly, it shows that the goal should not necessarily be to "find yourself" but rather to "create yourself." In reality, we don't ever find ourselves; each of us is a canvas at birth, and we undergo a perpetual process of painting throughout our lives from the bristles of our environment and choices. The self is not an unchanging entity, born into either privilege or poverty and forever enslaved to happenstance. Instead, the self is a fluid, dynamic, and ever-changing entity within which the freedom to "become" reveals itself. When we can accept this, we begin the process of *becoming* who we are and who we want to be. The Buddhist doctrine of non-self awakens us to the perpetual and dynamic process of inventing and reinventing ourselves. A rainbow is no less beautiful because it's an illusion, but expecting to chase after and capture one would lead to disappointment and distract from its beauty. This is why Eastern spiritual teachings emphasize direct experience rather than intellectualization.

The Finger Pointing to the Moon: The Map and the Territory

The technical explanation of the anātman in the previous section was set up as a sort of preface to the actual goal of experiencing it in meditative practice. Indeed, attempting to convince the reader that there is no self by revealing the absence of anatomical constancy may be a fun mental exercise, but it serves no purpose if not to motivate to pursue meditative practice and experience it firsthand.

Many experienced meditators and gurus talk about a realization they come to after practicing meditation for many years; this is often referred to as "pure consciousness." When I first began my meditation practice, I struggled with the innumerable incessant thoughts that barraged my mind; though the ruminations progressively lessened, they continued this way for a few years. However, one day, about two years after I had begun meditating, while sitting on my zafu (a round cushion used for seated meditation), I experienced something I can only barely put into words. It was as if I was looking at myself, except I was not me; I was inseparable from everything.

We commonly hear the clichéd phrase of being "one with everything," popular among new-age movements. However, as I've mentioned before, it's one thing to *think* you are one with everything and something wholly different to *feel* like you are one with everything. Indeed, during this experience, the feeling of "I" had disappeared, as did the usual sense of separateness from the world. In Zen Buddhism, this is known as "satori" or sudden enlightenment. I felt totally at peace, and afterward, I developed an insight that the ego is an illusion, that I am the universe, and that the universe is me. Indeed, we are all interconnected with each other in ways we cannot begin to imagine.

For this reason, Zen teachings de-emphasize reliance upon scripture and instead encourage direct experience of reality, a concept which is captured by the Zen saying, "A finger pointing to the moon is not the moon." This means that the only way to experience the insights contained in meditation is through practicing it rather than reading about it.[151] The abstract concepts and words we create to refer to the world and make life more convenient aren't the things themselves. At any rate, it's well known that meditation can generate stark insights that change your entire worldview. However, these states are transitory, at least from my perspective. Though spiritual texts like those of Buddhism teach of eventual attainment of a permanent state of bliss referred to as "nirvana," it's much more likely that states like satori will come and go. After all, Buddhism rejects the notion of permanency. Then again, there is no way to know for sure; there could be a Zen master sitting on a mountain somewhere who has achieved this mystical state of conscious awareness. At any rate, the non-self is an experience that can be gained through meditation, the topic of the next section.

9

Meditation and Mindfulness

The practice of meditation has existed for thousands of years. The origins of meditation, in general, are somewhat varied and obscure, but it's generally accepted that it can be traced back to early Indian religions, notably Buddhism. The practice of meditation has been and continues to be thoroughly researched. Western psychology has even adopted it as a therapeutic technique, often referred to as "mindfulness." It's often an element of CBT[152] and DBT, as well as ACT Therapy[153] which I mentioned previously.[154] Moreover, numerous psychological treatment methods are derived from Eastern meditative practices like yoga and Zazen.[155]

Though meditation is a facet of some religions, we do not need to believe any dogmas or doctrines to engage in the practice. Furthermore, anyone wishing to expand the horizons of their spirituality may do so by exploring mindfulness and different meditative practices. Interestingly, there is a lot of overlap between secular spirituality and psychology and self-help. While many authors discuss meditation within the context of spirituality, I will mainly be talking about it within a psychosocial framework; that is, by explaining how it can cultivate acceptance and increase autonomy. I am most familiar with Zen meditation, a practice devoid of any dogma; this is the one I will mainly discuss. At the end of this chapter, I will provide a broad overview of different meditative practices, which I have found helpful for myself and my patients.

Zazen

Zen is a branch of Buddhism belonging to the Mahayana tradition. It's believed to have originated when a man named Bodhidharma came to China, bringing the Buddhist doctrine of the dharma from India. Later, Buddhism was brought to Japan, eventually making its way to the United States through a Zen master named Shunryu Suzuki.[156] The fundamental practice of Zen meditation, called Zazen, relies on the concept of mindfulness, or focused awareness. Mindfulness is the process of bringing our attention to focus on the present moment without judgment. Since the 1970s, mindfulness practices have been adapted to treat a variety of mental health conditions. Although mindfulness is central to many Buddhist teachings, Zazen is not the only way to achieve this state, as I'll explain later.

Zazen is a process whereby you must sit still on a cushion or chair and count your breath. It's important to note that Zazen doesn't mean spacing out or not thinking, as is often assumed. The goal of meditation isn't to have your mind go completely blank. Additionally, the term meditation is most often used to describe relaxation techniques and visualizations; however, in the Zen tradition, meditation is simply a method for focusing on the present moment. It's a practice that is simple but not easy. During the period of meditation, the meditator should remain completely still. Most meditation teachers encourage the individual to return to their breath every time their mind begins to wander. The practice of meditation involves taking a nonjudgmental view of your thoughts, noticing them as they arise, and simply letting them go, returning to the breath. The purpose of meditation is to develop acceptance of the present moment and discern your thoughts as fleeting aspects of the mind.

Practicing mindfulness helps us gain experiential knowledge of the transitory nature of our positive and negative feelings and sensations. Mental states change like the tides in an ocean, so mindfulness is a method of acceptance because it helps us let go of our tight hold on individual states. The Buddhist meditative practices encourage acceptance through experiencing the emotions rather than pushing them away. In Buddhism, rational thought and emotion aren't seen as entirely separate; the Buddhists considered all mental phenomena to be a sort of feeling or emotional state. Neuroscientists have found that the same neural pathways activated during emotional states are also deeply connected with cognition.[157]

Zen practice reveals to us that our minds are full of different stories and thoughts. They remind us of our past failures incessantly and fill us with its frightening predictions of a future it cannot possibly know. We seem prone to catastrophizing, believing the worst possible outcome will occur in any given situation; or we remain stuck, pining over our pasts or bemoaning our mistakes. We begin to believe in and be imprisoned by our ruminations. We encounter painful thoughts and neglect to challenge them, often because we are unaware that we even can. Consequently, this allows unchecked fears to run amok in our minds, causing us anguish. Meditative techniques are employed to help us free ourselves from the prison of our worries and anxieties. The practice of sitting still during meditation also helps to cultivate patience and tolerance toward both ourselves and others. It's an act of non-acting and, in many ways, it forces individuals to confront their feelings rather than run from them. This practice is a tool that helps us learn to make peace with ourselves and, ultimately, to accept ourselves.

I often hear people talk about meditation in a manner that places it wholly out of their reach. Among the abdications, I have heard: "I can't meditate! I have too much going on in my head; I would go crazy." However, it's worth bearing in mind that mindfulness doesn't come naturally to any of us, and that is precisely the point. To sit in meditative silence for long periods aids in the realization that inner strength can be intentionally developed and is not just a quality instilled from birth. Meditation is a great teacher; it shows us that we don't have to be slaves to our thoughts. Often, continued practice helps to generate greater *acceptance* and *freedom* from being hijacked by our unruly minds.

The Forest Pool

The best analogy that I've heard that describes the experiential process you undergo while practicing Zazen is the metaphor of the forest pool. We are asked to imagine a forest pool or pond. As wind and rain stir and shake up the pond, the water will be disturbed. It will become cloudy and murky with sediment, and you will be unable to see the bottom. If you attempt to see the pond's contents or its bottom by swimming or paddling through the water, you will only create more debris and cloudiness, more agitation. The only way you can clear the water is to patiently sit and wait for the debris to settle on its own. According to Buddhism, our minds are much like this forest pool. When we become angry, agitated, or anxious, our minds begin to stir up thoughts and feelings, and we cannot see clearly. Often, when we are being "stirred up," the decisions we make in that state tend to worsen the problem. By sitting in meditation and focusing on the breath (a bodily function that conveniently occurs in the present moment), we allow the sediment of the mind to settle, allowing us to see the world with clarity once again.[158] Next, I will discuss the relationship between meditation, the brain, and free will.

Meditation and Free Will: How Meditation Increases Your Freedom

Emotion regulation is another important domain of self-control. It is the ability to respond to ongoing demands in a socially appropriate way and inhibit inappropriate reactions.[159] On the other hand, emotion *dysregulation* is defined as the inability to inhibit thoughts, actions, or behaviors that result from emotional arousal, causing someone to act in a way that is not in alignment with their higher-order goals or the demands of the social environment.[160]

Studies have correlated the capacity for emotion regulation

with activation of the prefrontal cortex, including the orbital prefrontal cortex, the ventromedial prefrontal cortex, and the dorsolateral prefrontal cortex, amygdala, and the anterior cingulate cortex. Moreover, irregularities in one or more of these brain regions or interconnections are associated with deficits in regulating emotions. Some of these findings suggest the activation of the prefrontal cortex as a major player in aspects of emotion regulation. Mindfulness meditation has been shown to improve emotional regulation abilities. It has been shown to help individuals gain awareness of the present moment, improve their self-awareness, and improve their control over their circumstances.[161] Additionally, it helps people manage fear[162] by reducing activity in the amygdala, thus making us less reactive to stress.[163] These findings suggest that mindfulness meditation increases autonomy and the ability to exercise free will because, when mindful, people can respond to their circumstances with more equanimity.[164]

In 2014, Professor Nicole Yuan from the University of Arizona conducted a meta-analysis which found that larger prefrontal cortex volume and greater prefrontal cortex cortical thickness correlated with enhanced executive functioning.[165] Improvements in this brain region increased one's capacity to control and coordinate thoughts and behaviors.[166] This is an important finding that is especially relevant to meditation and free will, as we will see. Based on these studies, we know that this brain region is vitally important for regulating our behaviors. It allows you to override impulses that would get you into trouble in social situations. It's what allows us to envision and plan for our future.

Moreover, Robert Sapolsky, a neuro-endocrinologist at Stanford University, has asserted that one of the main functions of the prefrontal cortex is to help us delay gratification. That is, it aids in making choices that are difficult in the moment but which pay off in the future.[167] If we define free will as the ability to consciously choose rather than be a slave to unconscious, automatic processes, it makes sense that the prefrontal cortex is the region of the brain we'd want to strengthen in order to increase our autonomy. Luckily, thanks to neuroplasticity, there are ways to strengthen connectivity throughout the brain and improve the size and functioning of the prefrontal cortex.

A wealth of neuroscientific evidence has emerged showing that meditation, in general, can change the structural plasticity in regions of the brain that deal with executive function. For example, in one study, researchers used structural magnetic resonance imaging to compare the gray matter volume between the brains of experienced practitioners of Sahaja Yoga meditation and non-meditators. They found that gray matter volume was larger relative to non-meditators across the whole brain. What's more, they found that gray matter volume was specifically greater in the insula, ventromedial orbitofrontal cortex, and ventrolateral prefrontal cortex.[168] In another study, forty-six meditators' brains were compared with the brains of non-meditators via magnetic resonance imaging. Compared to controls, the meditators showed significantly greater cortical thickness in the anterior regions of the brain, including the prefrontal cortex and superior frontal cortex.[169]

Admittedly, there is no way to know if the meditators had larger gray matter volumes before the study. However, a controlled longitudinal study investigated the pre- and post-study changes in gray matter concentration related to participation in a mindfulness-based stress reduction

(MBSR) program. This was an eight-week course based on Zen teachings developed in 1979 by American professor of medicine and Zen practitioner Jon Kabat-Zin.[170] Anatomical MRI images from sixteen healthy non-meditators were taken before and after attending the eight-week program. Compared to controls, the results showed increases in gray matter concentration within brain regions like the left hippocampus, posterior cingulate cortex, and temporoparietal junction. The subsequent interpretation of these results was that participation in MBSR was associated with increased brain volume in areas involving emotion regulation, perspective taking, memory, and more.[171] MBSR training correlates with decreases in right basolateral amygdala gray matter density and increases in gray matter concentration in the left hippocampus.[172]

Studies have also shown that brief periods of mindfulness meditation training increase the amount of gray matter in the hippocampus, parietal lobe,[173] prefrontal cortex region, and other brain regions associated with body awareness[174] as well as decreasing activity within the amygdala.[175] Moreover, experienced meditators had stronger coupling between regions of the brain like the posterior cingulate, dorsal anterior cingulate, and dorsolateral prefrontal cortices when both meditating and not meditating.[176] Additionally, it was shown that meditation increases the integrity of gray and white matter within parts of the brain responsible for self-regulation and behavioral control[177] as well as improving communication between the cortex and other areas within the brain.[178] A paper published by Sara N. Gallant examined the literature on mindfulness and also found evidence that the effects were strongest regarding aspects of executive function such as inhibitory control; this is the ability to veto an action (also known as "free won't") discussed in Part One.

Psychological tests have been developed to measure aspects of executive function in humans. The Stroop Color and Word Test (SCWT), for example, measures delays in reaction time between congruent and incongruent stimuli.[179] Results suggest that, when naming a color which is written in a different color, there is a slower reaction time as the incongruence provides a distraction for the brain – otherwise known as the Stroop effect. Researchers have also used the Stroop effect during brain imaging studies to investigate brain regions involved in planning, decision-making, and distractibility.[180] Interestingly, studies have shown a reduced Stroop effect following mindfulness meditation training.[181] One neuroimaging study found that higher levels of mindfulness were associated with greater proficiency in inhibiting distracting information. Participants with at least six years of meditating experience performed better on the SCWT compared to non-meditators.[182] The results of another study that measured the effects of mindfulness meditation on the Stroop effect showed that it might alter the efficiency of allocating cognitive resources, leading to improved self-regulation of attention.[183]

Practicing mindfulness helps quiet our sympathetic nervous system and allows us to learn to *respond* to provocative situations rather than *react* to them.[184] Beyond increased freedom, there are many benefits of acceptance-based practices like meditation documented in the scientific literature. Studies on meditation conducted by the US Agency for Healthcare Research and Quality have found that meditation reduces some negative aspects of psychological stress.[185] Additionally, systematic reviews and meta-analyses have shown mindfulness meditation to help improve depressive symptoms,[186] enhance mood, provide greater resilience to stress, and increase attentional control.[187] Research has shown that self-described meditators have higher levels of well-being than non-meditators[188] and that meditating helps people manage a range of mental and physical symptoms such as fibromyalgia, psoriasis, and general stress;[189] that it improves concentration and boosts the immune response;[190] and that it improves memory, empathy, and posture, lowers blood pressure, and supports better management of pain.[191]

* * *

When I was younger, I had trouble regulating my emotional state. Among other things, I struggled with impulsivity and outbursts of anger. Despite being told to "think before you do" by innumerable teachers and counselors, I just couldn't. Forethought is a skill that requires practice, just as much as learning to do algebra or playing an instrument. Though, after years of meditation, I started to notice something amazing happening. When something made me angry, I began to see possible responses appear in my awareness, like pop-ups on a computer browser, and I selected which behavior I wanted to use at that moment. Before I began my meditative practice, in contrast, I'd often find myself in hot water after losing my cool and then wondering in hindsight why I behaved that way. Now, I began to see potential courses of action appear in my conscious awareness and I was able to opt to either go with the impulse or veto it in favor of the more socially appropriate behavior. Thus, through meditation, I began to generate a sort of "behavioral delay," allowing me to consider my options before acting.

Meditation is also a technique that I use with my patients on the psychiatric inpatient unit to help them manage their mental and emotional states. Speaking from personal experience, I've noticed a significant difference in how I interact with others and experience the world after practicing meditation. Besides the numerous physical, mental, and emotional benefits of meditation and its many variations, it offers us freedom from unrestrained impulses, liberation from the self, and release from the prison of our minds, which is perhaps the greatest gift.

10

Enter the Human Shadow

"To confront a person with his shadow is to show him his own light. Once one has experienced a few times what it's like to stand judgingly between the opposites, one begins to understand what is meant by the self. Anyone who perceives his shadow and his light simultaneously sees himself from two sides and thus gets in the middle."
  Good and Evil in Analytical Psychology by Carl Jung[192]

Earlier, I discussed Carl Rogers, the notion of what it means to "be yourself," and how the process of self-acceptance can be facilitated by psychotherapy. But how exactly do we be ourselves in all aspects of our lives? How do we carry this philosophy outside of the therapeutic context? And why should we?

To flourish as an individual in a larger social environment, we all must conform in some way to various social contexts. However, confusion may arise when we are, in one instance, told to conform to social conventions and, in the next, told to "always be yourself." What's more, in thinking of times we are most authentic, we might consider our true selves to encompass who we are when we're with our friends or family. But if, for example, we acted at work the way we act with our friends, we'd risk saying or doing something inappropriate. Indeed, it is true that in the workplace, we are compelled to adhere to certain professional standards. However, if we adopt a rigid and overly serious attitude, we can become inflexible and risk losing our diversity and uniqueness. We may then think we can't always be ourselves; otherwise, we could lose our jobs, causing us to abandon the notion that we can preserve our individuality and instead begrudgingly endure the pain of self-polarization.

Indeed, social conventions can sometimes run counter to who we are fundamentally. The need we all share to fit in sometimes causes us to polarize our personalities, splitting ourselves completely among our varied social settings. However, when we contort our personalities to fit neatly into these confined behavioral spaces based on what we think is appropriate or inappropriate, it only causes more stress and discomfort. So how can we adapt to our varied social environments while simultaneously retaining our individuality? How can we be true to ourselves and free our spirits? Once again, the answer lies not in *polarization* but rather in integration. That is, integrating what Carl Jung referred to as "the shadow," which I will now discuss, gives us more detailed insight into repairing this inner polarization.

∗ ∗ ∗

Jung was a protégé of Sigmund Freud and is known for having expanded upon, and eventually departed from, his mentor's theories. Among several influential ideas, Jung is known for his theory of the "human shadow," which he defined as the hidden parts of ourselves, the ones we abhor and attempt to bury, which we may even enjoy but are forced to shield from society. However, these hidden aspects of ourselves cannot be eliminated; just like a shadow, no matter how much light you shine on it, it simply shifts from one side to the other. Those familiar with Freud's psychoanalytic concept of the id, ego, and super ego, can think of the shadow as the id. However, you need not be a psychologist to understand the shadow, as you are already intimately acquainted with it.

Much like Freud's belief that all people contain an id, ego, and superego, Jung believed all people have a shadow.[193] The contents of the human shadow can be positive or negative, but because people normally suppress their undesirable qualities, the shadow is seen in Jungian terms as mostly negative.[194] The reason for choosing this particular theory, among a multitude of similar ones, is that the concept of the shadow encapsulates the power of acceptance through the lens of the unacceptable and shows us how to find our way back to the "disowned self." The disowned self always finds its way out of its prison regardless of how much it's suppressed.

We perpetually hide away things we find unacceptable about ourselves. This forced suppression also arises because we must conform to the conventions of society. This desire to relinquish things we hate about ourselves is common, especially when improving ourselves after years of problems. However, many of the issues that compel us to desire change and improvement don't vanish simply because we become aware of them or try to hide them. And, ultimately, this forced suppression of our shadows causes a psychological split and leads to inner suffering.[195] It's the act of resisting aspects of ourselves and attempting, with futility, to annihilate them which causes us psychological turmoil.[196]

According to Jung, not only are these aspects of our psyche impervious to destruction, but if left unexpressed, they will eventually grow to a point where they cannot be contained and subsequently wreak havoc on our lives. This notion can be illustrated using a feeling we are all familiar with: anger. Someone with anger issues doesn't enter treatment to cure their rage; they enter treatment to learn to manage and express it safely. Hitting a punching bag to vent your frustrations will save you from hitting someone's face; the anger is still there, but the mode of expression has changed. This "change" in expression is what the shadow aims to achieve. One of my favorite metaphors to conceptualize the shadow is to use the example of a soda bottle. If you take a bottle of soda and shake it vigorously, what will happen? An extreme amount of pressure will build up, causing the bottle to harden. If the bottle is then quickly opened, the drink's contents will come bursting out, and much of it will end up spilling on you or the floor. However, suppose the bottle cap is slowly loosened in such a way as to allow little bits of air to escape until the built-up pressure is fully released. In that case, you may open the bottle without any unwanted explosions.

Jung posits that finding healthy or acceptable ways to express unhealthy or socially unacceptable urges prevents neuroses and psychological harm. He also suggests that, by integrating with our shadows, we achieve what he calls a state of "individuation," that is, a way of actualizing your *whole* self, thereby repairing the intrapsychic divide.[197] We give ourselves the freedom to be who we are. Acceptance of oneself, and acceptance of our circumstances, is possible only when our ordered selves and chaotic selves are seen as two parts of an inseparable whole.

The Jungian concept of the shadow allows us to conform to conventional norms (which we all must do if we want to function in society) while also bringing pieces of ourselves into every situation. When we sacrifice ourselves and lose our individuality for the sake of fitting in with our environment, we lose our freedom entirely and become, once again, enslaved. In this line of thinking, true self-indifference comes when we choose to be *all* shadow. In many ways, the concept of the shadow is just a variation of finding a middle ground between the extremes of self-restraint and disinhibition. Thus, to achieve individuation, we must merge with whatever part of ourselves is most starved, rather than starving one side or the other. The individuated person emerges when we end this internal battle.

Take once again the feeling of anger, for example. When we feel it, we can sometimes reframe a situation and see it differently, which can quell the anger. However, sometimes we are justified in our anger. It's not that our feelings are inherently "bad" in this situation; rather, it's the way we learn to deal with our feelings that can impact our functioning.

From an early age, however, many of us are discouraged from expressing our feelings. We are taught that anger is terrible, that crying is weak, and that anxiety is useless. We are encouraged only to act "appropriately." As mentioned earlier, we show only the highlight reels of our lives on our social media accounts and elsewhere. As a society, we are afraid of anything within the realm of chaos; we expect only perfection. So, we subsequently send our feelings into hiding, pretending that they don't exist. But we're constantly reminded of them as they're with us all the time. The shadow helps us to realize that these feelings are okay, accepted, and normal. It suggests to us that when we reconnect with those parts of ourselves that we were taught not to like, perhaps we will become more real than we were before.

For Jung, understanding our limits, expressing our hidden sides, and using our supposed "faults" to their maximum utility are essential steps toward achieving individuation. So often, we see people using this method without even realizing it. We see famous songwriters whose brushes with death or experiences of tremendous loss and heartache allow them to channel their pain into brilliant masterpieces. We observe the recovered alcoholic who uses their experience with alcoholism to relate to and help other addicts. However, it should be noted that not everyone who uses their weaknesses as strengths is individuated. Instead, we are individuated when our most disowned aspects are brought under conscious awareness and control in ways that don't interfere with our functioning. When you can accept your shadow, you achieve true genuineness and authenticity; this is what is meant by "being yourself."

My Shadow: Accepting the Unacceptable

"Be that self which one truly is."
   Søren Kierkegaard[198]

After learning meditation, I gained the power to tame my inner beast. With my newfound self-confidence, I sought to eliminate the beast entirely. I began to study and practice everything from biofeedback and psychotherapy, to martial arts and yoga. Through diligently studying these practices, I gained much greater self-discipline. I began to pursue my career path, and with each passing grade, my self-confidence was strengthened. Upon graduation, I was hired to work as a therapist at a psychiatric hospital, and it was at this time of my life where I first encountered my shadow. After starting my career, I had a lot of energy and kept a forward momentum in my new position. I learned quickly and excelled at my job, taking on new challenges and maintaining commitments. I had a healthy diet, slept the appropriate hours, exercised regularly, and meditated daily. Eventually, though, I began to feel burnt out. I couldn't understand what the problem was; I was doing everything right. A few inconclusive medical evaluations later and I was back in therapy to treat my idiopathic fatigue.

During sessions, I'd complain about how hard I worked to be my best, when it didn't seem to be getting me anywhere. I was always exhausted. It didn't take long for my therapist to figure out what the issue was. She said, "You are burning yourself out with this lifestyle; that is what is happening. You are overly rigid."[199]

Once again, I didn't believe it; I recoiled from my therapist's diagnosis of the issue. She suggested I factor in or rather "pre-commit" to rest times, once or twice a week. At first, I didn't like the idea of resting. I felt I got enough rest when I slept – why would I need more than that? However, a shift in my thinking came when she reframed the purpose of rest from a pointless endeavor to an essential aspect of mental and physical health. She likened mental rest to physical rest, which is necessary to achieve gains during workouts. I slowly started to turn around in my thinking.

My therapist maintained that factoring in indulgence or leisure relaxation must also be a priority of perhaps equal value.[200] Indeed, research has found that encouraging indulgence via pre-commitment positively impacts people who experience guilt during failures of self-control. Without the ability to permit ourselves to indulge, we eventually become high-strung, burnt out, or depressed.[201] Scheduling rest was my therapist's way of helping me course-correct the imbalance I created; I now saw that I had polarized my lifestyle. With much hesitation, I tried this strategy out, partly because I thought she might have a point and partly because my fatigue at this point practically forced me to rest. It took a few months before I was able to commit to this fully. I slowly began to schedule rest periods and leisure time into my week, thus alleviating much of my stress. Though spiritual and psychological practices like yoga and mindfulness are effortful generators of good health, we also require periods of non-effort to bring about balanced well-being.

I eventually realized that my shadow could be thought of as "laziness" or "indulgence." However, the shadow side of over self-restraint grows mightier and fiercer as time passes. With every rigid, inflexible decision, it comes closer to bursting out of its prison with a dangerous ferocity. This is what Jung meant about the enduring nature of the shadow; the longer you resist it, the bigger it grows until it erupts and wreaks havoc.

My futile attempt to "wish away" my "inner darkness" led to it tightening its grip on me.[202] I mistakenly thought that I could meditate away the unacceptable parts of me. In reality, they were inherent elements of myself that I could never expunge from my psyche, nor should I have wanted to. The resistance toward my shadow became a major source of my suffering. My psychotherapist acted as a mirror on to which I could project my inner psychological reflection, thus helping me repair the split. I now began to wonder. If I didn't see a problem so obvious to those around me, what else was I missing? Was there some other way I was unknowingly harming myself?

My Shadow: The Monk and the Wolf

Despite finding a solution to my initial problem, I felt something else was missing; my inner work wasn't quite finished. Now, I would go to therapy and complain about an "inner pressure." It was not exactly a headache, although I would get those too from time to time. It was a strong tension of a psychological variety. My grievances each session went something to the effect of, "I do everything right. I've learned how to manage stress, and I actively utilize what I've learned. What am I doing wrong?" I had even been incorporating rest into my schedule, in fact, even more than before. However, although I was allowing for times of rest, they were isolated to only those periods. At all other times, I was ultra-self-restricted. I wanted my new life to bear no resemblance to the one of profound suffering which characterized my youth.

When I was young, I lacked self-esteem. I had little to lose and had trouble holding onto what little I had. When my confidence began to improve, I started to see that I was capable of more. I built a new life for myself, but it was then that I became fearful of losing everything I had worked so hard for. These fears were not all imaginary; indeed, they had a basis in the reality of my past losses. Through therapy, I awoke to the painful reality that the majority of my problems were self-caused. Through this realization, I became ridden with guilt. I began to believe that *everything* was my fault and became overly apologetic. I wanted to be so far removed from my past that in my new life I'd do anything to be accepted, even if it meant apologizing when I wasn't wrong. At work, I was a rigid professional and took myself very seriously. At home and social functions, I allowed myself to have fun and let loose. I couldn't fathom even the slightest merging of these two worlds.

In therapy, it's sometimes helpful to assign a name to your inner conflicts, that is, to anthropomorphize them. So, after a while, it became relatively easy to notice an emerging theme. I had worked so hard on my self-discipline that I became something of a modern-day monastic. My life revolved around strict adherence to meditative practices to keep troublesome elements of my personality locked in a mental prison. All the while, I was failing to realize that I was locking myself into this prison. We began to call this highly ordered part of me "the monk."

The next task was to label or name this other, chaotic part of me, the one I kept hidden. That part was not so easy. I called this part of me "the monster." For a while, discussions of this imaginal duality took the form of "the monk and the monster." However, this "monster" was amorphous, and so it wasn't until I was able to define this entity that the healing began. At first, I struggled to put my finger on what encapsulated this "other" self until, one day, I saw a quote from an old Cherokee legend that goes something like this:

"One evening, an elderly Cherokee brave told his grandson about a battle that goes on inside people. He said, 'My son, the battle is between two wolves inside us all. One is evil. It's anger, envy, jealousy, sorrow, regret, greed, arrogance, self-pity, guilt, resentment, inferiority, lies, false pride, superiority, and ego. The other is good. It's joy, peace, love, hope, serenity, humility, kindness, benevolence, empathy, generosity, truth, compassion, and faith.' The grandson thought about it for a minute and then asked his grandfather, 'Which wolf wins?' The old Cherokee simply replied, 'The one that you feed.'"[203]

A wolf! Wolves are fascinating, wild creatures; some travel in packs while others travel alone. If my shadow was anything, it was a wolf; that is, the part of me that was wild and carefree. The part that, like the lone wolf, preferred to follow his own path. Finally, I was able to see these two selves more clearly; the monk and the wolf. I had locked this part of me in a cage in the deep recesses of my mind, ever-present but imprisoned and yearning to be free. The rattles of the wolf's cage were heard and felt as manifestations of my intrapsychic distress.

Initially, the wolf only came out when I was in social settings in my personal life, although he was kept on a short leash by the monk. In professional settings, the wolf returned to his cage, and the monk would make his appearance. Unlike the laid-back, carefree spontaneity of the wolf, the monk was very reserved; stoic and regimented. Constantly monitoring his thoughts, behaviors, and social interactions, the monk was preoccupied with making sure the wolf would never reveal himself at an inopportune time. Eventually, I saw that my rigid self-criticism was not improving my work and productivity but was impairing my ability to be an effective clinician. By putting a name and a face to my shadow, I was able to see the split I had created within myself. And insight is the first step to healing.

Eventually, I wondered what would happen if the monk and the wolf could understand each other. What if, rather than seeing the wolf as something of an unwanted child and a nuisance, I instead viewed him a companion to love, nurture, and accept? I subsequently made a determined effort to see him as such. It was then that my "disowned self" integrated with my "socially acceptable self," thus causing a merger of the shadow. This was an effortful and sometimes vulnerable process of gradually letting the wolf out of the cage and seeing that I was in control; that my genuine, authentic self was accepted. It was a process of surrender through the peaceful realization that not only can I never rid myself of the "bad" or flawed parts of my personality, but that I should be grateful for them. Indeed, it was only in resisting myself that pain and inner turmoil flourished for all those years.

Through this process, I became whole. I began to take the essential parts of myself freely and openly into professional interactions and vice versa. I became genuinely "me," no longer feeling I had to hide who I was. I felt the release of intense internal pressure. I began to experience what it means to accept yourself viscerally. Individuation occurs when the ordered self and the chaotic self stop pulling each other in opposite directions in a perpetual tug of war and finally meet in the middle.[204]

11

Nothing Good or Bad

Acceptance and the Extremes of Human Suffering

We now know what it means to accept oneself, but what does it mean to accept the pain associated with uncontrollable and unfortunate circumstances? Is it even possible to do so? Would we even want to? Are there not at least some life situations that are completely unacceptable? One can turn to a random page in any history textbook, and with very little effort, find instances of human suffering which seem unforgivable. Indeed, the extremes of suffering that have occurred worldwide throughout history would make anyone question the idea of accepting the awful parts of life. Is there a way for us to reconcile the concept of acceptance with the unacceptable?

Furthermore, when discussing the power of pain or aspects typically considered the "dark" parts of humanity, another important question reveals itself. How can we distinguish between an event that causes trauma and an event that generates growth and transformation? What is the difference, fundamentally? Why can some people experience these events as transformative, while others experience them as frightening and traumatic? What is more, what does freedom or acceptance have to do with it? These questions are crucial in determining how to help prevent the emergence of PTSD and other psychiatric illnesses and aid people recovering from traumatic experiences. They can also be helpful to anyone feeling distressed or overwhelmed by their life circumstances.

Right from the outset, I will acknowledge that several factors contribute to the development of traumatic stress, like lack of social support, genetics, perceived life threat, and prior trauma history.[205] Everyone has a threshold for how much they can "take," so to speak. Someone genetically predisposed to depression, for example, and placed in a high-stress environment without adaptive skills, is more likely to become depressed than someone in the same situation without that predisposition.[206] Based on the literature on trauma, we know that the developing years during childhood are vulnerable times for growing brains; that is to say, trauma in early childhood increases the likelihood of mental illness in adulthood.[207] Additionally, people are more likely to be traumatized in adulthood if they have experienced trauma in childhood.[208]

Certainly, there is much to be said about factors that make some people more vulnerable to PTSD and mental illnesses than others. However, the factors that affect people's perception and long-term outcomes after a traumatic event are many, and as far as we know, not yet reducible to precise causes. This remains a topic of debate within the mental health literature. Let's look at this through the framework of autonomy and self-determination.

While it may be the case that uncontrollable circumstances contribute to the development of psychological illnesses in the aftermath of adversity, it's also true that individuals have the power to consciously choose how they will perceive a certain event, which can have long-lasting effects on that person's life and overall well-being. Studies and anecdotal accounts reveal two fundamental differences between those who are shattered by adversity or grow from it.

Firstly, someone who actively attempts to find purpose during a traumatic event and engenders a sense of personal agency is at a reduced risk of developing PTSD and other stress-related illnesses. Secondly, we are more likely to grow or transform from adversity if we can sculpt some benefit out of the clay of disaster. This chapter will take a deeper look at what ancient and contemporary knowledge can teach us about dealing with even the most extreme situations. We will see how the concepts of autonomy, growth, and purpose intersect with adversity.

Transforming Adversity: The Perception of Willingness

Research shows that freedom of will plays an important role in developing psychological illnesses resulting from disasters and extreme events. In his book, *The Body Keeps the Score*, Bessel van der Kolk describes how victims of a catastrophe who saw themselves as helpless and powerless over their circumstances, that is, completely lacking control, ended up with traumatic symptoms later on as opposed to those who took initiative during the event (e.g., helping others, fighting off an attacker, etc.) Those who undergo chronic stress or a major, life-altering situation will more likely manifest PTSD if they feel trapped or completely hopeless during the event.

Conversely, those who experience such an event but consciously act with initiative, intention, and access a semblance of control are much less likely to experience long-term traumatic stress symptoms.[209] Indeed, we can lessen the devastating effects of extreme life experiences by attaining (to the degree possible) a sense of agency. Even those "genetically predisposed" to traumatization can rise above adversity; a testament to the fact that we aren't destined to conform to statistics. The act of changing the way we view our circumstances is sometimes powerful enough to determine the extent of our suffering.

Nothing Good or Bad

"There is nothing either good or bad, but thinking makes it so."
William Shakespeare[210]

When writing this book, I considered that some might be perturbed by the idea that a benefit, learning experience, or "bright side" can be found in almost any unpleasant situation. I will be the first to admit that certain extremes of human suffering could have and should have never happened. There is no "positive" side to events that have caused the needless loss of life through humanity's often barbaric history. And, certainly, if we could go back in time and stop those events from taking place, anyone in their right mind would. What can be said is that through the inexcusable horrors of our predecessors, humans have, collectively, continued to learn how to grow from and prevent similar calamities from happening in the future. While it's not my intention to minimize the experience of people who have been through trauma, I wish to provide an alternative, empowering perspective.

As I mentioned in the first part of this book, my initial introduction to understanding the malleable nature of the mind and cultivating the ability to change my perceptions consciously was through reading the Dhammapada and studying Buddhism. The Buddhist way of life focuses on the fact that the mind is the wellspring of most of what we think, feel, and do. In some ways, then, Buddhism was the first form of psychology; it proposed that the mind generates all experience, and thus, is the most important thing to master if we intend to alleviate our suffering.

The Buddhist doctrine that "our life is shaped by our mind, [and] we become what we think" is a central aspect of cognitive behavioral therapy, a form of psychotherapy that helps people change their thinking, improve their moods, and modify ineffective or unwanted behavioral patterns.[211] We know that learning how to change the way we think can profoundly affect our life, something the Buddha and other spiritual teachers before him have taught through meditation. However, meditation is just one of many ways to change our thinking and cultivate an attitude of acceptance. These other ways can be found through stoic practices, as I'll now explain.

Stoicism is a branch of Hellenistic philosophy founded by Zeno of Citium in the third century BC, in Athens. Like Buddhism, Stoicism can be described as a philosophy of living. Among its many teachings is the belief that happiness, freedom, and well-being can be found through acceptance and using our mind to understand and improve conditions for ourselves and others. Seneca the Younger, or simply Seneca, was a Roman Stoic philosopher who wrote many treatises on the Stoic way of life. Among these was *De Providentia*, or *On Providence*, which was an effort to reconcile the problem of evil. In his essay, Seneca points out that trial and tribulation often leads to strength, especially if we can learn from and find virtue in our misfortune. In psychology, this is similar to "cognitive restructuring," a technique that involves looking at a problem from a unique perspective or from an angle that has the effect of lessening our negative emotions.[212]

We have all heard (sometimes to our chagrin) the popular adage, "Look on the bright side," often said by friends or loved ones in the wake of some personal misfortune. Of course, it generally offers little consolation to someone suffering a loss or tragedy. However, there is a method that extends beyond banally looking at the bright side when facing adversity. The practice of looking at ways in which you've gained more than you've lost in any given tragedy, misfortune, or inconvenience can radically shift the way you perceive and respond to the world and can ultimately free you from self-defeating thoughts. Moreover, the more global and long-term payoff involves habituating this way of thinking. Shifting our perspective in this way is empowering and helps us grow from the obstacles that life puts in our way. The obstacles in life can either make or break us, and we can *choose* the former or the latter. When we learn of our ability to change our thinking in order to affect our behavior, we take care of the percentage of life in our control. But, when we learn to grow from, rather than resist, the negative experiences that aren't in our control, in a sense, we deal properly with the percentage that isn't. The goal of acceptance is to learn how to appreciate and grow from arduous experiences.

Trauma to Transformation: Post-Traumatic Growth

"What doesn't kill me, makes me stronger."
Friedrich Nietzsche[213]

Research shows that not everyone who experiences trauma will incur long-term impairments; studies have shown that some individuals report experiencing growth after adversity.[214] The process mentioned above whereby a person seeks a benefit, gain, or other learning experience from their misfortune is known as "post-traumatic growth," a term created by psychologists Lawrence Calhoun and Richard Tedeschi.[215]

Post-traumatic growth is defined as having a transformative experience in the wake of traumatic events and challenges of life via the practice of "benefit finding."[216] Without reducing this incredibly life-changing and powerful concept to the idea that "it could have been worse," it's essential to note right from the outset that post-traumatic growth has several meanings, but it can be roughly summarized as a cognitive reframing of negative events. In this way, you essentially rewrite the script of your reality. It's a basic acceptance practice because rather than remaining trapped in despair, we become empowered to overcome our pain. Those who can reframe their experience in such a way tend to have better relationships, greater levels of inner strength and resilience, and a total shift in the way they see the world.[217]

Research has shed light on the other factors that affect

post-traumatic growth like religion, spirituality, problem-focused coping,[218] education level,[219] and autonomous social support.[220] However, psychologists have found evidence that growing from adversity can be an intentional cognitive process.[221] The research consistently indicates that those who can shift from seeing themselves as a victim to taking on an empowerment perspective by consciously seeking what was gained rather than lost, experience greater levels of happiness and well-being. The literature indicates that, just as trauma can inflict psychological and social harm on a person, the freedom to heal rests in the hands of the individual; this is a strong field of interest among many academic disciplines like psychology and social work, so it warrants our attention.[222]

Research on heart attack survivors, arguably a very traumatic experience, has shown, for example, that those able to find the benefits of their ordeal or who focused on what they gained rather than what they lost had a lower rate of relapse and morbidity for as long as eight years after their illness.[223] Moreover, research conducted in laboratory settings found that post-traumatic growth was associated with lower levels of the stress hormone cortisol in healthy women[224] and in women with breast cancer.[225] Other research has shown that people who engage in benefit finding are less likely to have trouble with symptoms of PTSD.[226] When we feel trapped, like there is no way out and no choice left, we are in danger of succumbing to our circumstances. But, when we choose to find the benefit of an unpleasant or dire situation, to push forward instead of giving up when all hope seems lost, that is when we can grow, heal, and triumph. Through this lens, the only truly "bad" or "negative" events are ones in which nothing can be learned or gained, in which no higher purpose can be derived. Thus, choosing to view stressful events as challenges to persevere through and grow from, as well as finding a sense of meaning and purpose within them, can sometimes be enough to become transformed rather than traumatized.

Acceptance and Purpose: The Myth of Sisyphus

"The workman of today works every day in his life at the same tasks, and this fate is no less absurd. But it is tragic only at the rare moments when it becomes conscious."
Albert Camus[227]

The ancient philosophers grappled with trying to understand the senseless suffering in the world. What is it all for? What does it all mean? For some, the question of how to cultivate life acceptance pales in comparison to why, if life is purposeless (or seems that way), we should continue to exist at all. Through the lens of absurdism, it's not immediately apparent why we should not end our life if, indeed, reality has no meaning. In a world of seeming meaninglessness, the Greeks came up with the myth of Sisyphus, a story that was an attempt to wrestle with that very question. Adapted into an influential philosophical essay of the same name by philosopher Albert Camus, the myth of Sisyphus is seen as an antidote to the absurdity of life.

As the story goes, Sisyphus was a former king who the gods condemned for committing many transgressions. As punishment for his wrongdoings, he was sentenced by Zeus to spend eternity rolling a stone up a hill, only for it to eventually roll back down to the bottom. Each time the stone returns to the bottom, Sisyphus must roll it back up in an endlessly repeating cycle, for all eternity. He is forever condemned to a life of meaningless drudgery. In some ways, many of us may find this story highly familiar and even relatable. At times, we may feel we are in the shoes of Sisyphus when we complete the same morning routine, travel to the same places, and experience the same pains and momentary pleasures over what feels like an eternity. Philosophers have remarked at how closely this age-old tale resembles the current state of affairs for our daily existence.

Camus saw this striking similarity between the predicament of Sisyphus and the seemingly endless burdens of modern life. It's Sisyphus's ability not only to realize this existential absurdity but to thrive in it that makes Camus and other philosophers see him not as cruel and deceitful (as his subjects might have seen him) but rather as a dynamic protagonist. Camus believed that freedom for Sisyphus (and for people in general) is achieved through an honest acknowledgment of this futile existence. That is, it's through reconciliation and acceptance (not resistance) of his situation. Though Sisyphus is physically forced into a life of eternal labor, he consciously chooses to become mentally liberated. Camus saw that it's only in balancing suffering and happiness, the achievement at the end of a long struggle, that we derive our meaning.[228] He concludes that, rather than experiencing misery, the intended goal of Zeus, Sisyphus is instead happy.[229]

However, realization and acceptance aren't the only ways in which the futility of Sisyphus's existence can be transformed; rather, it's a necessary first step. That is, by making imaginal alterations to the story, we can begin to discern the emergence of purpose. In other philosophical adaptations, we are asked to imagine that each time the stones roll back down the hill, they organize themselves into a magnificent and elegant temple; this gives Sisyphus's life a purpose, one of which he is wholly unaware. Having a grand purpose but being unaware of it will change nothing from his perspective. However, when he begins to see the beautiful outcome of his painstaking work and realizes that it's not all for naught, he is once again free.

Sisyphus's story shows us the various ways in which we can learn and grow from adversity. It's not that the adversity carries with it an underlying meaning for us to figure out; rather, it's our job to *create* meaning. I often fail to think of a negative event that I could not view, in hindsight, as a learning experience. There is no doubt that I could have dispensed with some of what I would consider the more needless and extreme afflictions scattered throughout my life story. That is something that will always be true, but it does nothing to reduce the value contained in making honest appraisals whereby we can see what was learned and (sometimes inadvertently) gained.

It may be tempting for some to depreciate and reduce the myth of Sisyphus to something more banal and simplistic. Indeed, the saying, "When life gives you lemons, you make lemonade" is what comes to mind when we think about what it means to make the best of a bad situation. However, cheap catchphrases aren't enough to help us truly understand and, more importantly, live by these teachings.

It's glaringly obvious, especially from the pessimist's viewpoint, that it may be all well and good that Sisyphus has found meaning and comfort through acceptance, but that does nothing to change the fact that he is still enslaved in a life of eternal drudgery. We may think, how can he be happy or free in a situation that represents the exact antithesis of freedom? It may feel contrived to discern Sisyphus's predicament as anything other than hellish while he is quite apparently the unwilling actor in a horror scenario.

And this, dependably, brings us to the realization that Sisyphus's freedom is actualized through the realm of the mind. Indeed, our minds give us a unique property unshared by any material objects or elements; that property is the ability to choose. When we are physically constrained, we retain a level of freedom that is both profoundly intimate and unequivocally ours. Freedom must be a choice we make. It's with this recognition that we have arrived at the end of the chapter. Next, I will briefly discuss specific methods and practices that fall more or less into the category of acceptance.

12

Methods of Acceptance

By now, it should be clear that adopting an attitude of acceptance can help us live more freely. Now that we have a thorough understanding of this concept in the context of the self and of one's circumstances, this chapter will be dedicated to a cursory exploration of the various techniques and methods which can be said to fall, more or less, under the framework of acceptance. This chapter will focus on different approaches to acceptance from both ancient and contemporary thinkers, many of which lead to the same goal. As you may recall from earlier chapters, mindfulness is the practice of placing attention on the present moment. Although mindfulness is cultivated and strengthened during meditation, it can also be fostered across a wide range of other activities. I have also discussed Zazen, which belongs to the Zen division of Buddhism. However, many other beneficial meditative practices can help cultivate acceptance. This chapter will describe several that I have personally benefitted from and those supported by research.

Dzogchen

There is a meditative practice belonging to the Tibetan Buddhist tradition called Dzogchen; this is a lesser-known method espoused by author and neuroscientist, Sam Harris, in his book, *Waking Up*.[230] The aim of Dzogchen is to gain direct experience, rather than intellectual knowledge, of non-duality and for the mind to awaken to its true nature, often referred to as a state of "pure consciousness," that is, the continuous experience of a mind undivided. To achieve this state, you must attempt to turn attention in on itself rather than to a particular sensory experience. Simply, it's the practice of attempting to observe the mind itself, to "look at what's looking."[231] This realization exposes the meditator to the transitory nature of our thoughts and feelings, something that, once seen, cannot be unseen. By investigating our emotions, we realize that they are as transient as a gentle breeze, instead of resisting negative feelings or trying to replace them with positive ones.

The Buddhists saw emotional states as mirages. They look real, and can have actual effects on our perception; however, upon closer inspection, they seem to vanish. According to Buddhism, we are liberated from the prison of negative emotions when we see that feelings, like anger and sadness, aren't concrete but fundamentally empty. Some consider this practice to have many conceptual parallels with psychotherapeutic approaches that attempt to integrate aspects of the personality.[232]

Getting Started:

Whereas the practice of Zazen teaches mindful awareness of the breath for the entire session, some teachers encourage mindfulness of the breath as a preliminary grounding method preceding the primary practice. In Dzogchen, teachers may encourage beginning with mindful breathing as in Zazen. When the mind begins to stabilize, simply observe the mind by searching for your head. To gain insight into Dzogchen, some teachers like Douglas Harding recommend imagining you have no head, also known as "the headless way." Like Zazen, searching for the head by turning attention inwards toward the mind is the anchor with which to return once the mind inevitably wanders.[233]

See Hear Feel

See Hear Feel is a technique promoted by American meditation teacher and Buddhist monk, Shinzen Young. It's a technique whereby you "note" your sensory experiences by labeling them. This practice was taught to me by a psychotherapist who also studied Buddhism, and it greatly enhanced my meditation practice.

It's generally considered that all sensory experiences are fundamentally constituted of feelings, sounds, or sights (both internally and externally). The method involves naming each sensory experience that occurs in the present moment and switching to the next as it arises. The sound of a bird chirping can be labeled as "hearing," whereas the sensation of hunger or your back pressed up against your seat can be labeled as "feeling." Finally, the sights within your immediate environment or images in your mind can be labeled as "seeing." You will notice that your mind tends to switch back and forth between these basic sensations. Your only job is to notice and label them as they arise. This practice is especially helpful for those new to mindfulness as sensory events are always available as an anchor with which to return to the present moment.[234]

Getting Started:

To practice this, you may sit in a comfortable position on a chair or cushion. Whichever position you choose, it is important to remain grounded and still. We can center the mind by beginning with three to five mindful breaths. Next, bring attention to whichever sensory experience is occurring in the present moment. When the mind wanders, bring it back to your sensory experiences. Since the wandering mind is itself a sensory experience, when you become aware of it, you can note the thought. For example, noticing your mind wandered toward a visual thought of what you are having for dinner can be labeled "seeing"; if the next sensory experience is a gentle breeze, it can be labeled "feeling." You can alternate between noticing sensory experiences until the session is concluded; this can be anywhere from ten to thirty minutes.

Yoga

Yoga is a 3,000-year-old practice belonging to Indian philosophical and spiritual traditions that incorporates both mental and physical aspects. I've chosen to place it within the meditation paradigm because it's historically regarded and contemporaneously practiced as a spiritual discipline. Yoga helps you to build strength, endurance, flexibility, and self-control; however, it also improves our ability to manage stress and helps to foster greater calmness and well-being. Regular exercise (especially the kind that athletes at higher levels perform) certainly requires self-awareness, intense focus, and concentration. While yoga surely involves physical exertion, it's as much a meditative practice in that it emphasizes being mindful of your breathing and synchronizing breath with movement. Thus, yoga effectively encapsulates exercise for the mind *and* body.[235] As such, it has been found to help improve depression, anxiety, and insomnia.[236]

Getting Started:

Unlike seated meditative techniques, it is not feasible to provide a basic instruction of yoga practice in this brief overview. However, some simple suggestions can help beginners. Firstly, it is important to find an experienced and qualified yoga instructor. If you are new to yoga or physical exertion in general, look for beginner classes, most of which are easy to find as they are advertised accordingly. You may want to find a yoga class that is a good fit for you, based on your goals. Some forms of yoga are more meditative, like Hatha Yoga and Iyengar Yoga, whereas others are therapeutic, like Viniyoga. In contrast, some are more athletic and rigorous, like Ashtanga Yoga, Power Yoga, and Vinyasa Flow.[237] It all depends on what you're aiming to achieve. Thankfully, the internet makes it easy to find reviews and other details such as instructor credentials and experience. Word of mouth will also help you determine if a particular

Gratitude Practice

Gratitude is the practice of appreciating what we already have, rather than suffering the misery of wanting what we don't or can't have. The practice is as simple as writing down a brief list of things you are grateful for each night. Research studies have shown that this practice can have significant positive effects such as lowering blood pressure, strengthening the immune system, and improving our sense of well-being.[238]

Getting Started:

Each night, before bed, take a blank notebook or journal and write down three or four things for which you are grateful. You do not have to search for significant things to be grateful for (although you can). For example, it can be as simple as:

I am grateful for:
1. *The roof over my head.*
2. *The good friends in my life.*
3. *The fact I got through a tough day at work.*

Putting at least three on your list will train your mind to seek out the positive.

Zazen

This practice was discussed in depth earlier. However, I will provide a basic guide on how Zazen is traditionally practiced.

Getting Started:

Start by sitting in a chair or on a meditation cushion (zafu). If in a chair, make sure to keep the feet flat and the spine straight. If on a cushion, try to sit with your back straight and legs crossed (lotus or half-lotus). You may feel more comfortable in a kneeling position (seiza), with a cushion between you and the ground to avoid sitting directly on your calves. In most disciplines, correct posture is essential because it helps the practitioner feel centered and grounded, which facilitates stillness. Next, keep your hands rested in the center of your lap near your navel with palms facing up, bringing thumb tips together so that they are comfortably touching. You can close your eyes or keep them half-open while facing a blank surface like a wall. Close your mouth and bring the tip of your tongue to touch the roof of your mouth. Start to focus on your breathing. When your mind begins to wander, notice you've wandered and return to the breath. Importantly, a wandering mind is natural and takes many years to tame. Do not be harsh or self-critical; when the mind wanders, simply bring it back to the breath[239] without judgment.[240] Start with five-minute sessions and work your way up to fifteen minutes per day. The morning time or nighttime, right before bed, is best.

Relaxation Strategies

Normally, in the West, when people think about meditation, they immediately think of relaxation. While mindfulness and meditative practices can generate relaxation, they do so more in the long run. In the beginning, these practices require intentional effort; they demand patience and rigor. Similar to working out at the gym, mindfulness and focused awareness are workouts for the mind. Eventually, relaxation comes in the form of a life of peace and freedom from many problems that typically result from an untamed mind. That is not to discount the benefits of techniques that help us relax in the present moment, however. Indeed, psychology is a repository of many practices that help calm the mind and body, some of which have been adapted from Eastern philosophies like Hinduism and Buddhism, which we will explore.

Relaxation requires learning exercises that help to reduce muscle tension and calm the sympathetic nervous system during emotionally challenging times. These techniques and methods all have a wide research base which has demonstrated their effectiveness in managing symptoms of anxiety, panic, nervousness, and other fears. The subsequent physiological response of the lowering of heart rate and blood pressure generated when practicing these techniques has been called the "relaxation response," a term coined in 1975 by an American cardiologist, Herbert Benson. He observed that deep states of calmness and relaxation are physiologically incompatible with worry and anxiety, showing that intentionally inducing a state of relaxation is an effective method of naturally thwarting panic, anxiety, or overwhelm.[241]

As a final disclaimer, as is the case with any practice that shifts our perspective and opens us to greater insights, it is always recommended to find an experienced teacher. Books are excellent starting points, but inevitably, there are questions that only someone with years of experience can answer. Thanks to the internet, anyone can find a teacher or an associated community with little effort.

Getting Started:

When we experience stress, we often begin to tense our muscles in areas of our bodies without realizing it. Thus, we become "tense" and rigid, transferring our physical stress into other parts of our bodies. This technique allows you to locate and release stress and can be done lying down or seated. This practice can also be done after a round of whichever breathing exercises work best for you. Start at your head by squeezing the muscles of your eyes, nose, and cheeks and hold it for three to five seconds before relaxing for another three to five seconds. Make your way down to squeeze your neck and shoulders, scanning after the squeezing action to be sure there's no tension left and relaxing if there is. Then, tighten your biceps, forearms, and fists for three to five seconds, and relax. Make sure to inhale and exhale deeply as you perform this relaxation strategy. Next, move down to your lower body, flexing your abdomen and relaxing as you did with your face and arms. Now, bring your attention to your lower legs, flexing and relaxing. Finally, scan your body once more from head to toe to ensure there is no tension anywhere in the body. This technique can also be done without tensing the muscles; one can simply scan the body from head to toe, making sure the muscles are relaxed.

Diaphragmatic Breathing

This breathing technique is one that I practice and teach to my clients. It involves breathing through the diaphragm or the belly. The diaphragm is the most efficient but least used muscle for breathing.

Getting Started:

To practice this, place one hand on your belly, below the ribs, and the other on your chest, making sure to breathe in through the nose. The chest should be still, and your stomach should move upwards, so the hand placed on the diaphragm rises while the one on the chest remains stationary. You may practice this in a repeating cycle for however long feels right to you. Research has demonstrated that this technique helps improve sustained attention, reduce cortisol levels, and improve overall mental health.[242]

Floatation Therapy

Also known as floatation-REST (reduced environmental stimulation therapy), this is a combination of meditative and relaxation practice insofar as it achieves some of the goals of both. It's also a practice that is becoming more commercially available. Floatation therapy is a practice whereby someone lays face-up in a pool of water infused with Epsom salts contained within a dark tank, thereby significantly decreasing the information received by the nervous system through sensory experiences (although it's impossible to extinguish them completely.) Not many studies have been conducted on this form of therapy. However, research has shown that being cut off from sounds, touch, and smells has anxiolytic properties; that is, it can help lessen anxiety.[243] Some studies have shown floatation therapy to improve memory, lower blood pressure,[244] reduce cortisol levels,[245] relieve pain,[246] reduce stress, and increase subjective relaxation.[247] From personal experience, I can attest to the sort of mental defragmentation that seems to occur when the body and mind aren't being constantly bombarded by the often abrasive stimuli of our daily lives.

Getting Started:

Floatation centers are becoming more popular and can be found locally in most areas via the internet, community websites, or social media.

2:1 Breathing

This is perhaps my favorite breathing technique and one that I have taught my clients with much success. It's called 2:1 breathing, a practice whereby you exhale for twice the length of your inhalation, preferably in the same style as diaphragmatic breathing. Note that it is not important to exhale *precisely* twice as long as you inhale. As long as the exhalation is longer than the inhalation you will achieve the benefits. Thus, as a simple tool to remember it more easily, it can be referred to as "7/11" breathing. That is, inhaling for a count of seven and exhaling for a count of eleven. During inhalation, the sympathetic nervous system activates and the heart rate begins to increase; however, exhalation (governed by the parasympathetic nervous system) slows down the heart rate.[248] During the state of up-regulation, when someone is in a state of panic or anxiety, their physiological responses go into a heightened state. When we exhale for longer than we inhale, however, the body automatically relaxes, the heart rate slows down, and blood pressure begins to stabilize. This is a yogic technique studied extensively with markedly beneficial effects on high blood pressure and heart rate, and it's also incredibly helpful for stopping panic and anxiety attacks in their tracks.[249]

Getting Started:

Start by finding a comfortable place to sit and set your timer for five to ten minutes. Breathe in for a count of seven and breathe out for a count of eleven, and then repeat.[250] You can incorporate this as part of meditation practice, use it when feeling anxious or over-stimulated, or include it in your sleep routine to get you into a calmer state before bed.

Square Breathing

Square breathing is derived from a yogic breathing technique called Sama Vritti, or "even breath." It helps to produce states of relaxation, encourage positive mood, and reduce anxiety.[251] I have heard clients express that it's also useful as a sleep aid.

Getting Started:

Start by sitting on a chair or cushion and adjust your position until you feel grounded, or lay down if you feel more comfortable doing so. Note that laying down puts you at risk of falling asleep, which might not be a bad thing.
1. Inhale through your nose for a count of four.
2. Hold that breath for a count of four.
3. Exhale through your mouth for a count of four.
4. Hold for a count of four.
5. Repeat this cycle for as long as needed.

As with 2:1 breathing, this can be used as part of your meditation practice, when feeling anxious or over-stimulated, or as part of your sleep routine.

Massage Therapy

This is a natural way to help relieve tension and calm psychological distress. Being touched therapeutically mimics the feeling of being nurtured and secure that we experience as infants (without which a child's development would be negatively impacted[252]). The feeling of being touched by another human is a primal, instinctual feeling and can help us calm down when upset. Though we grow into self-sufficient adults, we still require this kind of affection for our well-being.[253]

Getting Started:

Numerous massage centers can be found locally via the internet, social media, or business directories.

III

Freedom through Change

The notion of "change" is both the opposite and counterpart of acceptance; it is a concept that our culture is more closely acquainted with. The promulgation of personal growth contained herein is meant to encourage change and improvement. —a promotion of self-belief and of using whatever resources are at our disposal to achieve a life of freedom.

13

Vision

Like acceptance, change is sometimes distorted by the media and within the public's perception. In Western culture, we are bombarded with messages of productivity, hard work, and attainment of financial wealth and material goods. Indeed, we are incessantly exposed to advertisements that depict the idea that a life of happiness comes about only by accruing wealth, physical beauty, and material possessions. It's often hard to tell how we can truly be freed from suffering.

The remaining two parts of this book are dedicated to understanding what it means to change and learning how to insulate oneself against the mixed messages of our society. In this way, we can free ourselves from the crippling hold of uncertainty and be liberated from the toxic idea that the accumulation of "stuff" is the only point to and value of our lives.

While writing this book, people close to me who saw the kinds of research I was doing would often ask if I was writing a self-help book. Indeed, this was not surprising as there is much conceptual intersection between psychology and self-improvement. Although self-help and personal growth, as I see it, belong to the "change" ethos and are interchangeable at times, the primary difference is that self-help is usually concerned with managing functional impairments, while personal growth may encompass deficits but also deals with improving an already functional life.[254]

Stated more clearly, the concept of self-help seems to be geared toward helping people overcome conditions, mostly without the help of a professional,[255] whereas personal growth focuses on continued advancement in the direction of cultivating our "best self," by whatever means. However, many self-help and psychotherapy methods are useful for personal growth and sometimes overlap, and I aim to encourage change and improvement through the explanation and utilization of multiple resources.

If I had to distill the fundamental traits that we require, as individuals, in order to change successfully (and grow), I would list the following:

1. Vision
2. The ability to pre-plan
3. Self-discipline
4. Self-knowledge
5. Problem-solving skills
6. Persistence

To get anywhere in life, you must first know *where* you are going (vision), chart your course (planning), develop the ability to resist temptations, delay gratification, and inhibit unwanted urges (self-discipline), and then cultivate a thorough understanding of your potential and capabilities (self-knowledge). After that, you must develop the necessary skills to help you along the journey to your destination (problem-solving), and finally, you must not stop, except for momentary breaks, until you arrive at your destination (persistence). These are the few attributes without which personal achievement may be difficult, if not impossible, to attain. Because self-knowledge is perhaps one of the most important aspects of acceptance and change, the concept of "understanding ourselves" requires its own segment which is the basis for part four.

Vision: The Shape of Our Life

"Our life is shaped by our mind; we become what we think."
  The Buddha[256]

In my view, "vision" is the most fundamental aspect of change, improvement, or goal accomplishment. Having a vision means having a clear understanding of the kind of person you want to be. You cannot reach a destination that doesn't exist or hit a target you can't see. When you have no higher vision or no vision at all, you remain aimless. You become trapped in a prison of ambiguity, missed opportunity, and untapped potential.

Imagine you are invited to a dinner celebration at a specific location; if you know the address, you'll eventually arrive at your destination, even if you get a bit lost along the way. The same is true of personal success. Going through life without a future vision is like receiving the dinner invitation and beginning your journey without learning the address. You will quickly realize that you have no idea where you are going, and it may be too late by the time you do.

Having a vision of yourself, on the other hand, grants you

the certitude that a map and compass provide the sailor. That is, knowing who you want to be and what you want for your life is the first step toward that end. Envisioning the person you wish to be helps you develop the parameters to direct your efforts. No longer will you drift, directionless; instead, your life will begin to take form and shape. Having a map doesn't guarantee you will not get lost or even get there at all; but it ensures that, unlike before, you now have a fighting chance.

The Buddha's words that our "lives are shaped by our minds" is more than just a call for people to practice mindful meditation. It's perhaps one of the first written realizations that all purposeful creations began first as thoughts before coming into physical existence.

Whenever I travel to Manhattan on the ferry, I am awestruck by the imposing and inspiring skyscrapers. One thought that astounds me the most is that every single one of those buildings began as simply a thought in one person's mind. A complex of infinitesimal brain cells and neuronal firings occurring within a three-pound glob of gray matter somehow gave birth to these beautiful, intricate, concrete and steel structures, hundreds of meters high; a true testament to the fact that we become what we think. If something as staggering, elegant, and inspiring can be created from just a thought, imagine what kind of person you can become by thinking it.

Except for those inclined toward spontaneity, most of us carefully plan out our vacations, day trips, parties, weddings, and other activities. Why do we not apply this same line of thinking with regards to our long-term goals? It seems that it's fine for us to put our brainpower toward fun things which aren't too far in the future. But, often, the moment we are tasked with envisioning and planning for our future and long-term ambitions, we tend to shut down.

Imagine the kind of life you'd have if you took the time to chart out the details of your future; if you envisioned the ideal version of yourself with as much effort as you apply toward constructing your weekend plans. Humans are the only species capable of detailed forethought and future planning; this is a unique gift that we ought not to waste. So ask yourself now, who do you want to be?

14

Planning and Preparation

"The only thing we have to fear is ... fear itself."
Franklin D. Roosevelt[257]

To achieve anything in life, we must cultivate a deep understanding of the obstacles we face on our journey. Many times, our obstacles are fear-based. Learning to overcome fear will help eliminate a substantial portion of the barriers to our success. There are many distinct types of fear; however, I want to make a critical distinction between two kinds.

Generally, fear is defined as an emotion elicited by the perception of a threat that causes physiological and behavioral changes like fighting, fleeing, and freezing. The first kind of fear is innate; these fears keep us alive and aren't necessarily the ones we want to relinquish. The second kind of fear is what we learn through conditioning (think Pavlov's dog). These fears are sometimes helpful; for example, learning not to touch a hot stove will save you from getting burnt in the future. However, learned fears that impair functioning or prevent goal achievement in non-threatening or otherwise innocuous situations are ones we can do without. These are sometimes called "phobias" or "irrational fears,"[258] which can be crippling. Fear also encompasses various emotions such as avoidance, apprehension, doubt, and resistance, which can inhibit personal growth and improvement. Thankfully, just as fear can be learned, it can also be unlearned. One way to effectively manage fear is to prepare for it, as I'll now explain.

The Neuroscience of Visualization and Extinction

Research in neuroscience has shown that the brain doesn't completely distinguish between real and imagined events. Many professional athletes and musicians[259] often visualize their outcomes to improve their performance and gain an advantage.[260] This is referred to as "mental practice;"[261] that is, the act of mentally rehearsing a motor activity, like playing basketball, will activate the same regions of the brain as if playing basketball. And it needn't be a sport or instrument; while mentally practicing or visualizing any function, the brain will signal to the body to release the same chemicals and hormones associated with performing the function in real life. Mentally preparing in the present will improve physical performance in the future because, according to your brain, you've practiced once before.[262]

Studies have shown that those who engage in regular physical performance, like athletes, physical therapy patients, and musicians, can benefit from mental practice.[263] In many instances, where someone successfully handles an extreme situation that is usually fear-provoking, we find that mental training was involved in preparing for that experience. This has important implications for the management of fear and paves the way to understand how to overcome it –visualizing your future in the present increases your likelihood of success because you've already practiced once in your head.[264]

The term "extinction" is used to describe the eventual result of repeated exposure to fearful stimuli, known colloquially as "desensitization." In some cases, extinction of a fear response occurs as an unintended consequence of our daily lives and occupations. We see desensitization happening all the time; for example, a pathologist who has performed so many autopsies that the grotesque details no longer produce an extreme reaction. Or perhaps an oncologist who's made so many cancer diagnoses that they can break the news to their patient without hesitation. This phenomenon, whereby an individual extinguishes a fear response, has formed the basis for exposure therapy. Therapists use exposure therapy to help a person overcome their fear by exposing them, with their consent, to the source of their fear in a safe environment. Many studies have detailed the effectiveness of exposure therapy to treat several fear-based disorders like generalized anxiety disorder, PTSD, and obsessive-compulsive disorder.[265]

There are several types of exposure therapy:

1. **In vivo (real-life):** A person is exposed to real-life, fear-inducing situations, albeit to a much lesser degree. For example, someone may overcome a fear of large social gatherings by gradually being exposed to smaller social gatherings.

2. **Imaginal:** An individual is tasked with visualizing or imagining a feared situation and gradually becomes desensitized to it. The brain and body generate the same response to an imagined threat as to the real danger. If you continue to imagine it in a safe environment or while practicing a stress management technique like abdominal breathing, the

physiological response becomes reduced or, in some cases, extinct. The advantage of imaginal exposure is that a person will overcome feared memories and practice quelling fears that aren't easily replicable in real life, like skydiving and public speaking.

3. **Interoceptive:** The individual confronts feared bodily symptoms such as increased heart rate and shortness of breath.[266]

I will be focusing on imaginal and interoceptive exposure, since they offer a greater degree of control. Several physiological changes occur in the body during the perception of a threat and subsequent experience of fear, such as hyperventilation, vasoconstriction, and sweating. However, those same physiological responses can be triggered just by thinking about or imagining a fear-triggering event. Just as imagining fearful events can put your body in a corresponding physiological state, imagining positive experiences can do the same; this is what makes exposure therapy convenient and effective.

The effectiveness of this behavioral strategy in helping people manage their fear is backed by evidence. A brain imaging study conducted by the University of Colorado Boulder and Icahn School of Medicine found that imagining dangerous or threatening stimuli can change how they are represented in the brain. In their study, sixty-eight healthy subjects were conditioned to associate a particular sound with an uncomfortable but minor electric shock. They were subsequently divided into three groups and either exposed to the actual threatening sound, asked to imagine the sound, or asked to imagine pleasant scenery without any further electric shocks. When the researchers measured the participants' brain activity using functional magnetic resonance imaging (fMRI), they found that brain activity in the prefrontal cortex, amygdala, and auditory cortex was similar in both the imagined and real threat groups.

Additionally, after repeated exposure to the sounds, they found that with the electric shock no longer present, both groups experienced extinction; that is, the formerly fear-provoking stimulus no longer generated a subsequent fear response. These findings are interpreted to mean that through exposure, the brain, or rather people, can unlearn fear.[267] Visualization seems to come in handy more often when the endeavor is not something you can realistically or reasonably practice beforehand, like, say, jumping out of an airplane or performing in front of a giant crowd.

Fear Prophylaxis: Preparation and Exposure

"The brave man is not he who doesn't feel afraid, but he who conquers that fear."
Nelson Mandela[268]

As we saw in Part Two, aside from genetic predispositions and other external causes, perception is a major factor in determining who will become traumatized. A person can become traumatized by a situation that another may willingly subject themselves to without any adverse effects. Those who perceive a loss of control and forceful subjection to painful and frightening circumstances are at greater risk. Moreover, I discussed post-traumatic growth, which can occur in the aftermath of adversity; those who consciously derive a sense of purpose during or after a catastrophe are least likely to sustain long-term psychological and emotional harm.

However, I believe there are also prophylactic measures we can take to alleviate and reduce fear's influence on us. Astronaut Chris Hadfield gave a TED talk about fear called, "What I Learned from Going Blind in Space."[269] In this video, he recalled that many people would ask him how he dared to ride a rocket into outer space, with a one in thirty chance of not surviving, and go on a "spacewalk" (leaving the spaceship while in earth's orbit to make repairs of satellites or other equipment). Regardless of the odds, fear of death is but one among a multitude of possible frightening experiences that could occur while sitting in a fiery tin can, hurtling out of the earth's atmosphere into the unknown. There are innumerable things that could go wrong, like Hadfield going blind during his spacewalk.

However, Hadfield's talk was not about how to scare people out of spaceflight or to brag about a brand of bravery afforded to only a lucky few, but rather it explored the fact that even crippling fears and terrifying circumstances can be vanquished.

Hadfield's method for overcoming fears of the rarest and most intense variety is achieved through planning and preparation. That is, he was not just allowed to waltz onto a NASA spacecraft simply by being a former fighter pilot with an engineering degree. Rather, he underwent intensive study and practice.

Astronauts typically train roughly seven hours underwater for each hour of their intended spacewalk. Hadfield trained via a combination of underwater practice, virtual simulations, and by learning everything that there is to know about his spacesuit and how to deal with various scenarios. It was so intensive that, by the time he was ready for the real thing, it didn't feel like anything out of the ordinary. His fears were quelled by having already prepared for most of what could go wrong.[270] Planning and preparing are the best safeguards against fear. But can this be applied to all fears? What about the fear of death?

Death is an eventuality that many of us ignore out of fear, though it's perhaps one of, if not the chief, executor of all fears. Indeed, researchers within the paradigm of terror-management theory (TMT) hypothesize that fear of death is a fundamental human motivation.[271] Ernest Becker, an anthropologist whose work in this area had a significant influence on TMT, believed that the fear of death is not usually present in daily life due to the defense mechanism of "repression." Repression is the process whereby we tuck away a psychologically painful or discomforting truth into our unconscious, thereby protecting ourselves from it. However, once buried in the unconscious, it continues to have adverse effects on our lives while remaining outside of our conscious awareness.[272] TMT researchers have studied the concept of "mortality salience" or "awareness of death"[273] and its effects on human psychological functioning.

The practices used to study mortality salience involve composing essays about death, going to a cemetery to engender thoughts of one's mortality, and contemplating death.[274] The results of many of these studies have shown that willfully activating the often-repressed thoughts about death and bringing them to the surface of our awareness can lead to positive changes in worldview and behavior. Studies have revealed that death awareness heightened impetus to pursue internal ambitions[275] and generated greater desires to pursue intrinsic life goals and priorities.[276] Furthermore, research has found more prosocial attitudes and a higher propensity to engage in charitable endeavors among those who induce mortality salience.[277]

Early Buddhism recognized this existential terror. According to the Maraṇasati Sutta, a part of Buddhist scripture called *Aṅguttara Nikāya*, the Buddha is said to have encouraged his followers to contemplate their mortality. In fact, in Buddhism there is a meditative practice called "Maransati," meaning "mindfulness of death," which is intended to inoculate you against the fear of death.[278] There hasn't been much research conducted on Maransati, but some believe it can be helpful. Indeed, it stands to reason that, if the contemplation of our mortality can positively affect existential anxieties, then cultivating mindful awareness of death through the practice of Maransati may also be of some benefit.[279]

15

Self-Discipline

"He who conquers others is strong; he who conquers himself is mighty."
Lao Tzu[280]

During one of his talks, my Zen teacher, Ken Byalin, said something that stuck with me for most of my life. After a moment of silence, he said, "Do first that which you fear most." So simple, yet so profound. Although not a new idea, this little titbit of wisdom has been indispensable to my time management and organizational skills, both personally and professionally. Often, we flourish at engaging in all the endeavors which exist in our comfort zone. The moment we are tasked with something that lives outside of it, we become paralyzed and, in some cases, unable to act. Often, this takes the form of procrastination, that phenomenon we are all familiar with, in which we save the uncomfortable task for last, or many times, avoid it entirely.

One pathway to personal growth is via venturing beyond the horizon of our sphere of safety and into less familiar but ultimately life-enhancing territory. This voyage, that is, the facing of our fears, involves something which causes many of us to become immobile. When we elect to succumb to our fears, we subsequently limit our potential. And make no mistake, surrender is always a choice. When we face our fears, we broaden our potential for further growth. Many of us would rather not deal with that sort of discomfort; we may have tried but swiftly returned to our comfort zones when encountering failure or pain. Often, this becomes a self-fulfilling prophecy, and failure becomes a reminder of why we should have never left our comfort zones from the outset.

However, it's these same limiting thought patterns that imprison us in our comfort zones and that ultimately bring us back to them. Those who remain unable to perceive their limitations as opportunities for growth are often equally unable to realize that they are the source of their own suffering. The primary issue involved is inaccurate expectations; pain and failure are necessary for the growing process. Indeed, the proponents of self-improvement often encourage people to continue to raise their standards and expectations.[281]

Many of our limitations exist nowhere else but our own minds, so it would help to cultivate a deep understanding of ourselves. The act of pushing past your mental boundaries generates more self-knowledge, and more self-understanding allows you to ascend to new heights; this is a cyclical process that embodies the process of personal growth. The *intentional* act of stepping outside of your comfort zone teaches you more about who you are. As you continue to raise the proverbial "bar" incrementally, you begin to develop more confidence in your abilities. The process of growth requires breaking down the person you thought you were and rebuilding into the person you want to be.

To be sure, stepping outside your comfort zone is scary; it involves acknowledging and facing fear, uncertainty, and discomfort. As with anything, there are inherent risks involved, though it's not risk or failure which matters most; what fundamentally colors the way one will perceive risky experiences is the extent to which it's done freely. One can achieve mastery through incremental and willful ventures beyond the stagnant realms of familiarity and into the unknown.

The Road Less Traveled

"I shall be telling this with a sigh
  Somewhere ages and ages hence:
  Two roads diverged in a wood, and I –
  I took the one less traveled by,
  And that has made all the difference."
Robert Frost [282]

I have observed a propensity for modern personal improvement mentors and coaches to, perhaps unknowingly, promulgate a superficial and potentially unhealthy form of improvement. However, the principles from which these movements have originated can be traced back to Aristotelian virtue ethics and Buddhist spiritual practices, none of which are superficial but rather vastly profound. They offer ways of living that extend far beyond their surface-level prescriptions, which, at best, offer unrealistic advantages like "unlimited success" and "endless wealth." At worst, they are nothing more than get-rich-quick schemes, in which the only person getting rich is the one selling the gimmick.

How many times have we tried and failed to maintain a commitment? Diets, exercise programs, and all of our New Year's resolutions eventually go down the tubes as the novelty of our new resolve fades. At any rate, true exemplars of our ancient ancestors' wise philosophies aim to encourage delaying of gratification, altruism, walking the middle path, finding meaning, and cultivating purpose. To truly free ourselves from the suffering brought on by living only for immediate gratification, we must think of concepts like delaying gratification and walking the middle path as *ways of life* rather than *temporary trends*.

It's a basic axiom that most of us wish to reduce the more unnecessary and needless sufferings we endure. Due to our entropic universe, we will inexorably experience adversity whether we want to or not; and while pain and problems are necessary for growth, there is a way of living which reduces avoidable and often self-caused problems. An integral property of this way of life is self-discipline.[283] It's very simple to understand but not always easy to put into practice. But, before we get deeper into self-discipline, it's important to touch upon its opposite: instant gratification.

The Puzzle of Instant Gratification

If there is anything we've learned from the study of human behavior, it's that people will always prefer pleasure now over pleasure later. However, this predisposition stands in direct opposition to self-discipline. To illustrate how instant gratification is adversarial to self-control, we will start with the perhaps more extreme example of alcoholism and problem drinking. Indeed, alcohol addiction, or addiction in general, is a perfect exemplar of a breakdown in self-control systems. In behavioral psychology, it's considered a general fact that a painful stimulus should decrease the frequency of any given behavior, while a rewarding stimulus will increase or reinforce it.[284] So, it seems a perplexing question as to why we continue to drink alcohol to the point of hangovers, blackouts, vomiting, and other ills which often stem from over-consumption, especially those suffering from alcoholism. Wouldn't it seem that a hangover and its associated unpleasantries like headaches, nausea, vomiting, and dizziness, which are all uncomfortable and even painful experiences, would prompt us to avoid over-consumption in the future?

Or take gambling, for instance. It doesn't take a behaviorist to realize that casinos, which exploit knowledge of human psychology, are designed to take much more money than they give.[285] We all know, or at least have heard, of someone who frequents a casino; they almost certainly (and knowingly) lose their money. We become perplexed as to why they would not just stop the first time they lost; wouldn't it be consistent with operant conditioning for them to quit after their first big defeat and the associated pain of being in debt? Indeed, when puzzling over this phenomenon, "touching a hot stove," a phrase colloquially used to describe the behaviorist notion of punishment, springs to mind. Shouldn't an aversive stimulus reduce rather than reinforce a behavior?

Indeed, in our society, we are often at a loss to understand why addicts keep touching the proverbial "hot stove." Worse, we are often critical of them as well. It's sometimes hard for us to reconcile the extreme cases of self-destruction that typically result from addiction without blaming it on "bad morals," a less mentally-taxing position to take. We are often unaware that we are struggling with our own inner demons that are perhaps equally difficult to control but less socially unacceptable or even noticeable.

This problem of overindulgence keeps us trapped in a downward spiral, as we perpetually attempt to gratify ourselves at the expense of our future, never fully realizing that after these transient pleasures fade, and they always do, we are left hungrier than before. It's not just the behaviors associated with addiction, cravings, and insatiable excess that we tend to question. Indeed, we wonder why some people repeatedly engage in criminal acts. While there are many external forces at play, some theoretical frameworks can help elucidate seemingly inexplicable and ineffective behaviors, and aid us in understanding how to change our own, as will be discussed in the next section.

Delayed Punishment and the "Hot Stove"

Operant conditioning, as described by pioneering psychologist B.F. Skinner, reveals that when a painful stimulus occurs immediately following a behavior, it's almost certain (with few exceptions) to reduce or inhibit that behavior (e.g., extinction). So, why then, if drugs, alcohol, and other addictions cause pain or adverse consequences, do so many people become addicted?

At some level, we all seem to desire freedom from our problems, addictions, maladies, and woes. It's also apparent that we desire more pleasure than pain. Yet, despite this, the paradox is that addiction, in particular, and destructive habits, in general, are evidence that we also choose pain. Indeed, we consider it a violation of our fundamental nature as humans when observing people engaging in actions that are sure to cause problems. If painful consequences reduce behavior, how come the consequences of addiction don't stop the addict? However, the reality of addiction and addictive behavior is much more complex than we realize. Though we think it runs counter to reason and basic psychology, several factors influence these behaviors which are common to us all and which run contrary to commonly held and judgmental views of addiction.

Let us imagine, for example, that a hangover immediately follows from your first alcoholic drink or that a gambler loses their entire life savings on just one crank of the slot. In this scenario, it becomes harder to imagine a recurrence of such an endeavor. That is, if consequences that are usually delayed occur immediately following the first use or abuse of any given drug, it stands to reason that few would repeat it. It seems that when small punishments occur within the context of potentially greater rewards, people continue to engage in unhealthy behaviors. However, being perpetually myopic or "nearsighted" prevents the addict or gambler from seeing that the gradual accumulation of small punishments will eventually lead to greater suffering in the future. Therefore, the "hot stove" analogy is not sufficient to explain how addictive behaviors persist despite the pain they cause, not unless this particular stove delivered an instant reward, followed by a delayed burn. If this were the case, I would bet that hot stoves would become a common cause of visits to the hospital emergency room (and stove addiction[286] recovery centers).

Designed by evolution, our primitive reward system gives us feelings of pleasure in the immediate moment, not in the future. This served as a protective function for early humans, as they relied on increasing attainment of resources that would help them survive while reducing contact with environmental threats and dangers. Thus, it would have been helpful to experience pleasure immediately upon retrieval of resources that supported survival and reproduction. However, this development, which occurred early on in our ancestral lineage, set us up for the kinds of problems we currently face with addiction, impulsivity, and self-control.

We evolved to be nearly indifferent toward future rewards because they are too far away temporally to trigger dopaminergic reward centers; this is why the hedonic pleasures we encounter during experiences – like sex, spending money, and eating tasty food – feel vastly different than the pleasures that delaying gratification brings. Scientific studies have validated the notion that the further away in time a reward will be given, the less desirable it becomes. For example, in one study, research participants reported that rewards they experienced as being too far away in time were not worth the wait.[287]

However, we don't have to study any scientific literature to understand this fact; most have learned this from experience. Indeed, anyone who has ever worked toward a challenging goal, like starting an intense diet and exercise program, for example, can attest to the fact that it's much more desirable to consume a pizza or pastry the moment it's offered, than to eat a salad, run on the treadmill, or perform endless weight-lifting repetitions knowing that the reward of losing weight and increased fitness is weeks in the future. We can all agree that present moment indulgence is a much more intense feeling than the pleasures associated with the eventual positive results of our diet and exercise program.

Furthermore, eating cookies in the present will feel better, qualitatively, than the feeling associated with the benefits of improved health and physique that may come from abstaining from sugary foods; this puts us at a disadvantage because if the easy path feels better than the hard path, we will often take the easy path. However, we know that, in most cases, what is easier *now* will cause hardship *later.* Unfortunately, that knowledge alone is rarely enough to help us change course.

The Savior within the Self

"You gain strength, courage and confidence by every experience in which you really stop to look fear in the face. You are able to say to yourself, 'I have lived through this horror. I can take the next thing that comes along.' You must do the thing you think you cannot do."
Eleanor Roosevelt[288]

Beyond problems with addiction and unhealthy habits, there are those of us who aren't finding our decisions and choices are effective in getting us further in life. We all want good things for ourselves like healthy bodies, stable minds, and financial security. We envision our idyllic selves in our minds, yet when put to the test, we tend to do the opposite of what will get us there. Because our neuroanatomy is structured to produce greater pleasures for present moment rewards than future rewards, we struggle endlessly with a dissonant incongruence between our desires and actions.[289] We tend to make *good enough* decisions rather than efficient ones. We tend to defer our problems to our future selves believing they will deal more efficiently with the fallout of our poor choices.[290]

It's perhaps unsurprising that we have cultivated this attitude toward ourselves. There are some aspects of our culture and society which bear some of the blame. For example, when we are children, our parents clean up after us. Usually, as we get older, we develop a sense of responsibility and clean up after ourselves. However, we continue to receive messages from the world around us that "someone else" will take care of our messes. When we finish eating at a restaurant, we leave our dishes for the staff to clean. Our hotel rooms are tended to by housekeeping staff; a room left untidy is spotless upon our return. Spill popcorn in a movie theater? Fear not, someone else will clean it up after we've left. We are taught to defer responsibility, leaving others to deal with debris left in our wake; rarely do we give a second thought to what we leave in disarray. "Someone else will deal with it, and that someone isn't going to be me," we tell ourselves. But what if the mess maker and the cleaner are the same person, i.e., you?

Indeed, research shows that we give about as much regard to our future selves as we do to strangers whose jobs are to clean up after us, which is often very little.[291] It's no wonder we often look back in regret at decisions we wished we would have made but now cannot. It's because our past selves couldn't see us or didn't want to. As we know, the prefrontal cortex is involved in imagining our "future selves."[292] We can begin to make better decisions when the present and future selves are seen as the same.[293] The decisions you do or don't make now will affect you at some point down the road. Even though you don't feel the pain of an unwise decision in the present, the "you" of the future will wish you did. Success in many domains of life is largely contingent upon this ability to care about "future you," as much as you care for "present you."[294]

When I was younger, I imagined that the "me" of the future would be far superior in every aspect to the "me" of the present. The me of the future would be responsible, would save money, and would buy a house. But if the present me could not harness those skills, what made me think that the me of the future would? The process whereby we defer present responsibilities to the future is known as "delay discounting."[295] It is similar to the concept of avoidance discussed in Part Two of this book; fear is seen as the primary cause of avoidance and resistance, the adversary of acceptance of ourselves and our circumstances. Delay discounting is no different; when we are afraid to face reality, we defer difficult challenges to our future selves.[296]

We idealize and romanticize our future selves, thinking of them as the disciplined heroes who will swoop in to save us. We can never be disciplined in the future if we don't begin to discipline ourselves in the present. In our mental projections, our future self always seems to be, in every way, superior to the present self. Each day that goes by, we imagine that "someday" we will harness and embody all of those idealized strengths and qualities we wish we had now. Forever chasing our shadow, we see it right before us but can never quite capture it.

It feels good to think this way, and the reason for this is an insidious one: by imagining a pleasant future while doing nothing to achieve it, we unknowingly give in to the temptations of instant gratification. We want to snuff out the guilt we experience for failing to put forth the effort to attain our higher goals; by imagining that some "super self" will eventually come to our rescue, we absolve ourselves of this guilt, thereby engendering in ourselves a sense of immediate comfort and relief. Somehow, we conjure up notions of a future self with the capacity for divine intervention of the sort that never arrives unless we *become* the intervention.[297]

The Tiger and Its Stripes: Strengthening Self-Control

Neuroscience has come a long way in helping to elucidate the mechanisms of the brain to give us insight into not only *what* is possible with regards to behavior change but also *how* it's possible. For example, studies conducted on children with attention deficit hyperactive disorder (ADHD) show that, at baseline, they are more impulsive than the average child. Researchers have demonstrated that impulsive behaviors can be improved through self-control training. For example, one study demonstrated that when children with ADHD are engaged in a verbal activity, their ability to delay gratification increases.[298] Studies have also shown that training in self-control in one area or task can extend to others.[299] Other research has shown that self-discipline and impulse control involve rewiring our neuroplastic brains, similar to how muscles are strengthened through weightlifting.[300] Indeed, it's possible to strengthen your mind as you strengthen your body. These self-control-enhancing techniques will be elaborated on in the last chapter of Part Three.

Self-Control Restoration

As we have discussed, self-control is defined as the conscious regulation *of* ourselves *by* ourselves. It's the process whereby we intentionally decide to either inhibit or express a desire,[301] bearing a strong similarity to "second-order volition" described in Part One. Self-control is required for almost everything we do, including delaying gratification.[302] Any time you stop yourself from acting on an urge, especially a contextually inappropriate one, you can be said to have exerted self-control (ergo: free will[303]).

Psychologist Roy Baumeister, of Florida State University, found that self-control is a limited mental resource and that, as previously mentioned, it functions similarly to a muscle. Despite our many cognitive abilities, we humans cannot determine when we are "out of gas," in a manner of speaking. We can generate rough approximations, but even those can be hugely inaccurate. Although our minds can sometimes feel like they are without limit, they have a finite amount of energy for any given task before requiring rest and rejuvenation.[304] Indeed, it's believed that the varied kinds of self-control are fueled by a central, though limited, reserve which is drained under certain conditions.[305] For example, Baumeister and colleagues have found that when a circumstance requires multiple instances of self-control exertion, we will have reduced willpower reserves for subsequent tasks, at least in the short-term.[306]

Research has shown that self-control is negatively affected by stress and can be impaired even after the cessation of the stressor.[307] Indeed, over-taxed self-control mechanisms can impair or disrupt functions such as impulse inhibition, thought suppression, and emotion control.[308] Even something as seemingly innocuous as foul smells can cause deficits in self-control functions.[309] Researchers have demonstrated that, while stress can reduce the availability of self-control resources, this internal reserve can also be refueled.[310] Dieting has been known to require a great deal of self-control, and people are more likely to give in to temptation when they are stressed or upset.[311] This fact maps well to an experience we are all familiar with when we're having a stressful day: desiring "comfort food." It's well known that stress can weaken willpower in the area of drug addiction. Recovering alcoholics sometimes relapse if they have trouble managing emotional disturbances.[312] Usually, this occurs when the stressor overwhelms their adaptive capacity. Heroin addicts are also more prone to relapse after having negative experiences or bad moods.[313] Research has also shown that a negative mood can reduce our capacity to delay gratification compared to positive or neutral moods.[314]

All this demonstrates that there are short-term depletions in self-control reserves. This is not surprising as energy is finite under any condition; we shouldn't expect our brains to break the laws of physics. But how can we strengthen our self-control reserves? Researchers designed an experiment to test the "willpower strengthening" hypothesis and see if self-control training combined with rest would increase our capacity for self-control exertion.

In this experiment, for two weeks, participants were given exercises designed to train their willpower capacity like mood regulation, using a meal diary, and posture correction. Afterward, these participants were shown to exhibit enhanced ability to clutch a handgrip for a duration that exceeded those who were not given willpower training exercises. These findings were interpreted as confirmation of the capacity for long-term self-control enhancements via training, similar to improving muscle strength at a gym.[315] Though this should be taken with a cautionary notice, as the continual taxing of self-control reserves, without adequate rest, can cause emotional exhaustion and attention burnout.

* * *

In the journey of life, we all must, at one time or another, contend with an unavoidable trade-off, namely, pleasure now, for pain later, or pain now, for reward later. However, we've seen that many worthwhile achievements usually require some degree of discipline and sacrifice to benefit our future. In order to practice and improve self-discipline, we must develop the habit of delaying gratification; living in this way ensures us a greater tomorrow. In chapter eighteen, I will discuss some methods for cultivating greater self-discipline. Next, we will begin an exploration of problem-solving.

16

Problem-Solving

The Blueprints of Ambition

There comes the point in everyone's life in which the universe tests them. We are continually presented with challenges from the time we are born until we pass on; this is an unavoidable fact of life. However, problems aren't inherently bad; they can be opportunities to grow. Within the ethos of "change," motivational speakers, gurus, and spiritual leaders all generally take the position that self-betterment is mostly a matter of error correction – more specifically, adjusting our course in the direction of becoming our "best self" or the "best version of ourself." When a solvable problem exists, developing a persistent and determined attitude toward finding a solution is generally considered a path to happiness and well-being. There can be no growth without challenge.

Things we usually consider bad, like pain, failure, and fear, are all required for growth; this is evident when we take our first steps. We start crawling, but we don't just accept we cannot walk like our God-like caregivers; indeed, we must eventually learn to walk. But no child leaps from crawling to walking without first taking a few falls, at least not in my experience. Indeed, this is one of the first circumstances we refuse to accept; the first problem we learn to solve.

In this way, we learn, from very early on, that failure is only a temporary state, provided we remain determined and persistent. We learn that to stay within our comfort zone is to become stagnant. To avoid pain is to relinquish pleasure, and to avoid failure is to prevent success. At this stage, we are given the very first blueprints for ambition. We would not be standing here (or walking) today if we had given up on this mission. At no point did we think it was time to quit because of our failures. Indeed, failure was not even a notion in our minds; we dealt with the pain and persevered until we got what we wanted. This childlike, unwavering confidence is what we should all remember that we once had and can have again. This persistence in the direction of our larger intentions, where failing is only a temporary setback, is the ultimate state of freedom.

So, one of the very first problems we learn to solve is how to walk instead of crawl, but from that point on, our problems usually get more complex. As you read this book, you may be thinking about how much better your life would be if you had no more problems or if you had never experienced problems in the past. Indeed, you may also be resentfully rebuking my claim that problems are gifts. I hold no argument against the claim that we can do without certain problems. I don't doubt that some extremes of human suffering could be eradicated from the timeline of history without significantly impacting civilization, except to reduce the needless torments people have experienced.

However, there are ways to transform the way we think about adversity and learn to use it to our advantage rather than allow it to defeat us. We can reach a state in which, to a large degree, our suffering can be alleviated and transformed by actively understanding, learning from, and changing our reality. Indeed, we will see how our thoughts and behaviors can either defeat us or empower us. Many experiments lend credence to the notion that positive emotions improve negative mood states and neutralize the effects of stress on the body.[316]

The Strength of Our Problems

For some reason, as we get older, we don't keep the same persistent attitude toward solving our problems as we did when we were learning how to take our first steps. Often, as adults, we encounter problems in our lives, and, to a greater or lesser extent, we avoid them once they become slightly more uncomfortable than expected. Many of us think that life is already painful enough; why add more pain on top by confronting them? We avoid facing our problems, preferring to stuff them away in a mental filing cabinet, or in a dark recess of our minds. Some of us are aware that, by doing this, we are gifting our future selves a world of torment, though we take temporary comfort in the moment of our problem deferral. Others remain unaware and presume that ignoring the problem will cause it to evaporate on its own.

To be fair to us all, life *is* difficult, and chronic and severe stress, as we have seen in previous chapters, can tax and overwhelm a person's ability to problem-solve; this becomes a cyclical process as the usual and familiar strategies we formerly employed to deal with life's difficulties are no longer enough. The subsequent hopelessness often results in depression and immobility. Living for so long in our comfort zones, we become well versed in the familiar landscape and its peaks and valleys.[317] However, this makes us unprepared for the almost certain times when we will be forced, for whatever reason, to leave the safety of our former repose. I have often reluctantly found myself on the receiving end of unwanted presents that my past self has gifted me as a direct result of avoiding a problem.

* * *

I often hear people say things like, "You don't need to get a college degree to be smart; anyone can learn things in a library or on the internet," and, "College is not necessary if you *really* want to make money." Indeed, when I first graduated college, I would sometimes wonder if I had retained anything I had learned. Moreover, if I happened to recall a fact, I'd then puzzle to determine its practical applicability to my life. How will I build credit with my knowledge of valence electrons? How can I mortgage a house with information about the Baroque music era? How can I learn to reduce stress and solve complex interpersonal problems with polynomials?

Clearly, it's not always easy to see the applicability of what we learn in school. There is certainly truth to the claim that you don't need a college degree to be smart, to make money, or to start a business. However, to consider college, or school in general, to be fruitless is to misunderstand its true value.

If you are pursuing a bachelor's degree, you will have

problem-solved your way through 120 credits worth of courses by the time you graduate. Thus, what you learn – and what you can apply to your life – are the problem-solving strategies that have been built up within you over the prior four (or more) years. When you graduate, it's almost certain that you would have (consciously or unconsciously) developed your own style for managing time and organizing your life to achieve academic success. You've no doubt learned to enlist the help of internal and external resources, the likes of which are valuable and applicable in virtually any other area of life.

Moreover, you have learned how to solve difficult problems by passing difficult courses. You have probably learned how to tolerate the arduous agony of studying for a class you loathed or in which you could see no value. This is a skill we all require as the world is full of mundane obligations. Whether it's starting a business, buying a house, building credit, fixing a faucet, or climbing a mountain, the development of self-confidence gained from learning how to solve problems is a tool that is arguably more valuable than any of the "facts" you might have learned in your courses.

Many of our difficulties are equations that we already know how to solve. We can draw on this ability in tough times simply by asking ourselves to recall a period when we persevered and triumphed through seemingly impossible or untenable adversity. We can learn to deal with present conflicts or dilemmas by recalling the skills, resources, and support we used in prior predicaments.

The ability to problem-solve, which we learn from infancy, stays with us throughout our lives. Unfortunately, we forget how to use these abilities, but we have them, nonetheless. It's now a matter of awakening the dormant potential, believing in ourselves, and realizing that we can access inherent capabilities, no matter how difficult the problem. All that is required is to embody the childlike persistence we all started with, allowing us to take our first few steps. We can use that persistence to confidently and freely walk through whatever challenges life throws our way.

17

Persistence

Making Friends with Failure

"It's not the critic who counts; not the man who points out how the strong man stumbles, or where the doer of deeds could have done them better. The credit belongs to the man who is actually in the arena, whose face is marred by dust and sweat and blood; who strives valiantly; who errs, who comes short again and again, because there is no effort without error and shortcoming; but who does actually strive to do the deeds; who knows great enthusiasms, the great devotions; who spends himself in a worthy cause; who at the best knows in the end the triumph of high achievement, and who at the worst, if he fails, at least fails while daring greatly, so that his place shall never be with those cold and timid souls who neither know victory nor defeat."
 Theodore Roosevelt[318]

"It is hard to fail, but it is worse never to have tried to succeed."
 Theodore Roosevelt[319]

As Teddy Roosevelt says, it's better to try and fail than to have never tried at all. In this sense, it's not in the event of failing after having put in the effort, but rather, it is in never *attempting* to attain your higher goals and desires that we are truly defeated.

Like many before me, I've come to see the mind as the first and perhaps most important obstacle to overcome regarding any given aspiration. Many times, when we fantasize about the things we want in life, and when we begin to imagine ourselves taking steps toward that target, we also tend to imagine the infinite ways we could fail rather than succeed. And, for most of us, just thinking about them is enough to stop us in our tracks. We quit before we even begin, and it all occurs not in reality but rather in a split-second thought process; our ambitions never get a fighting chance.

Failure, in my experience, often arises from this internal turmoil rather than from external struggles. The first obstacle we face shares the exact birthplace as our fears; they are cut from the same cloth. Indeed, the impediment known as "doubt," which we must surpass to achieve anything of value, originates nowhere else but in our mind. If you have the power to create both your dreams and your doubts, then you have the power to choose which one you will follow.

This all-too-familiar occurrence, whereby we quit before we begin, unfolds in the following manner. First, we envision working toward an undertaking that few ever dare to; then, almost immediately, rather than considering all the possible ways of attaining this objective, our minds instead reveal to us all the possible ways it can go wrong. It tells us why we aren't good enough, attractive enough, smart enough, or talented enough. This is called self-defeat; it's our mind attempting to protect us from pain. It essentially tells us that we are comfortable enough right where we are and that taking risks could interrupt that. However, while it makes sense to want to protect ourselves from pain, we are stronger and can handle more than we think.

Certainly, it's important to weigh the associated risks and benefits of any endeavor. Indeed, preparation and foresight are fundamental aspects of any achievement; stumbling blindly through the wilds of any journey is a recipe for disaster. On the other hand, it's impossible to avoid risk altogether, at least if we want to attain anything worthwhile in our lives.

One of the ways in which we allow self-defeat to envelop us is by viewing failure as adversity instead of as a necessary step toward growth. Instead of viewing challenges as opportunities for development and transformation, we see them as reasons to quit before we begin. The hedonic notions of maximizing pleasure and minimizing pain, influenced and promoted by Hegelian thinkers, fails to consider the indispensability of adversity. The proverbial "bumps in the road" are essential for any kind of achievement. There can be no learning or growth unless there is resistance. Although trite, it's true that if there is "no pain," there is "no gain." Hardship can either cause us to throw in the towel or become greater than we were before we started.

What I consider to be partially responsible for fostering self-defeat are misperceptions propagated by highlight reels on social media. Often, when the news and media report success stories,[320] they rarely share the innumerable struggles encountered on the path toward it. They only show the finished product, which has the unfortunate side effect of discouraging rather than inspiring others. Indeed, this produces a falsehood that some people possess inherent talents and aptitudes which enable them to achieve a rare status in life that others are utterly closed off from. In this way, we are unable to perceive the whole picture, and left to feel as though our higher ambitions are for other, more "capable" people. Moreover, we begin to believe that pain and failure are indications of our ineptitude and evidence that we should quit while we are ahead. After all, we see that such incompetence is not a quality our idols possess; thus, we think this must be proof of our inadequacy.

No, failure is not an accidental feature of achievement, nor an expression of our inherent value or capabilities (or lack thereof), but rather it's an essential aspect of success.

In this view, the only truly "bad" experience or circumstance is one in which nothing can be gained, learned, or from which no alternative perspective or purpose can be derived. It's not wanton failure and pain in isolation that creates purpose, though; rather, it's generated in our ability to adapt and find meaning from our misery.

Moreover, there are countless stories of incredible feats of human will to draw on; stories in which success had its roots in suffering. Through pain, these people have learned how to rewrite the script of their reality. In fact, they often use their pain to thrust them far beyond the bounds of what was considered "possible." They have broken the conventional paradigms and previously-held views regarding the unimaginable; thus, they have paved a clear path for others to do the same. In truth, *we* are those *other*, more "capable" people. We are separated from achieving similar successes only by a thin boundary called fear. Beyond this self-imposed perimeter fence we are otherwise indistinguishable from those who have what they want. It's an invisible barrier that only we can see, and only we can transcend.

From Pain to Purpose

"Persistence alone is omnipotent."
    Calvin Coolidge[321]

I have always believed that if you never give up, then you can never fail. However, we know that the real world doesn't always map neatly to our theories and principles. Though, what can be said is that the fundamental difference between those who give up versus those who continue after failure is that those who continue have not lost sight of their ultimate purpose. As we saw in the case of Viktor Frankl, having a purpose can free your mind from the horrors of imprisonment; it can transform you amid traumatic events and extinguish your thoughts of giving up, thereby activating your drive and persistence. Let us examine a few of those who seem to break the boundaries of generally-accepted physical and mental limits and learn what brought them to where they are now. For brevity, only two examples will be explored as they are sufficient to convey the main point.

Tommy Caldwell

Tommy Caldwell, an American rock climber, is a fitting example of someone who used his anguish to propel himself beyond the traditionally-accepted limits of his sport. He used the pain he experienced from a traumatic event and, later, a freak accident as motivation to push far beyond the boundaries of what was thought possible by experts in the fields of both medicine and rock climbing. In a documentary called *The Dawn Wall*, Caldwell recalls how he and his cohorts were taken hostage by rebels in Kyrgyzstan for six days while on a climbing expedition.

Caldwell recounts a story of pushing one of the rebels off a cliff in order to save himself and his friends. He and his fellow climbers watched the rebel fall, bounce off a ledge, and disappear, presumably to his death. Caldwell's girlfriend at the time, Beth Rodden, describes how, upon their return, she became traumatized and had difficulties processing what had happened in Kyrgyzstan. She began having nightmares and difficulty sleeping. However, Caldwell did not report such issues and quickly returned to rock climbing.

Why did they have two different reactions to the experience? Of course, there can be several relevant biological, psychological, and social factors, though we can make some assertions through the lens of freedom and self-determination. For example, when taken hostage, Caldwell was able to exert control over his circumstance, which led to saving his life and the lives of his friends. Rodden, on the other hand, while being saved and having escaped physically intact, may have had an external perceived locus of control. Seeing herself as the unwilling participant in an uncontrollable situation, she felt helpless, if not for the swift but risky actions of Caldwell. In this example, we are granted insight into the differences in outcomes between the intentional exertion of will versus the involuntary constraint of will during highly stressful and life-threatening situations.

About a year after the situation in Kyrgyzstan, Caldwell accidentally cut off his finger while working with a power saw and could not have it reattached. He described how the doctor that treated him, who also happened to be a rock climber, advised Caldwell to give up his profession as a free climber. Based on his medical knowledge and rock-climbing expertise, the doctor had considered a future of climbing for Caldwell to be an impossibility. However, Caldwell, instead of giving up, felt empowered by the prospect of continuing to climb. He subsequently began to retrain his hand and develop the necessary muscles required to begin climbing again. Through his unyielding persistence, he eventually climbed the Dawn Wall, a 3,000-foot section of El Capitan, the famous vertical rock formation located in Yosemite National Park and considered by many professional climbers to be unclimbable.

By doing this, Caldwell not only defied expert medical opinion regarding the limits of human physiology, especially in relation to rock climbing, but he also defied the consensus of expert rock climbers. This was truly an unimaginable feat which unequivocally demonstrated what can be achieved when we remain persistent.[322] It must be mentioned, though, that Caldwell did not emerge psychologically unscathed from the kidnapping after having accessed some mystical power of "inner freedom"; indeed, he too was in many ways haunted by that experience. Living a life of autonomy and self-determination doesn't grant one immunity from illness and injury. However, he was able to use the experience to empower himself and transform his pain into purpose.[323]

David Goggins

The next person of interest who I think exemplifies the power of persistence through pain and failure is David Goggins, an American ultramarathon runner, triathlete, ultradistance cyclist, author, and former Navy SEAL. In his book, *Master Your Mind, Defy the Odds*, Goggins describes the hellscape of his childhood and adolescence, having grown up poor, experiencing abuse, and subsisting on welfare checks. He talks about being broken and suffering regular beatings from his father, who he referred to as "the devil himself." He would have to stay home from school as he would be peppered with bruises all across his body, and he learned to dissociate in hopes of becoming invisible and being spared of his father's abuse.

He recounts how the consistent physical abuse caused him to give up hope. At times, he could only watch helplessly as his father relentlessly beat and abused his mother, which was unfortunately a frequent occurrence. He wrote about having been bullied and verbally assaulted with racist and derogatory insults. He became so strung out by toxic stress from being abused that he eventually developed a stutter.

Despite the abhorrent conditions of his upbringing, Goggins eventually accomplished seemingly impossible feats of human strength and endurance and has broken many world records. He formerly held the world record for the most pull-ups in twenty-four hours. Additionally, in 2005, he entered a twenty-four-hour ultramarathon in San Diego in which he was able to run 101 miles in nineteen hours and six minutes, despite having previously never run a marathon.[324] How did Goggins go from severe violence, poverty, emotional abuse, bullying, racism, and chronic stress, to breaking world records and achieving this level of success?

In his book, Goggins offers some insight into his mental state. He talks about how he used the pain he experienced in his early years to develop a "calloused mind" and transcend his limits.

He recalls a period of his life during the first phase of his Navy SEAL training, known as "Hell Week," where he had gone through extreme obstacles meant to test the apex of human mental and physical endurance. After having completed several challenges, sustaining an injury in the process, he recalls a moment when the extraordinary pain seemed to have evaporated and allowed him to break through the constraints of his anguish. He attributed this to his calloused mind, recalling his past challenges and refocusing on his former achievements.

Goggins describes how remembering the suffering you have experienced can eject you from self-limiting thoughts, enabling you to break through your limits. He believes that this process of refusing to quit, of remaining persistent, and of not giving in to one's pain, helps us to tap into the automatic fight-or-flight response. But rather than allowing this response to control you, instead, you are behind the wheel. In this way, Goggins conveys his method of harnessing our physiology's incredible power, which mostly lies dormant. He believes that people can learn to control their minds and access greater strength. To him, self-doubt is eliminated when we remind ourselves that we have always survived, despite "fear" and "doubt."[325]

Goggins doesn't necessarily encourage others to be *the* best, but rather to be *your* best. He is committed to a life of continually pushing himself beyond the safety and security of his comfort zone. He relentlessly pursues personal improvement and aims to test and surpass his limits. What is the limit to what he can achieve? What is the limit to what anyone can achieve? The jury is still out on this; however, Goggins is wholly engaged in the process of defining what that limit is for him. He serves as a testament to the fact that pain can be overcome with conscious intention, effort, and belief in the self. Moreover, his life and achievements demonstrate that when we believe we have reached the limits of our abilities, in fact, we have only just begun to tap into our ultimate potential.

The reason for having chosen to discuss those who have achieved success in athletic fields, rather than in finance or any other area, is because athletics has one of the broadest research bases. Furthermore, the same mindset that is required for success in athletics is needed for almost any other endeavor. Thus, if we can understand the blueprint for "limit-breaking" concerning physical achievements, we can extend that to other areas of our lives. There are very few peer-reviewed articles or experimental studies which have probed the nature of billionaires' success. Besides, I don't think that the accumulation of financial wealth is necessarily the ideal or the only kind of success. Ultimately, success is defined by the individual.

PERSISTENCE

From Adversity to Advantage

"I find that the harder I work, the more luck I seem to have."
  Thomas Jefferson[326]

Pain and adversity are often seen in a negative light and as something to be avoided entirely. Indeed, pain is something we are typically socialized to fear and flee from rather than face. As I mentioned above, we tend to see the highlight reels of people's lives on social media and elsewhere. We witness the fame and fortune of celebrities and are seldom privy to the many struggles encountered before achieving success. Usually, the message conveyed is that successful people are just lucky or happen to find themselves in favorable social and financial positions. Suppose we knew more about the adversity and less about the trivial aspects of fame. In that case, I think more people would feel empowered to access the power they have within.

Indeed, people who have attained success may, on the surface, appear to have done so effortlessly, but behind every true success story is a world of pain, failure, and adversity. An attitude of persistence doesn't mean that we will never encounter adversity or failure; rather, it ensures that failure will always be temporary. If we have learned anything thus far, it's that opposites are inseparable. It's not that we must always "grin and bear it" either. Of course, there will be times when pure endurance is demanded, but it's better to make friends with hardship and failure than to resist them. In earlier chapters, the idea of post-traumatic growth was discussed, and when it comes to the topic of change, the same line of thinking applies to the lesser (or greater) frustrations we encounter on our path toward our goals. Once we shift our perspective, we will begin to see most of our impediments less as a ferocious beast blocking our path and more so as an irritating fly, buzzing around and creating but a momentary distraction from the bigger picture.

Though it must be mentioned that the previous examples represent an extreme form of personal challenge that extends beyond the realm of what is usually required to develop self-awareness and self-understanding, it's not a requirement to achieve superhuman abilities or subject ourselves to potentially dangerous conditions to achieve personal growth. The athletes who describe their trials, tribulations, and triumphs, highlight the power of pain and the energy of suffering, which, when transformed, can be used for incredible and unimaginable feats. The abilities laid out for us by those brave enough to share their stories with the world act as the blueprints that can help bring us to new heights in our lives.

Though I say that if you never quit, you never fail, this doesn't mean that we should pursue our goals at the expense of our health. The key is to know when to pause, reevaluate, and then continue; this is the essence of persistence. Similar to how intentional effort toward developing a sense of agency during a traumatic event helps us to combat adversity, I believe the effort we take to feel safe, in control, and autonomous in our pursuits prevents *failure* from becoming *defeat.*

18

Methods of Change

At the end of Part Two, I listed several methods that I would consider as aligning with modes of acceptance. Those techniques or practices help us to accept aspects of ourselves or our circumstances and would be categorized accordingly. Similarly, techniques and practices that help us to learn to change ourselves or our circumstances, I would consider methods of change.

I consider these distinctions partially arbitrary because there is a considerable amount of overlap between the techniques in terms of what they ultimately provide to the practitioner. For example, yoga can be a method of change; however, it has a meditative component and thus can be considered an acceptance-based practice. If we consider self-improvement to belong to the dimension of "change," as I do, it's easy to see how the following methods help achieve that goal. The categorizations exist, although they aren't meant to be entirely precise, to provide a general guideline for balancing the order and chaos within our life and ultimately finding inner freedom and capacity for choice. In the end, what matters most is not what labels can be placed where but rather how we can use these practices to improve our lives.

Sleep Hygiene, Habits, and Sleep Deprivation

When discussing ways to get the most out of your life with energy, alertness, and clarity, there is no more important human habit than sleep. In 1989, a study was conducted in which experimenters wanted to determine the effects of sleep deprivation on living organisms by preventing lab rats from sleeping. They exposed ten rats to sleep deprivation and found that the rats that had been entirely prevented from sleeping died within just one month.[327]

It's also believed that sleep affects the immune system, and some data indicates that those who got a good night's sleep after receiving a vaccination were found to have had greater levels of antigen-specific immune defense than those who didn't sleep.[328] Some studies have found that sleep deprivation is also a risk factor for obesity and diabetes.[329]

Epidemiological research findings suggest that poor sleeping habits are associated with an increased risk of heart attack and strokes.[330] Sleep loss and poor sleep quality also negatively affect psychiatric functioning. Research has shown that people with persistent sleep deficits tend to report problems such as depression, substance use, anxiety, psychological issues,[331] and low self-esteem.[332] More and more, we are learning how important sleep is for restoration and healthy functioning.

In 2003, sleep researchers found that, when given a psychomotor test, people who reported only three hours of sleep per day had declining scores over a week and continued to have poorer functioning over as many as three days of regular sleep restoration. Moreover, the group that performed superiorly to all other participants in the experiment got approximately nine hours of sleep. People who think they can function on little sleep may be able to do so in the short term, but this demonstrates that sleep deprivation takes a heavy toll on mental and physical functioning over the long haul.[333]

Getting Started:

For years, debates concerning how much sleep someone should get each night have been raging on, but they all generally converge on a basic average of between eight to ten hours of sleep per night to support maximum performance.[334] For quality sleep, the US National Institute of Aging suggests regulating your sleep cycle by going to sleep and waking up at the same time every day (including weekends.) Also, they recommend avoiding taking naps close to bedtime, avoiding light from TV or cellphones, and abstaining from large meals, alcohol, and caffeine close to bedtime.[335]

Diet and Nutrition

Next is proper diet and nutrition. Research on the role of diet and nutrition on health and fitness continues to emerge and reveal that what we consume has a major impact on our mental and physical functioning. Often our diet can make or break our health and overall fitness more than exercise (although sleep trumps them both). But what exactly is a healthy diet? There are innumerable books devoted to proper diet, some of which agree with each other and many of which do not. It seems we have not quite gotten a handle on what the magic combination is. Indeed, some suggest that there is no one-size-fits-all diet and that everyone needs an individual, person-centered diet. While I think there is some truth to this claim, evaluating particular diet philosophies is unnecessary for the matter at hand. Rather, I will discuss diet as it relates to mental and physical functioning and some general emerging guidelines that can help us to feel better.

Probiotics and the Gut-Brain Axis

Within the last ten years, much research has emerged about the gut and the central nervous system, commonly referred to as the "gut-brain axis," and its connection to mental illness and the immune system. Probiotics are microorganisms normally found in fermented foods, like yogurt, kombucha, and kefir. There is evidence that psychological stress can exacerbate gastrointestinal permeability and cause imbalances within the microbiome, which is theorized to cause several physical illnesses and psychiatric illnesses. Moreover, emotional disturbances have been linked to alterations within the gut microbiome and comorbidities between mental illness and gastrointestinal maladies. It's thought that the therapeutic benefit of probiotics lies in restoring the natural gut bacteria in cases where there are microbial imbalances that can occur from stress or other reasons. Several studies have found improvements in mood symptoms like anxiety and depression among those who consumed probiotics. Along with probiotics, supplementing your diet with fish oil (containing omega-3 fatty acids) and vitamins D and B has been found to have a host of positive mental and physical benefits.

Healthy Diets

Researchers have found that Mediterranean and Japanese diets are some of the healthiest in the world. Unsurprisingly, these diets contain more whole foods rather than heavily processed or refined foods, and they naturally contain the previously mentioned vitamins, fatty acids and healthy bacteria. The Mediterranean and Japanese diets are high in natural foods like fruits and vegetables, grains, and lean protein sources and low in dairy and meat, although they don't exclude them.

Getting Started:

Though some research suggests that personalized diets will be the nutritional advice of the future,[336] we aren't quite there yet. Taken together, it seems the evidence points to the fact that diets that have shown some beneficial effects are those which, whether Mediterranean, Japanese, or otherwise, encourage whole, natural foods and a reduction or elimination of highly processed and refined foods.[337] Research suggests that these diets can, along with regular medications and medical advice, positively impact cardiovascular disease,[338] cancer,[339] type 2 diabetes,[340] and dementia.[341]

Exercise

Next on our list is exercise. Perhaps no activity has received more attention regarding ameliorating depressive symptoms and improving mood (without using traditional means like medication and therapy) than exercise. It's well-known but bears repeating that research has shown the beneficial antidepressant effects of exercise,[342] and in some instances, its antidepressant effects are comparable to the effects of psychotherapy.[343] Studies have found that moderate exercise for about thirty minutes a day reduced the risk of early death and morbidity.[344] It's generally known that exercise also has a positive effect on brain function and can enhance blood flow and cognitive function and improve neuroplasticity via something called brain-derived neurotrophic factor (BDNF). Exercise also helps the brain grow and form memories.[345]

Exercises like walking, running, and using an elliptical trainer or treadmill have been shown to help improve mood, and even low-intensity workouts and anaerobic exercise[346] can have a positive impact on depression and lead to enduring positive mood states.[347] The standard treatment for depression in mental health settings is a combination of psychotherapy and antidepressant medication; however, when exercise was compared with antidepressants, experiments revealed that although medications worked faster to ameliorate depressive symptoms, exercise was not only equally effective but provided longer-lasting remission.[348]

Getting Started:

There is no particular "right" way to get your heart pumping and reap the many benefits of exercise. For example, the CDC and the Physical Activity Guidelines Advisory Committee (PA-GAC) recommend 150 to 300 minutes of moderate exercise (brisk walking, yardwork, tennis) per week, or seventy-five to 150 minutes of intense physical activity (jogging, running, shoveling) per week for maximum health benefits.[349] One study found that walking just sixty minutes per week led to improvements in mood for participants.[350] For those with tight schedules, even just thirty minutes of exercise, three times per week can have positive effects.[351] I would always suggest doing something fun in your exercise routine because it helps it to go more quickly, gives you joy, and puts you in a better mood.

Socialization

In a book that has continually discouraged polarization, it would be negligent if I failed to mention that, while there is a substantial amount of freedom and well-being that we can attain independently, we humans did not evolve to be alone, and thus a great deal of our mental, physical, and spiritual functioning is dependent upon our social bonds. Unfortunately, there has been a gradual decline in social connectedness within Western culture, and there is some evidence that this is partially the reason for increases in mental illnesses and other issues.

There are echoes of the feelings I discussed earlier of mental imprisonment in the sphere of the social world. In his book, *Lost Connections*, Johann Hari points out that modern Western cultures have become increasingly individualistic, creating a sort of "ego prison" in which we are cut off from genuine connection, even though most of us aren't in any physical or objective enclosures.[352] Often, we are just feet away from our neighbors, but to engage with each other would mean to be interrupted from our cellphones. We prefer to stay buried in the safety of our social media worlds than risk engaging with the real world.

Getting Started:

We must begin to reconnect with each other; our well-being depends on it. There is an entire body of research on the beneficial effects of having positive social support. Where I work, patients without social support tend to have a worse prognosis than those who do. Of course, if relationships can cause suffering, then it stands to reason that they can also alleviate suffering. Indeed, research has documented the power of the healing relationship;[353] this maps onto my observation of people who I've seen heal in the context of therapeutic relationships. And this healing is not just isolated to the bond created in psychotherapy, but any interconnection in which we can feel safe and free from judgment. These relationships might include family members, friends, self-help groups, and religious communities.[354] Volunteering can also be a way to meet new people and improve health and well-being. Research has shown that those who engage in volunteering tend to have greater mental and physical functioning.[355]

Life and Time Management

In the academic literature, time management is defined as taking actions toward our goals to make optimal use of our time.[356] Our time must be proportioned to manage priorities and recognize and eliminate wasteful energy expenditure.[357] Improper management of our time can lead to disorganization and disruptions within our life. Articles and books have been written which encourage time-management practices such as setting goals, making to-do lists, scheduling obligations and commitments on a calendar, prioritizing (i.e., doing the hardest or more urgent things first), learning how to say "no," and delegating large tasks.[358] However, improvements in time management seem to have driven the economy to increase demands on students and workers, which, in my estimation, is not necessarily a good thing. However, it's still helpful to learn how to juggle multiple responsibilities to increase our autonomy and manage the curveballs that life sometimes throws at us.

Research has found that those who feel a sense of mastery over their time-management and organizational skills showed reduced role ambiguity, lower levels of somatic complaints, and fewer reports of feeling overwhelmed with their obligations.[359] These studies have shown that the resulting *perception* of "control" over our time leads to the improvements rather than the behaviors themselves.[360] In other words, we flourish when we *believe* in our freedom to self-determine our lives.[361] The time-management behavior which was most related to improvements in academic performance was "time-planning," which is defined as: weekly goal setting, daily planning, to-do lists, scheduling activities, clarity of goals for the week ahead as well as for the coming semester, holding on to potentially important documents, and a high level of confidence in our ability to manage the responsibilities of the coming week.[362]

Fundamentally, time management is less about time in particular and more about "life management." Whenever we have a big project ahead of us, it can seem overwhelming; this is not surprising as we tend to contemplate the completion of an enormous task as a whole rather than as a gradual, iterative process. Rarely are we expected to tackle the full breadth of a challenge at once; rather, it happens piecemeal if it is a truly achievable goal. Thus, it is helpful for us to view any significant challenge as a long journey instead of a day trip to a distant land. Seeing it this way will reduce the mental and emotional paralysis we sometimes experience when confronted by an unexpected problem or difficulty level.

Getting Started:

There are three ways that I find highly effective in managing time. These are:

1. A general to-do list: This can be done on virtually any piece of blank paper; however, it's often best to designate a particular notebook or writing pad to tasks. Begin to write down a few things you consider priorities (e.g., go back to school, save up for a house, improve health, lose weight, etc.); this will help you transform overwhelming responsibilities from an intangible rain cloud above your head into a concrete reality that you can see and control. The general to-do list is more of a broad overview of what needs to be done and should also contain big-picture goals.

2. Daily focused planning: This list breaks down the larger goals into steps and helps us achieve daily responsibilities (e.g., complete college application, make a doctor's appointment, buy healthy food, pay electric bill, go to the carwash, etc.). It is important to cross items off the list when they are completed; this provides us with feel-good neurotransmitters which correspond to achievement and helps to reinforce the habit of planning.

3. Weekly goal setting: Find a planner/scheduler that displays each week of the month for one year. Begin simply by listing routine obligations as well as intended plans. You can also extract items from your general and focused to-do list and spread them throughout the week; this way, you not only know *what* needs to be done but also *when* it's going to get done. You can also cross items out when they are completed. At the end of the year, you can look back and see how much you have accomplished.

Strengthening the Will

As previously mentioned, there are numerous ways to strengthen self-control, including meditation and exercise. Here are three more examples of change methods:

1. Begin a habit of waiting at least five minutes before engaging in your favorite activity (i.e., eating your favorite meal, etc.)

2. Find fun ways to do mundane tasks that you have to complete (e.g., going hiking or rock climbing instead of jogging on the treadmill in the gym, etc.)

3. When attempting to resist a temptation, try to imagine how one of your role models might handle the situation.

IV

Freedom through Understanding

Self-awareness is essential to regulate our emotions, for if we cannot understand the conditions occurring internally, we cannot manage them. And, without the ability to self-regulate, we become slaves to our unconscious drives, ergo: unfree.

19

Generating Self-Awareness

"Know thyself."
Socrates[363]

"Know thyself" is a popular phrase which we all seem to be familiar with, yet we often have no inkling of how to achieve it. Nonetheless, it's central to acceptance and change, and thus of utmost importance to personal growth. Self-knowledge is the balance scale on which they both hinge. Without the ability to know yourself, you cannot know your true capabilities. Without this understanding, you cannot know what needs to be changed and what should be accepted. Self knowledge allows us to use our understanding of our strengths and limitations to its full benefit. It increases the likelihood that we will achieve our goals.

Let's look at an example. With the invention and evolution of the automobile, its creators eventually began to realize the importance of installing gauges like an odometer, temperature gauge, tachometer, and oil pressure gauge, to name a few. The purpose of these additional installations was to monitor and correct problems with the engine and its other components if needed. Too much heat and the engine blows; too little oil and the engine stalls. These gauges help us know what we need more or less of to keep the car functionally stable in a balanced "homeostasis," if you will. Thanks to these gauges, we know with near exact precision when our vehicle's fuel is running low and when its oil requires changing. Gauges allow us to see how much heat the engine is accruing; without the guesswork, we can know, with confidence, if we need to add any antifreeze to keep it from overheating. This allows the entire system to maintain a functional state of equilibrium.

The same is not true for ourselves. Human beings don't have a built-in "dashboard of the mind," so to speak. For example, we don't have gauges showing how many calories we need before reaching nutritional sufficiency. Our stomachs are not reliable indicators; we can all probably recall times when we ate much more food than we needed without even realizing it. Our brains cannot give us an exact read-out of just how many reps we can do on the weight bench; this is apparent any time you felt like quitting, but then a workout buddy motivated you to push just past the bounds of your comfort zone. To your surprise, you find that your mind's doubt indicator was telling you lies.

Indeed, unlike cars and other electronics, which have become increasingly accurate and precise at displaying their needs, we don't have gauges that tell us how many miles we can run before getting injured, how much workload we can take on before burning out, or how much willpower we can utilize in saying no to cake, pastries, or junk food before we give in to temptation. I believe this is one of the key issues stunting our mental, physical, and spiritual growth. We all

GENERATING SELF-AWARENESS

want to step outside our comfort zones, but we aren't always sure how far is too far and how much is too much. And, as a result, we often give in to our fears and doubts before realizing our true potential.

If we all had built-in gauges, like automobiles, computers, and smartphones have, we would be able to perfectly balance our homeostasis while also pursuing our goals.

Human beings are a lot more complex than cars, however. And, although electronic devices provide useful analogies, to me the process of understanding oneself is a lot more like mapping the nuances of a complex and ever-evolving landscape rather than a process of developing better measuring instruments. Of course, a "map" *is* a kind of instrument, although a notoriously imprecise one; maps can be wrong and they certainly cannot match the accuracy of measuring instruments.

Though cartography is not quite the same as obtaining precise scientific measurements, the reasoning remains the same; we need to see where we are going. Being unable to view the path ahead will ensure that you will eventually get lost. We aren't always good at navigating through the terrain of our inner landscape, and it's no wonder why – self-insight and understanding are not skills that come naturally to us. These aren't abilities that our parents usually raise us to value, and are certainly not competencies within our schools' curriculums.

During his post-meditation talks, Zen master Ken sometimes discussed the Buddhist notion of "avidyā," which can be loosely translated as a type of delusion or a misunderstanding of the world.[364] However, Ken referred to these as merely "stories" that we often tell ourselves by listening to our fears and doubts – that is, whatever we tell ourselves about the nature of our capabilities is just a fable, one which may or may not be true. We often give up on a goal or task because we believe the thoughts that tell us that we "can't" accomplish the things we desire. But we don't have to believe thoughts which tell us when we should give up. Imagine how many times you may have quit or given into doubt because you told yourself, "I can't," when in reality you *can*. What would your world look like today?

On the other hand, we might be tempted to conjure up all kinds of problems with this reasoning. For example, "listen to your body" is a common utterance among those who believe that we should be sensitive to the messages we are getting from our bodies as they indicate what we truly need. And, of course, it may seem like nothing more than common sense to listen to your body when it's telling you what it requires.

Take running, for example. It may seem like common sense that becoming fatigued is your body's way of telling you to rest or stop. Or take weightlifting – to some, the feeling that you've reached your max repetition is a clear message from your body that you cannot lift any further. It's common and even normal to believe that a reliable way of knowing when to quit at a given task is the moment you "feel" like you can no longer continue. Unexamined, so many of us listen to the first thought in our heads which says, "I can't do this anymore." It's at this point that the majority of us, without any hesitation, give up.

However, the truth about what we can and cannot do is certainly not told to us by our minds. Timothy Noakes, a scientist and professor of exercise, found that exercise fatigue is not actually caused by the body's physical inability, but by a region of the brain charged with protecting us from harm. He and his fellow researchers found that, during the experience of muscle fatigue, there was no actual breakdown or failure of the muscle's ability to continue; it was just messages from the participants' brains that caused the muscles to give out.[365] At least with regards to exercise, physical limitations are just "stories," and much of our limitations are mental constructs that don't reflect the reality of what we can achieve. Left unchecked, it can make any of us complacent and unwilling to grow.

Though I use the example of exercise, the notion that we are physically capable of more than our minds lead us to believe is common across all types of endeavors involving human choice and decision-making, like dieting, meditating, learning, working, and other activities which require mental or physical endurance. It seems, instead, that what our minds tell us, for the most part, is what is painful and what we don't *want* to do, not what we actually *can* do. As previously mentioned, unlike our smartphones, we don't have a battery indicator to tell us when we're running low or when we have reached our total physical limit, but we can be sure that mental limitations aren't always accurate, and it's up to us to challenge them. Thus, to realize our true potential, we can never rely solely upon what our minds tell us. By challenging our limits, we gain insight, not into what they *are* but rather what they *aren't*.

When I first learned how to meditate, I gained insight into how the things my mind was telling me about my true potential and capabilities were a lie. Many negative thoughts told me how much I *couldn't* do, but until I took up Zen training, I never realized that those thoughts had no basis in reality. I began to challenge some core beliefs and started doing what I had formerly told myself I could not do. Eventually, with this newfound confidence, I began to take on an increasing number of challenges until, one day, I had burnt myself out. I became puzzled by this: *are there some things which my mind tells me I can't do that are false and some which are true?* Well, probably – I may have more potential than I gave myself credit for, but I am certainly not omnipotent. But then, how can I know the difference? Moreover, if I'm wrong when I think I've reached my limit, then what *is* my limit?

Indeed, we've all heard those struggling with stress utter statements like, "I don't know how much more of this I can take." How do we determine the boundary of human will? Is it just a gamble that our peers and mentors seem to be taking when they ignore the warnings and admonishments of their minds and bodies and pursue their goals regardless? To begin to understand this boundary, we must begin to understand ourselves. We must develop detailed and nuanced maps of our inner landscape.

To be able to increase our free will, that is, to enhance our autonomy and capacity for self-determination, we must be able to tolerate frustrations generated by our urges and our environment, and we must be able to self-regulate when our engine overheats or our fuel tanks are nearly empty.

Learning to understand what you're feeling and make sense of it, and the ability to reflect on your life in a meaningful way, are skills that people seldom develop unless they spend years in psychotherapy, long hours in meditation, or extended periods in any practice that presents safe and achievable challenges. However, these skills should not be seen as superfluous luxuries but rather as necessities. Learning to map our inner landscape is essential for cultivating the ability to traverse the rough terrain of reality and, ultimately, to become who we want to be. One vital component of self-understanding is known as "interoception," which can be achieved in numerous ways and is the main topic of the next section.

Interoception: Exploring the Inner World

"Knowledge is power"
   Francis Bacon[366]

When we're in school, we're told that understanding complex topics is just a matter of practice and study. We don't start, from birth, knowing how to divide and multiply fractions or determine the electron configuration of helium; instead, we are *taught* these skills. And, the more we practice them, the better we get. When we commit ourselves to learning something, then, with practice, we become more proficient at it; this not only occurs with math, science, and reading, but also with regards to inner awareness, also known as interoception.

Interoception is a scientific word for something we experience on a daily basis; our feelings and sensory signals that arise internally, like hunger, for example. It is sometimes divided into proprioception, the experiencing of our skin, muscles, and joints, and visceroception, the sense of our internal organs.[367] However, interoception also encompasses emotional experiences.

William James and Carl Lange created the James-Lange theory of emotion and posited that emotional senses are derived from physical sensations.[368] Thus, in this view, interoception is generated via the brain's ability to integrate and blend the numerous senses and signals originating from body regions into parts of the brain like the insula, cingulate cortex, orbitofrontal cortex, thalamus, prefrontal cortex, and amygdala.[369] For example, brain-imaging studies show that the insula, somatomotor, and cingulated cortices become engaged when participants concentrate on specific body parts like the heart.[370]

This interoceptive integration of sensory stimuli is considered part of how the brain forms a representational model of itself. Research has revealed that, in people with psychiatric disorders like PTSD, this ability to integrate sensory information is largely disrupted.[371] Indeed, distortions and interruptions within the brain's ability to integrate bodily signals have been implicated in several pathologies.[372]

Sensory integration and self-referential processing are considered part of a larger process called the "default mode network," of which the medial prefrontal cortex is a central brain structure.[373] Having disturbances in your ability to integrate sensory information means that your capacity for self-awareness is reduced, explaining why people with certain mental illnesses often experience difficulties generating a self-concept and self-awareness. For example, research has shown reductions in cardioceptive accuracy (heartbeat perception) among depressed patients.[374]

Neuroscientist Antonio Damasio posits that there are two different forms of self-awareness. One is the "core" self, which is transient and involves present-moment qualitative experiences. The second is the "extended" or "autobiographical" self, which is enduring and is responsible for our sense of personhood. The extended self contains memories of our past and constructs the story of our lives.

Damasio's research suggests that both the core and extended self are dependent on the brain's cortical midline structures (e.g., posteromedial cortices, medial prefrontal cortex, anterior cingulate cortices, thalamus, etc.)[375] Impairments in these regions, from chronic, acute, or traumatic stress, can cause disturbances in our sense of self.[376] For example, brain scans of patients with severe PTSD revealed significant disturbances in brain regions involved in self-referential processing.[377] Experiencing chronic stress that disrupts our ability to generate normal self-awareness is a major problem because it robs us of our freedom and keeps us trapped in fear. Without being able to understand ourselves intimately, our capacity to self-direct our lives becomes hampered. We are no longer able to fully understand and integrate our experiences, which leaves us confused and directionless. The map of our inner world becomes disordered, and thus we become lost.

Anyone who has ever lost their temper, only to regret later what they said and did, can be said to have had a momentary loss of freedom. Often, we give in to certain feelings and provocations out of avoidance and fear. Take rage, for example. Someone who becomes rageful is attempting to break free of whatever constraints have been unwillingly placed upon them. However, this is not a display of attaining freedom because it's almost always the case that, in retrospect, they behave in a manner they wish they hadn't. In our attempts to gain control over a situation, we subsequently lose that control.

In order to gain control over our behaviors, we must be able to understand what it feels like when our urges are attempting to express themselves without our conscious permission. As we become better at detecting and differentiating between different feelings, we generate greater mastery over our internal and external worlds. Methods for achieving this level of understanding will be discussed in the next chapter.

In his book, *The Body Keeps the Score*, psychiatrist Bessel van der Kolk (who I mentioned earlier) discusses a region of the brain called the medial-prefrontal cortex (MPFC), which he calls the "watchtower." He and other researchers consider this location to be where sensory information is subtly perceived by conscious awareness. He, too, believes that for us to begin to achieve agency and ultimately autonomy, we need to notice sensory experiences as they arise so that we may respond rather than react to internal and external stimuli.[378]

Another phenomenon whereby we become trapped by our mind and physiology is called a panic attack, sometimes known as an anxiety attack. A panic attack is the experience of intense and often irrational fear of things like dying or losing our mind. During a panic attack, you're essentially entering fight-or-flight mode; however, rather than being triggered by rational fear (e.g., being chased by a lion), it's triggered by the misinterpretation of a physical sensation you perceive as being unusual or insidious, such as brief light-headedness or heart palpitations. Once triggered, your brain begins to engage your fight-or-flight systems and discharges hormones like adrenaline into your bloodstream, preparing you for the perceived threat. However, going into fight-or-flight mode just increases the unnerving sensations that started the panic cycle from the beginning. The reactive state your body enters continues to produce a host of other symptoms that reinforce your anticipatory fears; you begin to feel depersonalized, spacey, and light-headed, leading you to mistakenly believe you are having a medical emergency.[379] If left unmanaged, this cycle can keep you paralyzed in a state of fear for extended periods. Panic attacks feel very real; they hijack your mind and body, and for those terrifying moments, you become convinced of impending doom. In truth, these are essentially problems with self-awareness, or lack thereof, rather than with any truly insidious malady.

People with panic disorders are often hyper-vigilant concerning observing bodily sensations. However, being in this constant state of worry virtually ensures the emergence of an eventual panic attack.[380] Cognitive behavioral therapists and others within the mental health field believe that panic attacks are outside of our control until we become proficient in interoceptive awareness. That is, we fear things that we perceive as abnormal and which we don't understand. Becoming an expert in self-awareness means becoming intimately knowledgeable about your body. For example, the adrenaline which is released during the beginning phases of the fight-or-flight response is quickly cleared from the body – it's estimated to last five minutes or less.[381] Thus, if you become aware of your physiologic reactions and notice when you are nearing the onset of an attack, you can thwart it before it begins. By becoming mindful and focusing on your breathing, you give your body time to metabolize the stress hormones before they can trigger a cascade of consternation.[382] I recommend trying 7/11 breathing as mentioned in Chapter 12, Methods of Acceptance. In my experience, it's helped many prevent or recover from a panic attack.

Research has shown that interoceptive awareness and other cognitive behavioral strategies are effective in providing long-term benefits for those with panic disorders.[383] In one method, known as interoceptive desensitization, a person with a panic disorder finds a safe way to face their feared physical experience to gradually reduce or completely sever the link between the sensation and the fear response. It's about learning to be comfortable with our fears so that they no longer wreak havoc on our lives. Bessel van der Kolk contends that PTSD and other traumas strip the victim of their sense of agency and perception of having control over their lives, which he calls "self-leadership." He helps people gain greater interoceptive awareness in therapy sessions by assisting them in noticing and articulating their inner experiences and helping them to map their physical locations like pain, tightness in the chest, or muscular tension. He asserts that recovery begins when his clients gain a greater ability to link their physical experiences with mental events.[384]

The less we understand our inner experiences, the more we allow them to take control of us. Freedom is actualized when we can tame the inner beast that resides within all of us.[385] We aren't born as, and we don't necessarily grow into, masters of interoception; this is probably because we are so focused on external stimuli, and there is rarely any impetus for us to explore our internal worlds.

For thousands of years, practitioners of contemplative arts have known that it's possible to better understand the self through different forms of meditation or intentional focus and concentration. However, neuroscientific research has shown that it's possible to influence our own emotions via cultivating interoceptive awareness.[386] The brain gets better at whatever it does repeatedly; solve hundreds of algebra equations and you will become proficient in algebra. Likewise, practice self-awareness regularly, and you will not only become a self-expert, but you will be able to live with greater free will. In trauma, a disorder in which the link between our senses and our conscious awareness is severed or weakened, research has shown that practices like yoga, neurofeedback, biofeedback, deep breathing, and any practice in which someone can learn to safely reconnect with themselves, is beneficial in improving interoception and body awareness, thereby increasing personal agency.[387]

Inner Cartography: Mapping the Inner Landscape

I studied martial arts for ten years and achieved a black belt in 2016. I credit martial arts for being one of many practices that helped me tame my "inner beast" and develop greater self-discipline. The challenges I faced in learning how to control my body and mind helped me in many areas of my personal and professional life.

For one, it helped me better understand my potential. In martial arts, there is a technique called "breaking," in which instructors challenge their students to break through several wooden boards.[388] Often this is done after first observing their instructors doing it with ease. Typically, a student will be tested with a smaller number of boards than the teacher. Upon seeing these wooden boards, however, the student is often apprehensive and unsure about their ability to perform such a feat. When the moment arrives for them to test their skill in this practice, they usually find that, to their surprise, they can break the wooden boards.

The purpose of this exercise in martial arts is not to show off or be brutish; rather, it's to demonstrate to the student that they can do more than they think. The boards represent mental walls, limitations that we can break through if we believe in ourselves and are given encouragement. Similar practices are performed all over the world and in many different self-help and personal development circles.

Another example is the "fire walk," whereby a person is challenged to walk barefoot across hot coals.[389] Again, the purpose is not to show that any individual is capable of mystical or superhuman feats, but rather that our fears are often illusions and we are capable of more than previously thought. These practices help us map out our inner worlds, and as we continue to challenge ourselves, our maps become increasingly refined. Self-doubt is defeated by learning the parameters of our former achievements or by understanding the limits of human physiology. However, these methods are not perfect in determining the limits of what is possible for us. As we have seen with people like Tommy Caldwell and David Goggins, people can go well beyond the bounds of what was previously thought "humanly possible."

Another way of stepping outside our comfort zone and improving upon the nuances and gradation of our inner maps is by doing "just a little bit more" than we thought we could in any given endeavor or pursuit within which we wish to grow or improve. In this way, we can avoid major risks while also beginning to chip away at the self-imposed cage we have constructed out of fear and doubt. Pushing beyond the bounds of self-doubt is a process whereby you either prove your mind wrong or force it to conform to new standards. You don't always have to over-work yourself; rather, you can intentionally extend just beyond the bounds of what you previously thought possible, especially when you feel like giving up.

The conscious act of accepting and pushing past perceived limitations involves learning more about your abilities and engaging in the process of continual self-reinvention. And, as we raise the bar higher, we begin to develop our own internal gauges; we may not be able to see how much fuel we have left in our tank or how far we can push past our boundaries, but with practice, we begin to develop a more accurate understanding. We begin to realize that when we receive the first signals from our mind that we are spent, we have in fact barely scratched the surface of our potential.

However, the signpost you must watch out for is that which indicates you are entering the realm of physical or mental dysfunction. If you notice that you are regularly experiencing illness or significant injuries, or even interpersonal conflicts, this is a warning that it may be time to pull back. While pushing ahead of our fears can help us grow, pushing too far can do the opposite; this means that the fundamental sensation you will experience when you have gone too far is the feeling of being trapped or, in some ways, constrained. The restraint of the will is the simplest and simultaneously most profound indication that you have fallen off the map. That is why free will is so important and central to all that we do; the notion of human free will is not mere intellectual ostentation for pensive armchair philosophers – rather, it's the key to our growth and advancement.

Stress and Human Limitations

Thus far, the notion of stress and its harmful effects has been discussed at length. Now that we know that stress can have devastating effects on our mental and physical functioning, and we know the factors that mediate and improve outcomes for those who experience chronic stress, is it the case that *all* stress is bad? Throughout my life, I would often wonder why some challenges or tragedies – like a stressful job or loss of a loved one – would break me down, and yet other challenges – like climbing a tall mountain or attaining a college degree – which seemed, in some instances, perhaps even more insurmountable, led instead to personal growth. Indeed, some people lament that stress has burnt them out, while others report stress as being good and, in some cases, even pleasurable. Understanding the important distinctions between good and bad stress is essential to helping ourselves determine the boundary of our mental and physical limits.

As we have seen, chronic stress and trauma can trigger or exacerbate symptoms of mental illness, though it seems to be yet another paradox, because to grow we must experience it. Moreover, to achieve success, we are often told that we need to push beyond the boundaries of what we think is possible; that is, we need to subject ourselves to stress to a degree beyond what we think we can handle. We need to be able to adapt to highly stressful events, a process known as "psychological resilience," or just "resilience."

Resilient individuals more or less have the ability to recover from an affliction or adversity[390] without incurring severe psychological impairments. So, the question is: if dysfunction and pathology often result from experiencing stress beyond what we can handle, and the key to personal growth is achieved through pushing beyond what we can handle, how can we know which type will be harmful and which will be helpful?

The answer is in the distinction between harmful stress, or

"distress," and good stress, known as "eustress," a term coined by endocrinologist Hans Selye. Eustress is defined in the literature as "when the gap between what one has and what one wants is slightly pushed, but not overwhelmed."[391] In contrast to eustress, distress is usually considered negative stress, that is, "persistent stress that is not resolved through coping or adaptation."[392] Notice that for something to be interpreted as eustress, it must depend on the perception of the experiencer pursuing what they "want" and not having it thrust upon them as in the case of most, if not all, traumatic or chronically stressful events. It's also essential to make the clear distinction between the kind of stress that causes dysfunction, which typically robs us of our freedom, versus the kind of stress that places us in the driver's seat of our destiny. The mindset of freedom and empowerment is a vital protective factor against a wide range of mental disturbances.

Studies have shown that eustress and distress produce different responses in the neuroendocrine system, which is particularly dependent on the amount of personal control (freedom) we feel over the stressor.[393] Although there is most definitely a genetic component that predisposes individuals to experience stress more intensely than others, the research is clear on the role that mindset plays in interpreting stressful events and their ultimate effects on the individual.[394]

Chronic stress is not a worthwhile challenge; it deprives you of the vital recovery period needed to grow. Without the healing time in between stressful events, we continue to break down, and thus growth is stunted. We don't know what the limits of human potential are for certain, but based on the accounts of those who have persevered through great adversity and seemingly impossible odds, limits extend only as far as the ability to maintain a sense of autonomy and intentionality.

Charting Your Own Course

We all want to do what we think is best for ourselves, but what is best isn't always clear. And, it's fair to say that, to some degree, what's best is a highly subjective and personal state that can vary from person to person. However, it's useful to remember that, when charting a course to a specific destination, we can look at our "map," which can help us decide the best route.

For example, there are many ways to get to a particular geographical destination by car. If the map is up to date, we will know which route has tolls, which has traffic, and at what time of day; we can see which route is shorter, which is longer, and which is economically preferable; we can identify road closures, detours, and other possible delays. These navigation systems are created by people who have done the work for us; they have analyzed the roads and routes to avoid paying tolls or getting stuck in traffic. Although imperfect, these systems are very reliable.

It seems clear that there may not be a one-size-fits-all map toward getting where we want to go in life, at least not as of yet. However, like the navigation system described above, there are myriad paths toward freedom. We can update these maps within ourselves through methods like interoception and self-understanding as well as other methods described in this book. We can learn the methods, teachings, and practices of those who came before us and whose trials and errors refined the maps of freedom, the routes of which have become more finely tuned over thousands of years and which helped to create the diverse maps we have today. How privileged we are to have these pathways outlined for us, created through the labors and toils of past philosophers, spiritualists, and, more recently, through natural and social scientists' hard work and effort.

Ultimately, we must chart our own course and find out what works for us, but this doesn't preclude the notion that the ever-changing and ever-updating itineraries currently available to us have much to offer as guides toward that end. Through the many profound literary works, scriptural texts, and scholarly teachings we have access to, we can learn which roads are worthwhile and which aren't. We can learn the peaks, valleys, potholes, weather conditions, and possible risks so that, before our journeys, if we are wise, we can be better prepared. For, as with any journey, as time propels you with increasing speed toward your future, aimlessly wandering will all but ensure you get nowhere fast; this is why it's important to get intimately familiar with the path you have chosen.

We realize that improving our lives and overcoming our fears involves a complex interplay between self-understanding and self-creation. Self-understanding allows us to install more reliable barometers to access our true potential and further paint the canvas of our lives. With practice, we can reach a point where we are more in touch with our inner world, a point at which we no longer overestimate what we can reasonably handle without overwhelming ourselves. And, similarly, a point at which we can more fluidly move through our lives knowing enough about our internal gauges; enough that we seldom give in to the limitations imposed by parts of ourselves that don't have the full story. Next, I will discuss the many ways to cultivate and develop better "maps" of our internal worlds.

20

Methods of Self-Understanding

Self-regulation, or emotion regulation, is exactly what it sounds like: balancing the conflict between order and chaos that arise internally. Stated less poetically, it's the capacity to stabilize our moods and manage our emotional states in a way that allows us to function well within the context of multiple dimensions, which include psychological, physiological, and interpersonal. Issues or deficits within our ability to regulate our emotions can impair proper functioning and reduce overall well-being.[395]

When I began writing this book, I was aiming to act as a guide for both mental health professionals and people seeking a way to free themselves from what is holding them back. In keeping with the theme of this book, the following is meant to be a basic guide to the practices that help us transcend our limitations and understand the intricacies of our vast inner territories. This self-knowledge is the light in the darkness of the unknown.

Psychotherapy: Mental Causation, Emotion Control, and Free Will

Before we jump into the methods of self-understanding, of which psychotherapy is one, I'd like to first explain psychotherapy and aspects of internal control as they relate to free will and autonomy. Researchers and clinicians consider the notion of agency and intentionality to be an essential component of successful psychotherapy outcomes. We may not yet know how subjective experiences influence our behaviors, but it has always been clear from a clinical point of view that when a person comes to therapy for help, they plan to change some aspect of their behaviors or beliefs; this presumes that choice is real and that, with help, we can increase their capacity for making self-determined choices.[396]

We all seem to feel like we are undeniably free and autonomous operators, yet some thinkers consider this to be nothing more than an illusion. Neuroscience has helped reveal how our experiences of volitional control and self-determined behavior, which occur in the context of psychotherapy, can map onto reality. Researchers have conducted imaging studies on the brain to investigate regions that become active during certain emotions, behaviors, and cognitive processes. Some researchers have even begun promising work in determining the neural correlates of intentional emotion control.

Unsurprisingly, studies have found that when a person consciously attempts to calm themselves down from something like anger or anxiety, increases in activity in areas of the brain like the prefrontal cortex and reductions in the activity of the amygdala are observed.[397] Further, this research has revealed that intentional recruitment of metacognitive processes can change the way emotional stimuli are interpreted and subsequently reacted to, demonstrating that we can consciously affect our feelings and behaviors.[398] There has been much research on the neural basis of voluntary regulatory mechanisms that has lent credence to the idea that mental events can affect neuroplasticity and exert physical alterations in brain structures based on our thoughts.[399] Our conscious minds aren't just along for the ride (as some people believe); instead, they play an active role in our behaviors and interactions.

Psychotherapy has long been known as one of the ways that a person can cultivate greater self-awareness and control over their emotional states. It is predicated on the fact that there is such a thing as mental causation; that changing the way we think can change the way we feel. It's also considered to be a major factor in a client's progress.[400] Improvements in emotional control occur within the therapeutic relationship built between the therapist and client. In therapy, the clinician provides a safe, nonjudgmental space for their client; these are the conditions under which new adaptive skills can be learned.[401] Some have hypothesized that learning new habits and skills during psychotherapy can cause structural alterations in neuronal connections within the brain.[402]

In addition to improving self-awareness and self-insight, research comparing psychotherapy and psychotropic medications has found that psychotherapy is roughly as effective for treating psychiatric conditions like depression, panic disorder, and obsessive-compulsive disorder. Moreover, combined treatment of psychotherapy and antidepressant medication is superior to either one alone.[403] Numerous meta-analytic studies have shown that psychotherapy and psychiatric medication treatment are equally beneficial in treating generalized anxiety disorder.[404] Moreover, psychotherapeutic interventions such as psychoeducation, cognitive behavioral therapy, family-focused therapy, and interpersonal and social rhythm therapy have shown significant benefits in reducing relapse rates among those with bipolar disorder.[405] Let's now look at the methods of self-understanding in detail.

Method 1: Psychotherapy

Psychodynamic Psychotherapy

Psychodynamic psychotherapy, in particular, fosters emotional expressiveness and supports the development of emotional insight. A psychodynamic therapist helps their clients articulate a comprehensive range of their inner feelings and experiences, including frightening ones. A client may lack or have reduced insight into the feelings which linger in their unconscious and which unknowingly wreak havoc on their lives until brought to the surface and dealt with, something which can be an uncomfortable process.

In Parts Two and Three, I discussed the process of accepting oneself and facing our fears. The purpose of psychodynamic psychotherapy is to enable us to do both.[406] Avoidance occurs often and manifests itself in the context of therapy in the form of consciously or unconsciously missing appointments, showing up late, or being guarded and not open or forthcoming during sessions. Psychodynamic therapists attempt to get to the root of what is causing intrapsychic distress or interpersonal dysfunction. It's believed that traumatic or extremely negative experiences in early childhood lay the groundwork for future psychological disturbances. Sometimes, this insight alone can help alleviate some of the client's suffering and open up pathways to recovery. The psychodynamic therapist aims to cease unhealthy behavioral patterns by exposing themes that continue to emerge, thereby increasing self-awareness and putting the client back in control of their lives.[407]

Cognitive Behavioral Therapy

As discussed in earlier chapters, cognitive behavioral therapy (CBT) is considered a highly successful form of treatment for various mental illnesses and other psychological disturbances that don't necessarily qualify as disorders.[408] Developed by psychologist Albert Ellis and psychiatrist Aaron Beck in the 1960s and '70s, CBT continues to be a popular treatment methodology within psychotherapy and other areas of mental health. Like psychodynamic psychotherapy, CBT is predicated on the notion that mental illnesses sometimes result from distortions in cognitive processes. Though being partially affected by conscious thought, CBT therapists believe that the same thoughts that cause distress can be changed through adaptive cognitive techniques to help alleviate such distress and elicit more adaptive behaviors that help foster well-being.[409]

Researchers have since developed a plethora of strategies within the CBT paradigm that target particular disorders. A strategy for changing thoughts to improve anxiety will differ from a strategy used to improve depressive symptoms. Although there is some overlap, overall stress reduction elicited from an intervention can help to improve a range of symptoms. The literature on CBT is huge, and numerous studies have found it effective for treating disorders such as depression, anxiety, panic, eating disorders, anger issues, and stress. Additionally, it has shown some benefits in treating personality disorders, insomnia, and chronic pain.[410] Note that the two types I listed are not the only effective forms of psychotherapy, and I suggest looking into various forms until you find the right fit for you.

Getting Started:

Years ago, when I sought out a therapist after college, I had several interesting experiences. I once went to see a therapist who apparently had many years of experience but who began falling asleep as I was telling my story. I ended that relationship quickly. Continuing on my journey, I met a therapist who dominated our conversation, showed no warmth, and appeared preoccupied with getting my money. Determined to find help, I met another whose garbage can was filled to the brim with energy drinks and who took back-to-back clients without breaks, from morning to afternoon until late into the evening. On our third meeting, I was shocked as he went from having a full head of hair and a beard to shaving his face and hair completely off. Although not obligated to share life details with clients, I think that warranted at least a brief mention. The following week after our fourth session, I received a letter in the mail that the office had closed and that I was on my own. Needless to say, I was discouraged. However, the fourth time was a charm; I finally met someone who was a perfect fit.

I often hear people say, "I tried therapy once, but it didn't work," or, "My therapist didn't understand me." Upon further questioning, they usually reveal that their search ended after one bad experience. It is important to remember that there are competent and incompetent therapists, just as there are competent and incompetent plumbers, accountants, and surgeons. Moreover, even "good" therapists are not the right fit for everyone. There is no one-size-fits-all therapist, which is why it's important not to give up on therapy based on one encounter. If possible, you need to continue seeking until you find someone who makes you feel comfortable and understood.

Signs of a competent therapist are:
1. Genuineness
2. Honesty
3. Empathy
4. Cultural competence
5. Self-awareness
6. A sense of humor
7. Warmth
8. They maintain healthy boundaries[411]

Ways of finding a therapist include:

1. If you have insurance, call or use their provider directory to find therapists in your area.

2. Look at reviews on the internet; reviews are a great way to get a rough idea of who you'll likely click with.

3. Ask family, friends, or coworkers. (Note: but just because someone found a good fit for themselves does not always mean the therapist will be right for you.)

4. Go with your gut. Schedule a consultation with a

therapist, and pay attention to your intuition and gut reactions. If you feel comfortable, then proceed; if not, continue looking.[412]

Method 2: Expressive Writing

Among mental health professionals, writing is considered to be an effective way to improve interoceptive capacities. Useful methods are journaling, diaries, expressive writing, and inventory. Journaling is the process whereby we bring our attention inwards and document our qualitative states. This is, in a sense, an internal mapping of the nuances, peaks, and valleys of our inner world, and is meant to increase our ability to be in touch with ourselves.[413] It allows the writer to tap into previously unavailable or unrealized feelings, thoughts, urges, and desires. It's used in diverse ways to help us gain deeper self-awareness and self-understanding, and even sometimes to communicate feelings or thoughts that are otherwise hard to verbally articulate.[414]

Research has found writing to be beneficial for emotional well-being[415] and overall mental health;[416] it can help improve goal attainment and lead to the refinement of our life values and ambitions. The subsequent parsing of life ambitions and objectives can also help reduce ambiguity and reduce potential medical problems arising from the stress of intrapersonal conflicts and confusion.[417] Research has found that expressive writing about goals helps enhance self-regulation[418] and leads to an improved sense of personal meaning and life-purpose.[419]

James Pennebaker, an American social psychologist at the University of Texas at Austin, pioneered the Expressive

Writing Paradigm, a therapeutic writing method. He has studied the relationship between expressive writing and its effects on mental and physical health. Pennebaker's findings support the notion that certain forms of expressive writing can positively impact our psychological and physical functioning[420].

Getting Started:

Often when we think of journaling, we are compelled to document the significant events of our day. However, the research supports following some method or structure that transcends simply recording life events. Instead, the literature encourages incorporating processing emotions, seeking alternative perspectives, and challenging limiting beliefs to gain optimal benefit from writing or journaling. Below are instructions for therapeutic expressive writing.[421]

1. It is helpful to have your own diary or journal instead of using something like a notepad or loose paper. Using an actual book acts as a sort of anchor, and it will help you feel like your thoughts and feelings matter and that you at least have a safe place to express them.

2. Find time once or twice a week to devote to your expressive writing and self-inquiry. It helps if you set aside a particular time of day for consistency and regularity, for example, every morning upon waking or every night before bed. Also, it is important to set a time frame, such as ten minutes, for which you will devote to this practice. If no time limit is placed, you may be compelled to close the book and give up on the practice altogether if nothing comes to mind. Selecting a specific allotment of time will ensure that you can

process your thoughts and feelings, which may take a while to make their way onto the pages.

3. Write about the most pressing concerns, thoughts, feelings, and experiences. This is not a college course, so feel free to write without regard for language/writing rules. Your inner psyche and emotions do not much care for proper grammar.

4. In a world with constant demands, little personal time, and less privacy, this is a time to focus only on yourself and to keep your writing private.

5. This is about relieving stress, not creating more; this is not a time to pressure yourself. If you feel that you do not want to or cannot write, then close the book and resolve to continue whenever you feel ready.

6. Exploring emotions and bringing to the surface issues we wish to ignore can be a jarring experience for anyone. Do not be hard on yourself if you feel upset during or after this practice; simply acknowledge your feelings and move on with your day. Grappling with different emotions can be challenging, but it can also help us grow. Remember that whatever you experience is normal.

7. Whether you decide to keep or get rid of them, it is entirely up to you what to do with your journal or diary entries. Remember, this is your personal process of which you have complete ownership.[422,423]

Method 3: Inventory

Often, I stumble across techniques or practices that were originally designed to treat a specific disorder or are isolated to a particular program, but which have applicability in many other areas. One such practice is what is known as "moral inventory" or just "inventory." This is a practice which originated within the twelve-step program of Alcoholics Anonymous (AA) and has since been extended to other anonymous groups (e.g., Narcotics Anonymous, Gamblers Anonymous, Overeaters Anonymous, etc.) It is a process whereby we can take stock of our intrapersonal and interpersonal troubles. This practice is placed at number ten on the twelve-step list and usually begins after other steps have been completed. AA members believe that taking an honest look at their feelings, behaviors, and interactions through inventory helps them reduce internal distress and prevents their relapse.

Engaging in inventory requires the individual, usually at the end of the day and before going to sleep, to write down certain details of the day, including what made them angry, what they are worried or afraid of, and if they had been thinking about only themselves or considering the feelings of others. Additionally, if they have been deceptive or underhand, they must consider whether or not an apology is owed to anyone. Toward the end of this review of the day, they can write what things they did right, where they helped another person, and what they might be grateful for. Finally, there is a section for what corrective action, if any, may be necessary. In the beginning, this is done with the help of a sponsor because they believe recovering alcoholics aren't yet proficient at taking responsibility for their actions.

AA literature and practices are rooted in a long history, a detailed account of which I can barely do justice to. Through inventory, we can learn to accept responsibility and to cease blaming our behaviors and reactions on others, seeing more clearly our role in circumstances.

Learning to accept responsibility can be a painful and difficult process because it requires a willingness to accept and admit selfishness, fear, and dishonesty; it can be especially difficult for someone who has never looked critically at their role in a dispute or considered another's perspective. The literature encourages a "balanced" review, as it's recognized that even the most troubled person has points during the day in which they should be proud or grateful.

I have personally found the practice of inventory to be indispensable to self-understanding and lament that this method isn't more widely known of outside twelve-step programs. Because, in truth, it's not just alcoholics and addicts who can stand to benefit from making accurate appraisals of their life and circumstances; we all can.

There isn't much research on the practice of inventory and its benefits; however, there are some things which can be said. Firstly, neuroscience research increasingly supports the notion that when we focus on a particular way of thinking, such as mindfulness or interoception, our brains form stronger connections in the associated regions; this is the reason that "practice makes perfect." So, we can say with some level of certainty that diligently accepting responsibility for our actions and making honest appraisals of our circumstances is a skill that will improve with practice.

Whereas meditation and exercise are effective ways to discipline and improve the health of the mind and body, I would consider inventory, or any similar practice, to be effective in disciplining and improving our "social health." It should be mentioned that certain forms of psychotherapy also aim at generating the skill of honest self-appraisal accomplished through inventory, but this is usually in the context of a dialogue rather than in written form. When we can regularly task ourselves with seeing the role that we have played in a given conflict, and there usually is a role, we can more readily address and prevent similar problems from occurring in the future and thus reduce our suffering.

As a final word, it should be noted that the practice of inventory doesn't encourage people to make up or fabricate the taking of accountability in situations in which they are victims of another's unprovoked, unjustifiable, and undue hostility. In such cases, it's recommended that we instead seek to empathize and make our best attempt to see things from the other's perspective. Inventory is not done to excuse the behavior or exculpate the aggressor; it's done to benefit the victim. That is, AA is rooted in spiritual principles, of which one is forgiveness. Forgiveness is not always necessary to exonerate someone's wrongdoing; instead, it allows the sufferer to make peace with the aggressor rather than continue to harbor anger and resentments which will only continue to corrode their well-being and possibly lead to relapse. Thus, taking inventory, in whatever way it allows us to step outside ourselves momentarily, is a valuable way to foster self-knowledge.

Getting Started:

A modified form of this that can be beneficial to the layperson is via answering the following questions at the end of each night, or however often you feel comfortable with.

1. Who or what made you angry or upset?
2. What is another way of looking at the situation? Is there

a way to see things from their perspective?

3. What do I fear? Is this fear rational? Did I let any of my fears prevent me from working toward my goals? Is there a more empowering way to view this situation?

4. Did I lie to anyone, or was I dishonest in a way that could cause harm to another? If so, can I bring myself to tell the truth?

5. Did I knowingly or unknowingly cause harm to another? If so, do I owe anyone an apology?

6. What, if anything, should I do to remedy or correct any issues or problems? How can I do this in the most effective way?

7. What did I do well today? Who did I help? Did I take effective steps toward being my best self?

Method 4: Biofeedback

Another tremendously valuable tool in fostering interoceptive awareness and self-regulation is biofeedback: the use of electronic devices to reflect a person's physiological functions to help them learn to control them consciously.[424]

Biofeedback research has shown that certain human physiological processes can be consciously controlled and regulated, such as heart rate, pain perception, and brain waves.[425] There is evidence that biofeedback can positively affect mental and physical health[426] and research has shown its effectiveness for treating migraine headaches, anxiety, ADHD, and other disorders.[427] Biofeedback helps to improve what is known as heart rate variability (HRV), which is the variation of the time interval between heartbeats. HRV has traditionally been studied within medical settings as a predictor of heart attack, heart disease,[428] and even cancer.

However, research has shown that HRV is also a significant factor in mental illnesses like depression and PTSD.[429] For example, HRV is decreased among individuals who experience anxiety[430] and are under acute stress.[431] Research has also shown that activity in the prefrontal cortex mediates heart rate variability.[432] HRV has been found to moderate the relationship between the parasympathetic and sympathetic nervous systems (PNS and SNS). The literature on HRV suggests that increases in HRV may be associated with increased PNS activation, while increased SNS activation has been associated with lower HRV.[433]

Moreover, increased HRV has been found to correlate with improvements in self-regulation, impulse control, and judgment,[434] whereas low HRV is associated with poor decision-making.[435] Additionally, biofeedback helps manage the symptoms of depression and anxiety.[436] Much like the improvements observed in mindfulness practice, biofeedback training allows us to gain greater levels of control over our impulses, our moods, and our decisions.

Getting Started:

Biofeedback doesn't necessarily have to involve an electronic feedback device. *Natural biofeedback* is possible and encouraged. For example, try to get into the habit of not resisting your feelings. When angry, where do you notice the feeling? Is it in your chest? Your stomach? Although they are painful, paying close attention to them and locating where they reside in the body can have profound effects. It can help you reconnect with and understand yourself much better than before. Listen to and acknowledge your feelings instead of pushing them away or feeling the urge to act on them immediately; this will give you a greater sense of personal control. There are also some commercially available biofeedback devices that are relatively cheap, reliable, and can be purchased online.

21

The Middle Path between Acceptance and Change

The Galton Board

One day, I walked through the New York Hall of Science with my friend and fellow Zen practitioner, Kevon. We made our way through the various exhibits, marveling at the beauty and complexity of nature. As we were nearing the end of our tour, we began to walk through what is called the "Mathematica" exhibit, which displays a range of models designed to show the impact and changes that mathematics has made in contemporary society, such as with cellphones, computers, music, architecture, and so on.

A display called "The Probability Curve" caught our attention.[437] This exhibit displays a contraption known as a "bean machine" or "Galton board," named after its creator, Sir Francis Galton. The Galton board is a vertical board with interlaced columns of pegs that hold round pellets directly above it. When the pellets are released from the top portion of the device, they bounce off a series of ascending rows of pegs (usually a total of twelve rows). The first row has one peg, the second row has two pegs, and this pattern continues to the bottom. The pellets have an equal probability of bouncing either left or right as they hit each peg on their way to the bottom of the board. Once all the pellets reach the bottom, it forms what is known as a normal distribution or bell curve.

No matter how often you reset the pellets, the majority of them will always accrue in the middle, while a minority of them will end up on either the right or the left of the middle base.[438] The Galton board is a physical representation of order generated from chaos.

Much like Galton, the board's creator, Kevon and I were also fascinated by the seeming order that emerged from the chaos. We looked at each other in unspoken mutual understanding of what it meant to us as students of Buddhism, and remarked at the phenomenon whereby nature seemed to prefer the middle path. Though no existential or philosophical implications are typically meant to be drawn from the Galton board or the concept of normal distributions, this seemed to be a serendipitous validation of the Eastern spiritual principles we had been learning about at the time. It was a moment that showed us that any event, no matter how small or seemingly unremarkable, can act as a catalyst to help foster new insights when looked at from a unique perspective.

The Middle Way of Acceptance and Change

"God, grant me the serenity to accept the things I cannot change,
  The courage to change the things I can,
  And wisdom to know the difference."
Reinhold Niebuhr[439]

The serenity prayer, shown above, is commonly used by members of self-help groups. In just three lines, it encapsulates the precise essence of what it means to balance acceptance and change in the simplest terms. There is a kind of serenity in the act of acceptance, a mental and physical catharsis generated when we humbly surrender to the immutability of our circumstances. There is courage in the act of and process of change, which, for many of us, can sometimes be frightening, unfamiliar, and dysregulating. Finally, profound wisdom is contained in understanding what acceptance and change mean and how they fit into our lives.

On one end of the spectrum, we have the idea of acceptance – that is, laying the groundwork for growth and understanding by letting go of our fear of looking inward. On the other end of the spectrum, we have the concept of change; the belief that we should strive for growth and work toward becoming better than we were yesterday. However, attempting to push acceptance or change to their respective extremes will create disharmony and loss of free will. Self-help, self-improvement, and personal development attitudes and movements exist within the realm of change. However, polarizing the dimension of change can sometimes result in a sort of "toxic productivity" that causes the subsequent pursuit of unrelenting "achievement," and often leads to increased neuroticism, depression, and self-loathing, especially if we repeatedly fail to achieve our goals or feel the need to set unrealistic ones.

However, all-encompassing and indiscriminate acceptance can be just as harmful as the extremes of this "hustle culture," because the misinterpretation of acceptance as "giving in" and the subsequent excess of acceptance attitudes and behaviors can produce detachment and indifference. This is not indicative of any fatal glitches inherent in either view; rather, it's reflective of a misunderstanding of them. Change, growth, and improvement are just as crucial for human flourishing as self-compassion and self-acceptance; the key is finding the balance between them.

Like order and chaos, acceptance and change are inextricably interwoven, both aiding and opposing each other; they work in tandem atop the foundation of understanding. They are tools, skills, and strategies, which can be utilized in different contexts and situations. Pure acceptance in the face of that which is uncontrollable sets us free from turmoil, from ceaselessly attempting to push past the boundary of our uncomfortable reality. Acceptance means deliberately coming face to face with what we find intolerable about ourselves, both internally and externally, and making peace with what we see.

Accepting who we are requires that we fully understand our pasts and face our demons. It requires that we look unflinchingly at our history and attempt to forgive the injustices perpetrated against us, and equally, reconcile with our own actions, both the good and the bad. Indeed, an uncontrollable aspect of yourself or your situation, by its very definition, will remain that way whether you accept it or not, and thus the conscious and deliberate act of acceptance is the source of your freedom.

Self-acceptance works best when used in situations where the information available gives us only two choices: either allow the stress of an uncomfortable situation to disempower you or use it as the fuel to transcend your suffering. In either case, the choice to change your perspective is yours, and yours alone. On the other hand, the central space in which we can build the courage to change our lives in the direction of our choosing is through personal development; this reflects our innate ability to refuse to accept the issues and problems in our lives, especially the ones that there are clear solutions to, and strive to build, rebuild, or better ourselves. As the serenity prayer so eloquently articulates, the key is to know whether and when we must accept a situation, and when we can change it. We attain wisdom and understanding only after learning what we stand to gain or lose in any given situation.

* * *

One of the main goals of this book was to provide the basic knowledge and methods needed to "course-correct" between extremes to access personal freedom. Knowing how to course-correct, using the various tools contained herein, and being willing to do so, represents the human potential for change.

Sometimes, an inability to adequately balance acceptance and change will cause us anxiety and distress. When we worry, it's usually because we anticipate an uncertain future, which can leave us feeling trapped in the immobility of ambiguity. For example, if I know I have no choice but to accept something, at least my concerns are alleviated by letting go of my futile struggle for control and I can instead seek to adapt to the situation as best I can. If, on the other hand, I'm presented with a situation that has a clear solution or at least a malleable nature, all worries evaporate at my resolve. However, when a situation hangs somewhere in between, confusion seems to follow not far behind, which, I imagine, is another cause of our tendency to polarize.

Just as there will be events and circumstances in life that, despite our strongest efforts, will remain unacceptable to us, there will also be times in life in which polarizing is unavoidable. When we are worried about uncertainty, we feel we can alleviate much of our anxiety by choosing a side and infusing our identity with it. Feeling confident about this decision, any challenge to our identity is essentially a threat to our sense of self and security. Clinging to one side affords us an amelioration of our fears, and so we may fend off attempts made by others to join the opposing side, and also ignore appeals to the uncertain and scary middle ground where our identity, our very existence, is threatened.

When we attempt to balance or test our internal dialogue regarding our intentions or goals with external feedback, we get closer to meeting somewhere in the middle; however, getting too much input from our environment, like friends and family, and not enough from our own intuition can lead us to lose our autonomous selves and reinforce our dependency upon others. Similarly, relying too much on our internal systems to guide us can lead us to become unable to see how our actions affect others and even ourselves. To truly assess which path to take when determining any major life decision, we must integrate both internal and external feedback.

Admittedly, the middle path is not always clear; there will always be times when life presents us with situational gray areas. These may be difficult, if not impossible, for us to understand and will remain a source of discomfort. However, the gray areas don't have to be so frightening; indeed, we can learn to become comfortable with uncertainty. It's possible to cultivate the ability to accept that, though life will not always give us answers, our growth occurs through developing a tolerance of this ambiguity and unpredictability.

The wisdom of "knowing the difference" between acceptance and change empowers and enables us to accept our pain deliberately and use it as our motivation for change. It's precisely this sort of wisdom that unites acceptance and change and is integral to adequately navigating the middle path between order and chaos. It grants us the ability to select the appropriate course of action instead of it being chosen for us; this is the essence of self-determination. Through understanding how to balance acceptance and change, we gain access to our ultimate freedom.

The Map of Freedom

But what about freedom itself? Thus far, this book has talked endlessly about the importance of and methods of attaining free will. How can this stay consistent with the notion of balance? It's true that, as I've said before, freedom exists on a spectrum, at least from my perspective. And we must avoid polarizing free will, just as much as we should avoid believing it wholly nonexistent. However, it's easy to see that adopting a framework that consists of attaining absolute freedom can be just as limiting, if not more so, as constraining oneself within the notion that our lives are solely at the mercy of fate, luck, or happenstance, and that choice is an illusion. Attempting to obtain perfect freedom is essentially a descent into extremism. Freedom is both the quality as well as the practice of choosing the middle path.

Open-world video games can provide surprising insight into whether there is such a thing as "too much freedom" and help us gain a glimpse into the possible dynamics of human purpose. Admittedly, this is a rather unorthodox method of elucidation; however, sometimes profound wisdom can come from the most unlikely sources. Anyone who has ever played an open-world video game will be able to recall what it feels like to have too much freedom. If you have ever "beaten" or "won" a challenge in a video game, you've undoubtedly realized that, once you achieve every mission and have no more left to achieve, you are left roaming around in utter boredom. At this point, you either find a new goal, create one, or move on to a new game.

One day, I was playing a popular open-world video game in which, at a certain point, you reach a level where you can attain infinite power over the world. Once you have this you can do whatever you want, within the parameters of the game's physics, of course. During my downtime, or while bored, I would turn this game on, despite having "beaten" the final mission, and I would fly around and utilize my abilities. However, to my surprise and frustration, I'd often find that I could only do this for a very short time before again becoming incredibly bored.

Why was that? How could it be that when I achieved

virtually everything possible in a simulated world, I found myself less happy than when I had a mission to accomplish? How can having all the power and freedom in the "world" be… *boring?!* The answer was simple. It was precisely because there was nothing left to do after the game had been completed: there was no new level or higher goal to be attained and no purpose left. Essentially, there was nothing left to look forward to. This was just a further realization for me, among many, that having it "all" can feel shockingly similar to having "nothing" at all.

One can argue that it's unrealistic to compare a simplistic video game with the complexities of real life. And, fair enough, video games aren't real life. However, even "real," non-simulated life follows this formula. These games may not encapsulate all of the nuances of reality, but they help represent similar phenomena that occur in the process of struggle and attainment; that is, the feeling of boredom that inevitably sets in due to having nothing left to achieve. Individuals without a purpose find themselves despondent, spiritless, and perhaps even indifferent toward their lives.

It's important to note that you need not have ever played a video game in your life to understand this feeling. It might be any game in which you have developed mastery of the sort that left you feeling bored and unchallenged. Regardless of modality, we have all known what it's like to feel stagnant, like there's nothing left to pursue. This concept brings to mind the phrase, "It's the journey, not the destination." Indeed, it's the pursuit of goals, the excitement of challenges, and the hard-won victories where life satisfaction is found. Thus, freedom must be balanced, because you can feel as restrictive with too much freedom as with none at all.

In this perpetual drama we call life, a production of both comedic hilarity and abhorrent tragedy and everything in between, a story unfolding since the early days of humanity, we are continually trying to make sense of the confusion we have been born into. The suffering caused by this existential confusion extends for many layers, an incalculable depth into which even the most trivial squabbles are rooted. However, the stories of most major world religions and the philosophical quandaries found in many texts throughout history reveal something powerful and profound which can be discerned through the timeless and immutable nature of order and chaos.

Since the dawn of civilization, humankind has grappled with parts of themselves they abhor and detest while seeking to sharpen the parts that are seen as "good" and "right." Though it's apparent that this world consists of both happiness and suffering, it's the balance of both forces that is the key to wholeness. Rather than run from, avoid, or push away from our fears and suffering, we can learn to embrace them and see them as natural elements of our existence. I believe that the dots begin to connect more coherently when we view the world through this lens.

It's a mystery so far as to what constitutes life's ultimate or universal purpose, and I don't claim to know the answer. My aim is not to solve this complex problem, it's to provide a guide toward freedom, which is enhanced by cultivating individual purpose. Though we probably have a long journey ahead of us untangling the deep questions of human experience and existence, some exciting and profound insights can be observed where the avenues of empiricism and reason intersect. Indeed, I believe there are truths to be found and abundant common ground across every system of thought.

It should be noted that "the map is not the terrain" with any formula, concept, or theory. For example, when following a good map on a hiking trail, you may use it as a guide, but the actual trail may differ. If you only follow the map, you may be unable to see parts of the trail that have changed since the map's creation, or rather parts of the trail that a map cannot properly depict.

"Theory" is a type of map, and maps are only approximations of the real world. It can help you get where you need to go, but ultimately, you must use your own judgment and discretion to navigate the terrain. Fundamentally, this is the difference between theory and practice. Following theory too closely will cause you to ignore your own intuition, while practicing without theory may get you lost. Therefore, a healthy balance of the two is necessary to get to the top of the mountain and back.

There will be times in life when you will have to pick a side; times when, despite your best intentions, you will fall into extremes. However, if you have a detailed enough map, you will always be able to find your way back to the center. Ultimately, our journey to our destination has multiple navigational options. Some routes will get you there safely and expediently, some will get you lost, while others may bring you back to where you started. Other paths may take excessively long or be unreasonably difficult, but will still get you there eventually. Nonetheless, in my view, which is just one of many, irrespective of wherever, whenever, or however one may find it, the middle path of balance and equanimity is the path that opens the door to freedom.

Acknowledgements

I began writing the first draft of my manuscript after a conversation with my grammar school classmate Edward J. Flora, who I unexpectedly ran into while selling one of his books at a convention in Atlantic City, NJ, in 2018. At this time, I had written just thirty pages before I lost my confidence and gave up. Edward encouraged me to push forward; his words liberated me from the unfounded fears which had imprisoned my ambition and creativity. This conversation was critical, and without his inspiration, I probably wouldn't have written it.

This book is the product of my journey out of suffering and the idea was first conceived when I began to seek answers to how it all came to be. It is the tying together of years of observations within my personal life as a Zen student, martial arts practitioner, and the lives of my patients who have been my real teachers throughout my professional career. Their courage and endurance has inspired me, and I can only hope to give back some of that gift I've been given.

I want to express my deep appreciation to the clinicians, professors, authors, and scientists whose painstaking work has contributed to and shaped the current body of knowledge we are privileged to access. Your work has allowed me to answer many of the burning questions that led me to my current field and helped me bridge the gap between experience and textbook knowledge. With regards to all referenced material, I have worked hours on end and sacrificed much time to make sure I fully understood and have presented your hard work as accurately as possible. I sincerely apologize if I failed to do so. Please feel free to reach out to me and let me know if anything I've written misrepresents your work, and I will gladly fix it for future versions.

I want to express gratitude for the ancient and contemporary spiritual teachers and philosophers who have laid the foundations onto which we further our understanding of how to find meaning, purpose, and freedom in our lives. It is essential for me to note that, as information passes to different groups, cultures, individuals, it sometimes takes on a different flavor or interpretation. Mine is one of many different takes on these subjects, and thus it is meant as an introductory guide to motivate others to pursue the teachings and information provided herein. For those topics that one finds fascinating, or if one desires to learn more, I suggest going directly to the source, which is diligently cited and can be found in the *notes* section.

I want to thank my editors and designers at Reedsy, whose impressive work was humbling and made this book the absolute best it could be: Sarah Busby, Andy Dawson, Anna Krusinski, Megan Zavala, and Natalia Junqueira.

My friends and colleagues who endured me constantly talking about this book, whose insights, comments, and challenging questions acted as a sounding board that dramatically helped shape the book. Their honest and challenging feedback helped me feel more confident that the details of my message were being accounted for. More helpful than constructive criticism were their validating remarks and assurance during the many times I felt insecure and unsure and wondering if my message made sense, which gave me the fuel I needed to continue. I cannot list everyone, but know that I am grateful to those who I have not or could not mention. I thank especially Kevin J. Storburg, Christopher LaSalle, Philip D'Amico, Jeffery Goldman, and Cory Ann Cook.

My inspirational teachers, guides, and mentors who have shared with me their wisdom and steered me in the right direction: Ken Byalin, Eugene Isola, Andy Vetland, James Amberger, Hector Rosales, Joann Reetz, Lacey Sloan, Gregory Brown, Sergey Profis, Lauren Rogers-Sirin, Mike Buttermark, Cameron Searle, Joe Falbo, Patricia Correll-Dunphy, and Eli Shalenberg.

Also, in alignment with the theme of this book, I must also express gratitude for the negative experiences, all of which have shaped my life and current understanding. Along with the professors, doctors, senseis, therapists, and spiritual teachers, I must also thank the disciplinarians whose harsh treatment inadvertently helped me grow. Although it was probably not always their intention (to put it kindly), the difficult process of learning to triumph over those adversities gave me invaluable fortitude I may not have otherwise attained. I must also note that the 2019 COVID pandemic was a major source of stress for me, especially in the beginning. I worked twenty-four-hour shifts on the inpatient unit to ensure the safety and continued treatment of my patients. Indeed, this public health crisis continues to have significant impacts on many levels, including political, economic, social, environmental, and interpersonal. However, though I continued to work throughout the pandemic, the quarantine period, which caused closures and cancellations of most of my other obligations, allowed me to spend the extra free time working on the manuscript, which greatly sped up the process. One might say I was enabled to create some order out of the chaos.

Finally, I am eternally grateful to my parents, Karen and Frank, and my sister, Alana, for their unwavering love, support, and encouragement. They have helped provide me with the necessary foundation on top of which I have constructed the life of freedom I have today. Without their support, not only would this book not have been possible, but I may not have been around to write it. I am grateful for their patience and compassion towards me throughout the years as I struggled to find my own middle path between the order and chaos of my life. It is to them, my family, who I love deeply, to whom I've dedicated this book. Thank you from the bottom of my heart.

Notes

THE BEGINNING

1   Harari, Y. (2018). 21 lessons for the 21st century. London: Jonathan Cape. And Harris, S. (2012). Freewill. New York: Free Press. And Coyne, J. (2020, July 23). You don't have freewill. Retrieved January 02, 2021, from https://www.chronicle.com/article/you-dont-have-free-will/. And List, C. (2020, February 06). Science hasn't refuted freewill. Retrieved January 02, 2021, from http://bostonreview.net/science-nature-philosophy-religion/christian-list-science-hasnt-refuted-free-will.

2   Harris, S. (2012). Freewill. New York: Free Press. And Wegner, D. M. (2018). The illusion of conscious will. Cambridge, MA: The MIT Press. And Miles, J. B. (2015). The freewill delusion: How we settled for the illusion of morality. Kibworth Beauchamp: Matador.

THE CAUSES OF SUFFERING

3   Pleasants, S. A. (1966). The declaration of independence. C.E. Merrill Books

4   Rodziński, P., Rutkowski, K., & Ostachowska, A. (2017). Progression of suicidal ideation to suicidal behavior from a perspective of selected uicidological models. Progresja myśli samobójczych do zachowań samobójczych w świetle wybranych modeli suicydologicznych. *Psychiatria Polska, 51*(3), 515-530.

5   Throntveit, T. (2011). The fable of the fourteen points: Woodrow Wilson and national self-determination. *Diplomatic History, 35*(3), 445-481.

6   Deci, E. L., & Vansteenkiste, M. (2004). Self-determination theory and basic need satisfaction: Understanding human development in positive psychology. *Ricerche di Psicologia, 27*(1), 23-40.

7   Lee, L. (2010). Do patient autonomy preferences matter? Linking patient-centered care to patient–physician relationships and health

outcomes. *Social Science & Medicine (1982)*, *71(10)*, 1811–1818. And Ntoumanis, N. (2020). A meta-analysis of self-determination theory-informed intervention studies in the health domain: effects on motivation, health behavior, physical, and psychological health. *Health Psychology Review*, 1-31.

8 Fischer, B. (2011) What Is More Important for National Well-Being: Money or Autonomy? A Meta-Analysis of Well-Being, Burnout, and Anxiety Across 63 Societies. *Journal of personality and social psychology 101.1*, 164-184.

9 Black, A. E., & Deci, E. L. (2000). The effects of instructors' autonomy support and students' autonomous motivation on learning organic chemistry: A self-determination theory perspective. *Science Education*, *84(6)*, 740-756.

10 Code of Ethics of the National Association of Social Workers. (2005). *Journal of Aggression, Maltreatment & Trauma*, *11(3)*, 395-422.

11 Hollis, F. (1955). Principles and assumptions underlying casework practice. *Social Work (1939-1970)*, *12(2)*, 41-55.

12 Van der Kolk, B. (2015). The body keeps the score: brain, mind, and body in the healing of trauma, 54-55. Penguin.

13 Vohs, K.D., Schooler, J.W. (2008). The value of believing in freewill: Encouraging a belief in determinism increases cheating. *Psychological Science*, *19(1)*, 49-54.

14 Baumeister, R., Crescioni, A.W., Alquist, J. (2009). Freewill as advanced action control for human social life and culture. *Neuroethics*. *4*, 1-11. And Baumeister, R.F., Masicampo, E.J., DeWall, C.N. (2009). Prosocial benefits of feeling free: Disbelief in freewill increases aggression and reduces helpfulness. *Personality and Social Psychology Bulletin*, *35(2)*, 260-68. And Stillman, T. F., Baumeister, R.F., Vohs, K. D., Lambert, N.M., Fincham, F.D., Brewer, L.E. (2010). Personal Philosophy and Personnel Achievement: Belief in Freewill Predicts Better Job Performance. *Social Psychological and Personality Science*, *1(1)*, 43-50. And Miles, J.B. (2011). 'Irresponsible and a disservice': The integrity of social psychology turns on the freewill dilemma. *British Journal of Social Psychology*, *52(2)*, 205-18.

A BRIEF HISTORY OF FREE WILL

15 Libet, B., Gleason, C. A., Wright, E. W., & Pearl, D. K. (1983). Time

of conscious intention to act in relation to onset of cerebral activity (readiness-potential). The unconscious initiation of a freely voluntary act. *Brain: A Journal of Neurology*, *106 (Pt 3)*, 623-642.

16 Colman, A. (2015). psychical determinism. A dictionary of psychology. Oxford University Press.

17 Libet B., Gleason C.A., Wright E.W., & Pearl, D.K. (1983). Time of conscious intention to act in relation to onset of cerebral activity (readiness-potential): the unconscious initiation of a freely voluntary act. *Brain: A Journal of Neurology*, *106 (Pt 3)*, 623-642.10.1093/brain/106.3.623.

18 Ibid.

19 Libet, B. (1985). Unconscious cerebral initiative and the role of conscious will in voluntary action. *The Behavioral and Brain Sciences, 8*, 529–566..

20 Fisher, C.M. (1993). Concerning mind. *Can J Neurol Sci,20(3)*, 247-53. And
    Fisher, C.M. (2003). The reach of neurology. *Arch Neurol, 60(2)*, 173-177.

21 van Duijn, B. (2005). On the Alleged Illusion of Conscious Will. *Philosophical Psychology, 18(6)*, 699-714. And Roth, G. (2003). The interaction of cortex and basal ganglia in the control of voluntary actions. In S. Maasen, W. Prinz, & G. Roth (Eds.), Voluntary action: Brains, minds, and sociality, 115-132. New York: Oxford University Press. And Harris, S. (2012). Freewill. New York: Free Press.

22 Libet, B. (1985). Unconscious cerebral initiative.

23 Dennett, D.C. (2007). Freedom Evolves. London: Penguin.

24 Csikszentmihályi, M. (1990). Flow: The psychology of optimal experience. New York, NY: Harper and Row.

25 Corsini, R. (2002). flow. A dictionary of psychology. Routledge. https://doi.org/10.4324/9781315781501

26 Csikszentmihályi, M., & Larson, R. (2014). Flow and the foundations of positive psychology: The collected works of Mihaly Csikszentmihalyi. (Vol. 10, pp. 978-94). Dordrecht: Springer.

27 Bion, W. R. (1994). Learning from experience. Jason Aronson.

28 van Riel, R. (2017). Freewill, Foreknowledge, and Future-Dependent Beliefs. *The Southern Journal of Philosophy, 55(4)*, 500-520.

THE PHENOMENON OF POLARIZATION

29 Kernberg, O. F. (1975). Borderline conditions and pathological narcissism. New York, NY: Jason Aronson.

30 Lakritz, K. (2009). Kernberg's borderline conditions and pathological narcissism. *Psychiatric Times, 26(2)*, 15.

31 Perry, J. C., & Herman, J. L. (1992). Trauma and defense in the etiology of borderline personality disorder." In J. Paris (Ed.), Borderline personality disorder: Etiology and treatment, 123–139. Washington, DC: American Psychiatric Press.

32 American, P. A. (2013). *Diagnostic and Statistical Manual of Mental Disorders (dsm-5®)*.

33 Moscovici, Z. (1969). The group as a polarizer of attitudes. *Journal of Personality and Social Psychology, 12(2)*, 125-135.

DEGREES OF FREEDOM

34 MacCallum, G. (1967). Negative and Positive Freedom. *The Philosophical Review, 76(3)*, 312-334.

35 Hume, D. (2012). Treatise of Human Nature. Dover Publications.

36 Often, when the terms "positive" and "negative" are used in different contexts they can be confusing. In some contexts, "positive" means "good" and in others it means the presence rather than absence of something. So, to be clear, when discussing "negative freedom," it means freedom from restriction.

37 Hume, D. (2012). Treatise of Human Nature. Dover Publications.

38 Cormier B., Williams P. (1966). Excessive deprivation of liberty. *Can. Psychiatr. Assoc. J. 11*, 470-84. And Cullen F. (1995). Assessing the penal harm movement. *J. Res. Crime Delinq. 32*, 338-58.

39 Grassian, S., & Friedman, N. (1986). Effects of sensory deprivation in psychiatric seclusion and solitary confinement. *International Journal of Law and Psychiatry, 8(1)*, 49-65.

40 Haney, C. (2009). The social psychology of isolation: Why solitary confinement is psychologically harmful. *Prison Serv J. 181*, 12-20.

41 Bukstel, L. H., & Kilmann, P. R. (1980). Psychological effects of imprisonment on confined individuals. *Psychological Bulletin, 88(2)*, 469.

42 Deaton, J., Berg, W., & Richlin, M. (1977). Coping activities in solitary confinement of U.S. Navy POWs in Vietnam. *Journal of Applied Social Psychology 7*, 239-57.

43 Frankl, V. E. (2018). Man's search for meaning. Noura Books.

44 Frankfurt, H. (1971). Freedom of the will and the concept of a person. *The Journal of Philosophy, 68(1)*, 5-20.

45 VandenBos, G. R. (2007). impulsivity. APA dictionary of psychology. American Psychological Association.

46 Schumann, C. M., Bauman, M. D., & Amaral, D. G. (2011). Abnormal structure or function of the amygdala is a common component of neurodevelopmental disorders. *Neuropsychologia, 49(4)*, 745-759.

47 Rakic, P. (2009). Evolution of the neocortex: a perspective from developmental biology. Nature Reviews. *Neuroscience, 10(10)*, 724-735. https://doi.org/10.1038/nrn2719

48 Murray, E., Wise, S., & Graham, K. (2018). The evolution of memory systems: Ancestors, anatomy, and adaptations (First edition). Oxford University Press.

49 Amunts, K., Kedo, O., Kindler, M., Pieperhoff, P., Mohlberg, H., Shah, N. J., Habel, U., Schneider, F., & Zilles, K. (2005). Cytoarchitectonic mapping of the human amygdala, hippocampal region and entorhinal cortex: intersubject variability and probability maps. *Anatomy and Embryology, 210(5-6)*, 343-352.

50 Siever, L. (2008). Neurobiology of aggression and violence. *American Journal of Psychiatry, 165(4)*, 429-442.

51 Goleman, D. (1995). Emotional intelligence: why it can matter more than IQ. New York: Bantam Books.

52 Siever, L. (2008). Neurobiology of aggression and violence. *The American Journal of Psychiatry, 165(4)*, 429-442.

53 Jensen, F., & Mullen, S. (1982). C.G. Jung, Emma Jung and Toni Wolff: A collection of remembrances. San Francisco, CA: Analytical Psychology Club of San Francisco.

54 Taylor, J. Stacey (2017, June 20). Autonomy. Encyclopedia Britannica. https://www.britannica.com/topic/autonomy

55 Ibid.

56 Britannica, T. Editors of Encyclopedia (2020, May 27). humanistic

psychology. Encyclopedia Britannica. https://www.britannica.com/science/humanistic-psychology.

57 Schneider, K. J., Pierson, J. F., & Bugental, J. F. (2014). The handbook of humanistic psychology: Theory, research, and practice. Los Angeles, CA: Sage.

58 Deci, E. L. (1971). Effects of externally mediated rewards on intrinsic motivation. *Journal of Personality and Social Psychology, 18,* 105-115. 10.1037/h003064

59 Ryan, R.M., Kuhl, J., Deci, E.L. Nature and autonomy: an organizational view of social and neurobiological aspects of self-regulation in behavior and development. *Dev Psychopathol. 1997 Fall, 9(4),* 701-28.

60 Ryan, R., Patrick, H., Deci, E., & Williams, G. (2008). Facilitating health behaviour change and its maintenance: Interventions based on self-determination theory. *European Psychologist, 10(2).*

61 Gagné, M., & Deci, E. L. (2005). Self-determination theory and work motivation. *Journal of Organizational Behavior, 26,* 331-362.

62 Haggbloom, S. J., Warnick, R., Warnick, J. E., Jones, V. K., Yarbrough, G. L., Russell, T. M., ... & Monte, E. (2002). The 100 most eminent psychologists of the 20th century. *Review of General Psychology, 6 (2),* 139-152.

63 Rotter, J.B. (1966). Generalized expectancies for internal versus external control of reinforcement. *Psychological Monographs, 80(1),* 1-28.

64 Weiner, B. (2006). Social motivation, justice, and the moral emotions: An attributional approach. *Psychology Press.* https://doi.org/10.4324/9781410615749.

65 DeCharms, R. (1968). Personal causation: the internal affective determinants of behavior. New York: Academic.

66 Self-determination theory contains a quadrumvirate motivation grouping. This converges into a spectrum of *perceived* "locus of causality" in which feelings and behaviors can be situated from wholly externally motivated to completely internally motivated.

67 Ryan, R. M. (1982). Control and information in the intrapersonal sphere: An extension of cognitive evaluation theory. *Journal of Personality and Social Psychology 43,* 450-461.

68 Seligman, M.E.P. (1991) Learned optimism. Knopf: New York.

69 Shapiro, D.H. Jr., Schwartz, C.E., Astin, J.A. (1996). Controlling ourselves, controlling our world: Psychology's role in understanding positive and negative consequences of seeking and gaining control. *American Psychologist, 51(12)*,1213-1230.

70 Allen, D. G., Weeks, K. P., Moffitt, K. R. (2005). Turnover intentions and voluntary turnover: The moderating roles of self-monitoring, locus of control, proactive personality, and risk aversion. *Journal of Applied Psychology, 90(5)*, 980-990.

71 Connolly, S. (1980). Changing expectancies: A counseling model based on locus of control. *The Personnel and Guidance Journal, 59(3)*, 176-180.

72 April, K., Dharani, B., & Peters, K. (2012). Impact of locus of control expectancy on level of well-being. *Review of European Studies, 4(2)*.

73 Sheldon, K. M. (2001). The self-concordance model of healthy goal-striving: Implications for well-being and personality development. In Schmuck, P., & Sheldon, K., (Eds.), Life goals and well-being: Towards a positive psychology of human striving, 17–35. Seattle, WA.: Hogrefe and Huber.

74 Seligman, M. E. P. (1975). Helplessness: On depression, development, and death. San Francisco: W. H. Freeman.

75 Maier, S. F., & Seligman, M. E. (2016). Learned helplessness at fifty: Insights from neuroscience. *Psychological Review, 123(4)*, 349-367. And Maier, S. F., & Watkins, L. R. (2005). Stressor controllability and learned helplessness: the roles of the dorsal raphe nucleus, serotonin, and corticotropin-releasing factor. *Neuroscience & Biobehavioral Reviews, 29(4-5)*, 829-841.

76 Hiroto, D. S. (1974). Locus of control and learned helplessness. *Journal of Experimental Psychology, 102(2)*, 187-193.

77 Hiroto, D. S., & Seligman, M. E. (1975). Generality of learned helplessness in man. *Journal of Personality and Social Psychology, 31(2)*, 311.

78 Henry, P. C. (2005). Life stresses, explanatory style, hopelessness, and occupational class. *International Journal of Stress Management, 12(3)*, 241-256.

79 Greenwood, B. N., & Fleshner, M. (2008). Exercise, learned helplessness, and the stress-resistant brain. *Neuromolecular Medicine, 10(2)*, 81-98.

80 Barker, R. L. (2003). The social work dictionary. Washington, DC: NASW Press.

81 Frankl, V. E. (2018). Man's Search for Meaning. Noura Books.

ORDER AND CHAOS: DYNAMIC SHIFTS

82 Peterson, J. B. (2018). 12 rules for life: An antidote to chaos. Random House Canada.

83 Peterson, J. B. (2018). 12 rules for life: An antidote to chaos. And Biblical Series II: Genesis 1: Chaos & Order Transcript. (2018, April 17). Retrieved January 11, 2021, from https://www.jordanbpeterson.com/transcripts/biblical-series-ii/.

84 Wang, R. (2012). Yinyang: The way of heaven and earth in Chinese thought and culture. In Yinyang (Vol. 11). Cambridge University Press.

85 Simpson, J. A., & Speake, J. (1992). The concise Oxford dictionary of proverbs. Oxford: Oxford University Press.

86 The terms "middle way," "middle path," and "golden mean" will be used interchangeably to avoid repetition.

87 Ellis, R. M. (2015). Middle way philosophy: Omnibus edition. Lulu.com.

88 Nicomachean ethics. (2019). Hackett Publishing.

89 Harvey, P. (2013). An introduction to Buddhism teachings, history and practices. Cambridge: Cambridge University Press.

90 Christian Art Publishers. (2013). The holy bible: King James version.

91 Kahneman, D., Diener, E., and Schwarz, N. (eds). (1999). Well-being: The foundations of hedonic psychology. New York, NY: Russell Sage Foundation.

92 Kierkegaard, S. (1992). Either/or: A fragment of life, trans. Alistaire Hannay, 46. London and New York: Penguin..

93 Nietzsche, F. (2001). Nietzsche: Beyond good and evil: Prelude to a philosophy of the future. Cambridge University Press.

94 Ryan, R. M., and Deci, E. L. (2001). To be happy or to be self-fulfilled: a review of research on hedonic and eudaimonic well-being. *Annual Review of Psychology, 52*, ed. S. Fiske, 141-166. Palo Alto, CA: Annual Reviews.,

95 Rée, J., & Urmson, J. O. (Eds.). (2004). The concise encyclopedia of western philosophy, 152.

96 Rogers, C. (1961). On becoming a person. Boston, MA: Houghton Mifflin Co. And Rogers, C. (1963). The actualizing tendency in relation

to "motives" and to consciousness. In M. R. Jones (Ed.), Nebraska symposium on motivation (Vol. 11, 1-24). Lincoln, NE: University of Nebraska Press.

97 Sheldon, K. M., & Niemiec, C. P. (2006). It's not just the amount that counts: Balanced need satisfaction also affects well-being. *Journal of Personality and Social Psychology, 91*, 331-341.

98 Seligman, M. E. P. (2002). Authentic happiness. New York, NY: Free Press.

99 Fredrickson, B. L., & Losada, M. (2005). Positive affect and the complex dynamics of human flourishing. *American Psychologist, 60*, 678-686.

100 Peterson, C., Park, N., & Seligman, M. E. P. (2005). Orientations to happiness and life satisfaction: The full life versus the empty life. *Journal of Happiness Studies, 6*, 2-41.

101 Small, D. M., Zatorre, R. J., Dagher, A., Evans, A. C., & Jones-Gotman, M. (2001). Changes in brain activity related to eating chocolate. From pleasure to aversion. *Brain, 124*, 1720-1733.

102 Brickman, P., Coates, D., & Janoff-Bulman, R. (1978). Lottery winners and accident victims: Is happiness relative? *Journal of Personality and Social Psychology, 36(8)*, 917-927.

103 Sheldon, K. M., & Lucas, R. E. (Eds.). (2014). Stability of happiness: Theories and evidence on whether happiness can change. Elsevier.

104 Frey, B. S., Benesch, C., & Stutzer, A. (2007). Does watching TV make us happy? *Journal of Economic Psychology, 28*, 283-313.

105 Olds, J. (1970). Pleasure centers in the brain. *Engineering and Science, 33(7)*, 22-31.

106 Christian Art Publishers. (2013). The holy bible: King James version.

107 Benatti, F. (2003). Classical and quantum entropies: Dynamics and information. Entropy, 279-298.

108 Hawking, S. (1998). A brief history of time: Updated and expanded tenth anniversary edition. Bantam Books.

109 Sheldon, K. M., Joiner, T., & Williams, G. Self-determination theory in the clinic: Motivating physical and mental health. New Haven, CT: Yale University Press.

ACCEPTANCE AND CHANGE

110 Neff, K. (2015). The 5 myths of self-compassion. *Psychotherapy Networker, 39*(5). And Hastings, M. (2017, February 01). 5 myths about self-acceptance you should stop believing right now. Retrieved January 25, 2021, from https://medium.com/@marissa.hastings/5-myths-about-self-acceptance-you-should-stop-believing-right-now-e3baed5e4e18.

111 Graham, C. A. (2013). Carpe diem. *European Journal of Emergency Medicine: Official Journal of the European Society for Emergency Medicine, 20*(2), 71-71.

112 Miller, S., & Krauser, M. (2012, June 01). Parents, students: Hoffman estates school overreacted to Senior prank. Retrieved January 19, 2021, from https://chicago.cbslocal.com/2012/06/01/parent-teachers-swore-at-hoffman-estates-students-over-senior-prank/.

113 Dryden, W. (2013). Unconditional self-acceptance and self-compassion. In the strength of self-acceptance, 107-120. New York: Springer.

114 Hayes, S. C... Acceptance & commitment therapy (ACT). ContextualPsychology.org

115 Hayes, S. C., Strosahl, K. D., Wilson, K. G. (2012). Acceptance and commitment therapy: The process and practice of mindful change (second ed.), 240. New York: Guilford Press..

116 Hewitt, P. L., Flett, G. L., & Mikail, S. F. (2017). Perfectionism: A relational approach to conceptualization, assessment, and treatment. Guilford Press.

117 Watts, C. T. (1988). Hamlet. Twayne Publishers.

118 Vlahopoulos, B. A. (1986). The relationships between psychological well-being, self-acceptance, client status, and counselor facilitative behaviors (self concept). University of Cincinnati.

119 Sheldon, K. M., Ryan, R. M., Rawsthorne, L., & Ilardi, B. (1997). "True" self and "trait" self: Cross-role variation in the big five traits and its relations with authenticity and well-being. *Journal of Personality and Social Psychology 73*, 1380-1393.

120 Rogers, C. R. (1957). Becoming a person. In Symposium on emotional development, Oberlin College, Oberlin, OH. This chapter represents a lecture by Dr. Rogers given at the aforementioned symposium. Association Press.

121 Ibid.

122 Wegner, D. M., & Erber, R. (1992). The hyperaccessibility of suppressed thoughts. *Journal of Personality and Social Psychology, 63*(6), 903-912.

123 Sweller, J., Ayres, P., & Kalyuga, S. (2011). Cognitive load theory (first ed.). New York: Springer.

124 He speculated that it might be possible that directed and intentional thought suppression could lead to an improved ability to control unwanted thoughts over time.

125 Aurora, S. T. (2006). The paradoxical effects of suppressing anxious thoughts. *Cognition, Brain, Behavior, 10*(4), 599.

126 Purdon, C. (1999). Thought suppression and psychopathology. *Behaviour Research and Therapy, 37*(11), 1029-1054.

127 Erskine, J. A., Georgiou, G. J., & Kvavilashvili, L. (2010). I suppress, therefore I smoke: Effects of thought suppression on smoking behavior. *Psychological Science, 21*(9), 1225-1230.

128 Borton, J. L., Markowitz, L. J., & Dieterich, J. (2005). Effects of suppressing negative self–referent thoughts on mood and self–esteem. *Journal of Social and Clinical Psychology, 24*(2), 172-190.

129 Goldin, P., Ramel, W., & Gross, J. (2009). Mindfulness meditation training and self-referential processing in social anxiety disorder: Behavioral and neural effects. *Journal of Cognitive Psychotherapy, 23*(3), 242-257.

130 Giuliano, R. J., & Wicha, N. Y. (2010). Why the white bear is still there: Electrophysiological evidence for ironic semantic activation during thought suppression. *Brain Research, 1316*, 62-74.

131 Lisa Dietz (2003). DBT Skills List. Retrieved April 26, 2010, from https://www.dbtselfhelp.com/html/dbt_skills_list.html.

132 Van Dijk, S. (2012). DBT made simple: A step-by-step guide to dialectical behavior therapy. New Harbinger Publications.

133 Pederson, L. (2015). Dialectical behavior therapy: A contemporary guide for practitioners. In Dialectical behavior therapy. John Wiley & Sons.

134 Öst, L. G. (2008). Efficacy of the third wave of behavioral therapies: A systematic review and meta-analysis. *Behaviour Research and Therapy. 46 (3)*, 296-321.

135 Wilson, H. (2000). Exploring compatibilities between acceptance and commitment therapy and 12-step treatment for substance abuse. *Journal*

of Rational-Emotive and Cognitive-Behavior Therapy, 18(4), 209-234.

136 Wang, X. (2011). Zhi Mian and existential psychology. *The Humanistic Psychologist, 39(3),* 240-246.

137 Wilson, H. Exploring Compatibilities between

138 Ryff, C. D., & Singer, B. (1996). Psychological well-being: meaning, measurement, and implications for psychotherapy research. *Psychotherapy and Psychosomatics, 65,* 14-23.

FINDING NON-SELF

139 Sutta, A. L. (2010). The discourse on the not-self characteristic, Saṃyutta Nikāya, 22.59, edited and translated from the Pali by Ñanamoli Thera. Access to Insight.

140 Suzuki, S. (1970). Zen mind beginners mind. John Weatherhill. INC. New York and Tokyo.

141 Rohn, J. & de Bruyn, E. (2017). Choosing a trustworthy boss: Management. *The Dairy Mail, 24(4),* 54-55.

142 Kelman, H. (1958). Compliance, identification, and internalization: Three processes of attitude change. *Journal of Conflict Resolution, 2(1),* 51-60. And Wood, W., Lundgren, S., Ouellette, J., Busceme, S. & Blackstone, T. (1994). Minority influence: A meta-analytic review of social influence processes. *Psychological Bulletin. 115(3),* 323-345.

143 Colman, A. (2015). social influence. A dictionary of psychology. Oxford University Press.

144 Taylor, R. (1992). Metaphysics, 127. Prentice-Hall.

145 Broks, P. (2003). Into the silent land: Travels in neuropsychology. New York, NY: Atlantic Monthly Press.

146 Tononi, G., Boly, M., Massimini, M., & Koch, C. (2016). Integrated information theory: From consciousness to its physical substrate. Nature Reviews. *Neuroscience, 17(7),* 450-461. https://doi.org/10.1038/nrn.2016.44

147 Watts, A. (1999). The way of Zen. Vintage.

148 Hsu, L.. (2013) Relational Buddhism: An Integrative Psychology of Happiness Amidst Existential Suffering. in Oxford Handbook of Happiness. Vol. 1. Oxford University Press.

149 Khyentse, D.. (1993). The heart treasure of the enlightened ones: The practice of view, meditation, and action. (Padmakara Translation Group,

Trans.). Boston, MA: Shambhala Publications.

150 Gergen, K. J. (2009). Relational Being. Oxford: Oxford University Press. And Gergen, K. J. (2010). The acculturated brain. *Theory & Psychology, 20*, 795-816.

151 Okumura, S. (2010). Realizing genjokoan: The key to Dogen's Shobogenzo. Simon and Schuster.

MEDITATION AND MINDFULNESS

152 De Silva, M. W. P. (2005). An introduction to Buddhist psychology (fourth ed.). London: Palgrave-Macmillan.

153 Walsh, R., Shapiro, S. L. (2006). The meeting of meditative disciplines and western psychology: A mutually enriching dialogue. American Psychologist.

154 Seligman, M. E. (2004). Authentic happiness: Using the new positive psychology to realize your potential for lasting fulfillment. Simon and Schuster. And Pederson, L. (2015). Dialectical behavior therapy: A contemporary guide for practitioners. John Wiley & Sons.

155 Fitzpatrick, L. (2019). The monk who taught the world mindfulness awaits the end of this life. *Time 193(4)*. Chicago, IL.

156 Suzuki, S. (2020). Zen mind, beginner's mind. Shambhala Publications.

157 Damasio, A. R. (1994). Descartes' error. New York, NY: Avon Books. And Davidson, R. J. (2000). Cognitive neuroscience needs affective neuroscience (and vice versa). *Cognition and Emotion, 42*, 89-92. And Davidson, R. J., & Irwin, W. (1999). The functional neuroanatomy of emotion and affective style. *Trends in Cognitive Science, 3*, 11-21.

158 Landaw, Jonathan, et al. (2019) Buddhism for Dummies, 152. John Wiley & Sons.

159 Cole, M. (1994). The development of emotion regulation and dysregulation: A clinical perspective. *Monographs of the Society for Research in Child Development, 59(2/3)*, 73-100.

160 Zeman, J., Cassano, M., Perry-Parrish, C., & Stegall, S. (2006). Emotion regulation in children and adolescents. *Journal of Developmental & Behavioral Pediatrics, 27(2)*, 155-168.

161 Chawla, N., Collins, S., Bowen, S., Hsu, S., Grow, J., Douglass, A., & Marlatt, G. A. (2010). The mindfulness-based relapse prevention adherence and competence scale: Development, interrater reliability, and validity. *Psychotherapy Research, 20(4)*, 388-397.

162 Craig, A. D. (2003). Interoception: The sense of the physiological condition of the body. *Current Opinion in Neurobiology, 13*(4), 500-505.

163 Banks, S. J., Eddy, K. T., Angstadt, M., Nathan, P. J., & Phan, K. L. (2007). Amygdala-frontal connectivity during emotion regulation. *Social Cognitive and Affective Neuroscience, 2*(4), 303-312.

164 Brown, K. W., & Kasser, T. (2005). Are psychological and ecological well-being compatible? The role of values, mindfulness, and lifestyle. *Social Indicators Research, 74*(2), 349-368.

165 Yuan, R. (2014). Prefrontal cortex and executive functions in healthy adults: A meta-analysis of structural neuroimaging studies. *Neuroscience and Biobehavioral Reviews, 42,* 180-192.

166 Elliott, R. (2003). Executive functions and their disorders. *British Medical Bulletin, 65*(1), 49-59.

167 Sapolsky, R. M. (1998). Why zebras don't get ulcers: An updated guide to stress, stress-related diseases, and coping. New York: W.H. Freeman and Co

168 Hernández, S. E., Suero, J., Barros, A., González-Mora, J. L., & Rubia, K. (2016). Increased grey matter associated with long-term sahaja yoga meditation: A voxel-based morphometry study. *PloS One, 11*(3), e0150757.

169 Kang, J. (2013). The effect of meditation on brain structure: Cortical thickness mapping and diffusion tensor imaging. *Social Cognitive and Affective Neuroscience, 8*(1), 27-33.

170 Kabat-Zinn, J. (2003). Mindfulness-based stress reduction (MBSR). *Constructivism in the Human Sciences, 8*(2), 73.

171 Hölzel, C. (2010). Stress reduction correlates with structural changes in the amygdala. *Social Cognitive and Affective Neuroscience, 5*(1), 11-17, And Hölzel, C. (2010). Mindfulness practice leads to increases in regional brain gray matter density. *Psychiatry Research. Neuroimaging, 191*(1), 36-43.

172 Ibid.

173 Jensen, D. (2014). Neuromodulatory treatments for chronic pain: Efficacy and mechanisms. Nature Reviews. *Neurology, 10*(3), 167-178.

174 Fox, N. (2014). Is meditation associated with altered brain structure? A systematic review and meta-analysis of morphometric neuroimaging

in meditation practitioners. *Neuroscience and Biobehavioral Reviews, 43,* 48-73.

175 Reive, C. (2019). The biological measurements of mindfulness-based stress reduction: A systematic review. *Explore, 15(4),* 295-307.

176 Brewer, J. A., Worhunsky, P. D., Gray, J. R., Tang, Y. Y., Weber, J., & Kober, H. (2011). Meditation experience is associated with differences in default mode network activity and connectivity. *Proceedings of the National Academy of Sciences, 108(50),* 20254-20259.

177 Tang, Y. Y., Lu, Q., Fan, M., Yang, Y., & Posner, M. I. (2012). Mechanisms of white matter changes induced by meditation. *Proceedings of the National Academy of Sciences, 109(26),* 10570-10574.

178 Baer, R. (Ed.). (2010). Assessing mindfulness and acceptance processes in clients: Illuminating the theory and practice of change. New Harbinger Publications. And Chambers, R., Lo, B. C. Y., & Allen, N. B. (2008). The impact of intensive mindfulness training on attentional control, cognitive style, and affect. *Cognitive Therapy and Research, 32(3),* 303-322.

179 Stroop, J. (1992). Studies of interference in serial verbal reactions. *Journal of Experimental Psychology. General, 121(1),* 15-23.

180 Root-Bernstein, R (2007). Brain aging: Models, methods, And mechanisms. *The Journal of the American Medical Association. 298(23),* 2798-2799.

181 Moore, A., Malinowski, P. (March 2009). Meditation, mindfulness and cognitive flexibility. *Consciousness and Cognition. 18(1),* 176-86.

182 Fabio, F. (2018). Long-term meditation: the relationship between cognitive processes, thinking styles and mindfulness. *Cognitive Processing, 19(1),* 73-85.

183 Moore, G. (2012). Regular, brief mindfulness meditation practice improves electrophysiological markers of attentional control. *Frontiers in Human Neuroscience, 6,* 18.

184 Kabat-Zinn, J. (1990). Using the wisdom of your body and mind to face stress, pain, and illness. New York, NY: Bantam Doubleday Dell. And Fosha, D. E., Siegel, D. J., & Solomon, M. F. (2009). The healing power of emotion: Affective neuroscience, development & clinical practice. WW Norton & Company.

185 Goyal, S. (2014). Meditation programs for psychological stress and well-being: A systematic review and meta-analysis. *JAMA Internal Medicine,*

174(3), 357-368.

186 Jain, W. (2015). Critical analysis of the efficacy of meditation therapies for acute and subacute phase treatment of depressive disorders: A systematic review. *Psychosomatics, 56(2)*, 140-152.

187 Walsh, S. (2019). Effects of a mindfulness meditation app on subjective well-being: Active randomized controlled trial and experience sampling study. *JMIR Mental Health, 6(1)*, e10844-e10844.

188 Keune, P. M., & Perczel Forintos, D. (2010). Mindfulness meditation: A preliminary study on meditation practice during everyday life activities and its association with well-being. *Psihologijske Teme, 19(2)*, 373-386.

189 McKay, M., Davis, M., & Fanning, P. (2011). Thoughts and feelings: Taking control of your moods and your life. New Harbinger Publications.

190 Carlson, L. E., Speca, M., Faris, P., & Patel, K. D. (2007). One year pre–post intervention follow-up of psychological, immune, endocrine and blood pressure outcomes of mindfulness-based stress reduction (MBSR) in breast and prostate cancer outpatients. *Brain, Behavior, and Immunity, 21(8)*, 1038-1049.

191 Corey, G., & Corey, M. S. (2013). I never knew I had a choice: Explorations in personal growth. Cengage Learning.

ENTER THE HUMAN SHADOW

192 Jung, C. G. (1960). Good and evil in analytical psychology. *Journal of Analytical Psychology, 5(2)*, 872

193 Jung, C. G. (1960). Psychology and religion. Yale University Press.

194 Young-Eisendrath, P., & Dawson, T. (Eds.). (2008). The Cambridge companion to Jung. Cambridge University Press.

195 Jung, C., & Storr, A. (1983). The essential Jung. Princeton University Press.

196 Jung, C. G. (2014). The archetypes and the collective unconscious. Routledge.

197 Zweig, C., & Abrams, J. (Eds.). (1991). Meeting the shadow: The hidden power of the dark side of human nature. TarcherPerigee.

198 Pörn, I. (1984). Kierkegaard and the study of the self. *Inquiry, 27(1-4)*, 199-205.

199 There are several different terms for this phenomenon of internalized productivity, but ultimately, it was just another form of polarizing.

200 Kivetz, R. & Simonson, I. (2002). Self-control for the righteous: Toward a theory of precommitment to indulgence. *The Journal of Consumer Research, 29(2),* 199-217. And Haws, K. L., & Poynor, C. (2008). Seize the day! Encouraging indulgence for the hyperopic consumer. *Journal of Consumer Research, 35(4),* 680-691.

201 Shirom, A. (1989). Burnout in work organizations. In C. L. Cooper & I. T. Robertson (Eds.), International review of industrial and organizational psychology, 25–48. John Wiley & Sons.

202 Giannini, A.J. (1991). Fatigue, chronic. In Taylor, Robert B. (Eds.). Difficult diagnosis 2, 156. Philadelphia: W.B. Saunders Co. And Hockey, R. (2013). The psychology of fatigue: Work, effort and control. Cambridge University Press. And Styles, E. A. (1997). The psychology of attention. Psychology Press. And Pashler, H. (1998). The psychology of attention. A Bradford book. MIT Press.

203 Homeyer, F. (2017) Two wolves. *Ranch and Rural Living, 98(6),* 13.

204 Anyone wishing to meet their shadow can do so with the help of a qualified therapist. It can help you connect to who you are fundamentally, especially if you feel your issues stem from being forced to be who you aren't.

NOTHING GOOD OR BAD

205 Ozer, B. (2003). Predictors of posttraumatic stress disorder and symptoms in adults: A meta-Analysis. *Psychological Bulletin, 129(1),* 52-73.

206 Salleh M. R. (2008). Life event, stress and illness. *The Malaysian journal of medical sciences : MJMS, 15*(4), 9–18.

207 Zlotnick, C., Johnson, J., Kohn, R., Vicente, B., Rioseco, P., & Saldivia, S. (2008). Childhood trauma, trauma in adulthood, and psychiatric diagnoses: results from a community sample. *Comprehensive psychiatry, 49(2),* 163–169. https://doi.org/10.1016/j.comppsych.2007.08.007

208 Rodriguez, N., Kemp, H. V., & Foy, D. W. (1998). Posttraumatic stress disorder in survivors of childhood sexual and physical abuse: A critical review of the empirical research. *Journal of Child Sexual Abuse, 7*(2), 17-45.

209 Van der Kolk, B. (2015). The body keeps the score: brain, mind, and body in the healing of trauma, 54-55. Penguin.

210 Watts, C. T. (1988). Hamlet. Twayne Publishers

211 McKay, M., Davis, M., & Fanning, P. (2011). Thoughts and feelings: Taking control of your moods and your life. New Harbinger Publications.

212 Colman, A. M. (2015). cognitive restructuring. A dictionary of psychology. Oxford University Press.

213 Nietzsche, F. W., Saintilan, P., & Grünwald, M. (2000). What doesn't kill me makes me stronger. Sydney: Ice Calm.

214 Lechner, S., Stoelb, B., & Antoni, M. (2008). Group-based therapies for benefit finding in cancer. In S. Joseph & A. Linley (Eds.), Trauma, recovery, and growth: Positive psychological perspectives on post-traumatic stress, 207-231. Hoboken, NJ: John Wiley & Sons.

215 Calhoun, L. G., Cann, A., Tedeschi, R. G., & McMillan, J. (2000). A correlational test of the relationship between post-traumatic growth, religion, and cognitive processing. *Journal of Traumatic Stress, 13,* 521–527.

216 Tedeschi, C. (2004). Posttraumatic growth: Conceptual foundations and empirical evidence. *Psychological Inquiry, 15(1),* 1-18.

217 Shaw, A., Joseph, S., & Linley, P. A. (2005). Religiosity, spirituality and post-traumatic growth: A systematic review. *Mental Health, Religion, and Culture, 8,* 1-11.

218 Linley, P. A., & Joseph, S. (2004). Positive change processes following trauma and adversity: A review of the empirical literature. *Journal of Traumatic Stress, 17,* 11-22.

219 Sears, S. R., Stanton, A. L., & Danoff-Burg, S. (2003). The yellow brick road and the emerald city: benefit finding, positive reappraisal coping and posttraumatic growth in women with early-stage breast cancer. *Health Psychology, 22,* 487-497.

220 Cadell, S., Regehr, C., & Hemsworth, D. (2003). Factors contributing to posttraumatic growth: A proposed structural equation model. *American Journal of Orthopsychiatry, 73(3),* 279-287.

221 Frazier, P., Conlon, A., & Glaser, T. (2001). Positive and negative life changes following sexual assault. *Journal of Consulting and Clinical Psychology, 69,* 1048-1055.

222 Hefferon, Joseph. (2013) Post-traumatic growth: Eudaimonic happiness in the aftermath of adversity. Oxford handbook of happiness. Vol. 1. Oxford University Press.

223 Affleck, G., Tennen, H., Croog, S., & Levine, S. (1987). Causal attribution,

perceived benefits, and morbidity after a heart attack: An 8-year study. *Journal of Consulting and Clinical Psychology, 55(1)*, 29-35.

224 Epel, E. S., McEwen, B. S., & Ickovics, J. R. (1998). Embodying psychological thriving: Physical thriving in response to stress. *Journal of Social Issues, 54(2)*, 301-322.

225 Cruess, D. G., Antoni, M. H., McGregor, B. A., Kilbourn, K. M., Boyers, A. E., Alferi, S. M., Carver, C. S., & Kumar, M. (2000). Cognitive-behavioral stress management reduces serum cortisol by enhancing benefit finding among women being treated for early stage breast cancer. *Psychosomatic Medicine, 62(3)*, 304-308. https://doi.org/10.1097/00006842-200005000-00002

226 Linley, P. A., Joseph, S., & Goodfellow, B. (2008). Positive changes in outlook following trauma and their relationship to subsequent post-traumatic stress, depression, and anxiety. *Journal of Social and Clinical Psychology, 27*, 877-891.

227 Camus, A. (1955). The myth of Sisyphus and other essays. New York: Alfred A. Knopf.

228 Ibid.

229 Ibid.

METHODS OF ACCEPTANCE

230 Harris, S. (2014). Waking up: A guide to spirituality without religion. Simon and Schuster.

231 Ibid.

232 Wickramasekera, I. E. (2020). Hypnotic-like aspects of the Tibetan tradition of Dzogchen meditation. *International Journal of Clinical and Experimental Hypnosis, 68(2)*, 200-213.

233 Harding, D. E. (2014). On having no head: Zen and the rediscovery of the obvious. The Shollond Trust.

234 Young, S. (2016). The science of enlightenment: how meditation works. Sounds True.

235 Raub, J. A. (2002). Psychophysiologic effects of Hatha Yoga on musculoskeletal and cardiopulmonary function: A literature review. *The Journal of Alternative & Complementary Medicine, 8(6)*, 797-812. And Collins, C. (1998). Yoga: Intuition, preventive medicine, and treatment. *Journal of Obstetric, Gynecologic, & Neonatal Nursing, 27(5)*, 563-568. And

McCall, T. (2007). Yoga as medicine: The yogic prescription for health & healing: A yoga journal book. Bantam. And Desikachar, K., Bragdon, L., & Bossart, C. (2005). The yoga of healing: Exploring yoga's holistic model for health and well-being. *International Journal of Yoga Therapy, 15*(1), 17-39. And Arora, S., & Bhattacharjee, J. (2008). Modulation of immune responses in stress by yoga. *International Journal of Yoga, 1*(2), 45.

236 Pilkington, K., Kirkwood, G., Rampes, H., & Richardson, J. (2005). Yoga for depression: The research evidence. *Journal of Affective Disorders, 89*(1-3), 13-24.

237 Veterans Affairs. Go to VA.gov. (2019, October 30). Retrieved September 21, 2021, from https://www.va.gov/WHOLEHEALTH/veteran-handouts/docs/Yoga-508Final-9-4-2018.pdf.

238 Emmons, R. A., & Stern, R. (2013). Gratitude as a psychotherapeutic intervention. *Journal of Clinical Psychology, 69*(8), 846-855.

239 It is important to note that, when discussing meditation and associated breathing techniques, unless otherwise stated, the way to breathe is through the diaphragm (i.e., diaphragmatic breathing).

240 Hagen, S. (2012). Meditation now or never. Penguin.

241 McKay, M., Davis, M., & Fanning, P. (2011). Thoughts and feelings: Taking control of your moods and your life. New Harbinger Publications.

242 Ma, X., Yue, Z. Q., Gong, Z. Q., Zhang, H., Duan, N. Y., Shi, Y. T., ... & Li, Y. F. (2017). The effect of diaphragmatic breathing on attention, negative affect and stress in healthy adults. *Frontiers in Psychology, 8,* 874.

243 Feinstein, J. S., Khalsa, S. S., Yeh, H. W., Wohlrab, C., Simmons, W. K., Stein, M. B., & Paulus, M. P. (2018). Examining the short-term anxlolytic and antidepressant effect of Floatation-REST. *PloS One, 13*(2), e0190292.

244 Fine, T. H., & Turner Jr, J. W. (1982). The effect of brief restricted environmental stimulation therapy in the treatment of essential hypertension. *Behaviour Research and Therapy, 20*(6), 567-570.

245 Turner, J., Gerard, W., Hyland, J., Nieland, P., & Fine, T. (1993). Effects of wet and dry flotation REST on blood pressure and plasma cortisol. In Clinical and experimental restricted environmental stimulation, 239-247. New York: Springer.

246 Suedfeld, P., & Bow, R. A. (1999). Health and therapeutic applications

of chamber and flotation restricted environmental stimulation therapy (REST). *Psychology & Health, 14(3)*, 545-566.

247 Bood, S. Å., Sundequist, U., Kjellgren, A., Norlander, T., Nordström, L., Nordenström, K., & Nordström, G. (2006). Eliciting the relaxation response with the help of flotation-rest (restricted environmental stimulation technique) in patients with stress-related ailments. *International Journal of Stress Management, 13(2)*, 154.

248 Russo, M. A., Santarelli, D. M., & O'Rourke, D. (2017). The physiological effects of slow breathing in the healthy human. *Breathe, 13(4)*, 298-309.

249 Adhana, R., Gupta, R., Dvivedii, J. & Ahmad, S. The influence of the 2:1 yogic breathing technique on essential hypertension. *Indian J Physiol Pharmacol. 2013 Jan-Mar, 57(1)*, 38-44.

250 7/11 breathing. The Wellbeing Thesis. (2019, December 20). Retrieved September 21, 2021, from https://thewellbeingthesis.org.uk/foundati ons-for-success/stress/711 breathing.

251 Zaccaro, A., Piarulli, A., Laurino, M., Garbella, E., Menicucci, D., Neri, B., & Gemignani, A. (2018). How breath-control can change your life: A systematic review on psycho-physiological correlates of slow breathing. *Frontiers in Human Neuroscience, 12,* 353.

252 Ardiel, E. L., & Rankin, C. H. (2010). The importance of touch in development. *Pediatrics & Child Health, 15(3)*, 153–156. https://doi.org/ 10.1093/pch/15.3.153.

253 Van der Kolk, B. A. (2015). The body keeps the score: Brain, mind, and body in the healing of trauma. Penguin.

VISION

254 David, S. A., Boniwell, I., & Ayers, A. C. (Eds.). (2014). The Oxford handbook of happiness. Oxford University Press.

255 Amen, D. G. (2000). Change your brain, change your life: The breakthrough program for conquering anxiety, depression, obsessiveness, anger, and impulsiveness. Times Books. And McKay, M., Davis, M., & Fanning, P. (2011). Thoughts and feelings: Taking control of your moods and your life. New Harbinger Publications.

256 Carter, J. R., & Palihawadana, M. (2000). The Dhammapada. New York: Oxford University Press

PLANNING AND PREPARATION

257 Houck, D. W. (2002). FDR and fear itself: The first inaugural address (No. 7). Texas A&M University Press.

258 Britannica, T. Editors of Encyclopedia (2019, August 20). Phobia. Encyclopedia Britannica. https://www.britannica.com/science/phobia

259 Freymuth, M. (1993). Mental practice for musicians: Theory and application. *Medical Problems of Performing Artists, 8(4)*, 141-143.

260 Ungerleider, S., & Golding, J. M. (1991). Mental practice among Olympic athletes. *Perceptual and Motor Skills, 72(3)*, 1007-1017.

261 Pascual-Leone, A., Nguyet, D., Cohen, L. G., Brasil-Neto, J. P., Cammarota, A., & Hallett, M. (1995). Modulation of muscle responses evoked by transcranial magnetic stimulation during the acquisition of new fine motor skills. *Journal of Neurophysiology, 74(3)*, 1037-1045.

262 Moran, A., & O'Shea, H. (2020). Motor imagery practice and cognitive processes. *Frontiers in Psychology, 11*, 394.

263 Driskell J. E., Copper C., Moran A. (1994). Does mental practice enhance performance? *Journal of Applied Psychology, 79*, 481-492.

264 Kappes, H. B., & Morewedge, C. K. (2016). Mental simulation as substitute for experience. *Social and Personality Psychology Compass, 10(7)*, 405-420.

265 Huppert, J. D., & Roth, D. A. (2003). Treating obsessive-compulsive disorder with exposure and response prevention. *The Behavior Analyst Today, 4(1)*, 66.

266 Foa. (2011). Prolonged exposure therapy: past, present, and future. Depression and Anxiety, 4(12), 1043–1047. https://doi.org/10.1002/da.20907

267 Reddan, M. C., Wager, T. D., & Schiller, D. (2018). Attenuating neural threat expression with imagination. *Neuron, 100(4)*, 994-1005.

268 Abbasi, K. (2014). The path of non-conformity. *BMJ: British Medical Journal, 349*. https://doi.org/10.1136/bmj.g5036

269 Hadfield, C. (2014, March). What I learned from going blind in space. Retrieved February 06, 2021, from https://www.ted.com/talks/chris_hadfield_what_i_learned_from_going_blind_in_space?language=en.

270 Ibid.

271 Becker, E. (1973). The denial of death. New York: The Free Press.

272 Ibid.

273 Burke, B. L., Martens, A., & Faucher, E. H. (2010). Two decades of terror management theory: A meta-analysis of mortality salience research. *Personality and Social Psychology Review, 14*(2), 155-195.

274 Moon, H. G. (2019). Mindfulness of death as a tool for mortality salience induction with reference to terror management theory. *Religions, 10*(6), 353.

275 Vail III, K. E., Juhl, J., Arndt, J., Vess, M., Routledge, C., & Rutjens, B. T. (2012). When death is good for life: Considering the positive trajectories of terror management. *Personality and Social Psychology Review, 16*(4), 303-329.

276 Sheldon, K. M., & Kasser, T. (2008). Psychological threat and extrinsic goal striving. *Motivation and Emotion, 32*(1), 37-45.

277 Jonas, E., Schimel, J., Greenberg, J., & Pyszczynski, T. (2002). The Scrooge effect: Evidence that mortality salience increases prosocial attitudes and behavior. *Personality and Social Psychology Bulletin, 28*(10), 1342-1353.

278 Thera, N. (1999). Anguttara Nikaya (Vol. 42). Edaf.

279 Moon, H. G. (2019). Mindfulness of death as a tool for mortality salience induction with reference to terror management theory. *Religions, 10*(6), 353.

SELF-DISCIPLINE

280 Laozi, Gia-fu Feng, and Jane English. 1972. Tao te ching

281 Robbins, T. (2008). Unlimited power: The new science of personal achievement. Simon and Schuster.

282 Frost, R., Cosgrove, J. O., & Untermeyer, L. (2002). The road not taken: A selection of Robert Frost's poems, 270.

283 Self-discipline and self-control are used interchangeably here.

284 McSweeney, F., & Murphy, E. (2014). The Wiley-Blackwell handbook of operant and classical conditioning. Wiley Blackwell. And Roane, H. S., Ringdahl, J. E., & Falcomata, T. S. (Eds.). (2015). Clinical and organizational applications of applied behavior analysis. Academic Press.

285 Friedman, B. (2000). Designing casinos to dominate the competition: The Friedman international standards of casino design. Institute for the Study of Gambling and Commercial Gaming.

286 The effects of drugs hack the very nature of our biology; addiction is not always a problem of failing to learn from experience (i.e., learning to avoid things that cause us pain, like hot stoves). These commonly-held reductionistic views create a general notion that addiction is always a willful act rather than a medical disorder; indeed it is actually a much more complicated problem.

287 Critchfield, T. S., & Kollins, S. H. (2001). Temporal discounting: Basic research and the analysis of socially important behavior. *Journal of Applied Behavior Analysis, 34*(1), 101-122.

288 Roosevelt, E. (2011). You learn by living: Eleven keys for a more fulfilling life.

289 Mullainathan, S., & Thaler, R. H. (2000). Behavioral economics (No. w7948). National Bureau of Economic Research.

290 Selten, R. (1990). Bounded rationality. *Journal of Institutional and Theoretical Economics (JITE)/Zeitschrift für die gesamte Staatswissenschaft, 146*(4), 649-658. And Gigerenzer, G., & Selten, R. (Eds.). (2002). Bounded rationality: The adaptive toolbox. MIT press. And Kahneman, D. (2003). A perspective on judgment and choice: mapping bounded rationality. *American Psychologist, 58*(9), 697.

291 Pronin, E., Olivola, C. Y., & Kennedy, K. A. (2008). Doing unto future selves as you would do unto others: Psychological distance and decision making. *Personality and Social Psychology Bulletin, 34*(2), 224-236.

292 Mitchell, J. P., Schirmer, J., Ames, D. L., & Gilbert, D. T. (2011). Medial prefrontal cortex predicts intertemporal choice. *Journal of Cognitive Neuroscience, 23*(4), 857-866.

293 Ainslie, G. (1975). Specious reward: a behavioral theory of impulsiveness and impulse control. *Psychological Bulletin, 82*(4), 463.

294 Weber, E. U., Johnson, E. J., Milch, K. F., Chang, H., Brodscholl, J. C., & Goldstein, D. G. (2007). Asymmetric discounting in intertemporal choice: A query-theory account. *Psychological Science, 18*(6), 516-523.

295 Anokhin, A. P., Golosheykin, S., Grant, J. D., & Heath, A. C. (2011). Heritability of delay discounting in adolescence: A longitudinal twin study. *Behavior genetics, 41*(2), 175-183.

296 Madden, G. J., Begotka, A. M., Raiff, B. R., & Kastern, L. L. (2003). Delay discounting of real and hypothetical rewards. *Experimental and Clinical Psychopharmacology, 11*(2), 139.

297 Polivy, J., & Herman, C. P. (2002). If at first you don't succeed: False hopes of self-change. *American Psychologist, 57*(9), 677.

298 Neef, N. A., Bicard, D. F., & Endo, S. (2001). Assessment of impulsivity and the development of self-control in students with attention deficit hyperactivity disorder. *Journal of Applied Behavior Analysis, 34*(4), 397-408.

299 Neef, N., Marckel, J., Ferreri, S., Bicard, D., Endo, S., Aman, M., Miller, K., Jung, S., Nist, L., & Armstrong, N. (2005). Behavioral assessment of impulsivity: A comparison of children with and without attention deficit hyperactivity disorder. *Journal of Applied Behavior Analysis, 38*(1), 23-37.

300 Baumeister, R., & Juola Exline, J. (1999). Virtue, personality, and social relations: Self-control as the moral muscle. *Journal of Personality, 67*(6), 1165-1194.

301 Muraven, M, & Baumeister, R. F. (2000). Self-regulation and depletion of limited resources: Does self-control resemble a muscle? *Psychological Bulletin, 126*(2), 247.

302 Catania, A. C., Shimoff, E., & Matthews, B. A. (1989). An experimental analysis of rule-governed behavior. In S. C. Hayes (Ed.), Rule-governed behavior: Cognition, contingencies, and instructional control, 119-150. Plenum Press.

303 Shallice, T., & Burgess, P. (1993). Supervisory control of action and thought selection. In A. Baddeley & L. Weiskrantz (Eds.), Attention: Selection, awareness. and control, 171-187. Oxford: Oxford University Press.

304 Muraven, M. & Baumeister, R. (2000). Self-regulation and depletion of limited resources: Does self-control resemble a muscle? *Psychological Bulletin, 126*(2), 247-259.

305 Ibid.

306 Baumeister, R. F., Bratslavsky, E., Muraven, M., & Tice, D. M. (1998). Ego depletion: Is the active self a limited resource? *Journal of Personality and Social Psychology, 74*(5), 1252.

307 Glass, D. C., Singer, J. E., & Friedman, L. N. (1969). Psychic cost of adaptation to an environmental stressor. *Journal of Personality and Social Psychology, 12,* 200-210.

308 Wegner, D. M., & Pennebaker, J. W. (1993). Handbook of mental control. Prentice Hall.

309 Rotton, J. (1983). Affective and cognitive consequences of malodorous pollution. *Basic and Applied Social Psychology, 4,* 171-191.

310 Cohen, S. (1980). Aftereffects of stress on human performance and social behavior: A review of research and theory. *Psychological Bulletin, 88,* 82-108.

311 Greeno, C. G., & Wing, R.R. (1994). Stress-induced eating. *Psychological Bulletin, 115,* 444-464.

312 Hodgins, D. C., el Guebaly, N., & Armstrong, S. (1995). Prospective and retrospective reports of mood states before relapse to substance use. *Journal of Consulting and Clinical Psychology, 63,* 400-407.

313 Bradley, B. P., Phillips, G., Green, L., & Gossip, M. (1989). Circumstances surrounding the initial lapse to opiate use following detoxification. *British Journal of Psychiatry, 154,* 354-359.

314 Knapp, A., & Clark, M. S. (1991). Some detrimental effects of negative mood on individuals' ability to solve resource dilemmas. *Personality and Social Psychology Bulletin, 17,* 678-688. And Muraven, M. (1998). Mechanisms of self-control failure: Motivation and limited resources. Unpublished doctoral dissertation, Case Western Reserve University, Cleveland, Ohio.

315 Muraven, M., Baumeister, R. F., & Tice, D. M. (1999). Longitudinal improvement of self-regulation through practice: Building self-control strength through repeated exercise. *Journal of Social Psychology, 139,* 446-457. And Muraven, M., & Baumeister, R. F. (2000). Self-regulation and depletion of limited resources: Does self-control resemble a muscle? *Psychological Bulletin, 126(2),* 247-259.

PROBLEM-SOLVING

316 Fredrickson, B. L., Mancuso, R. A., Branigan, C., & Tugade, M. M. (2000). The undoing effect of positive emotions. *Motivation and Emotion, 24,* 237-258.

317 McKay, M., Davis, M., & Fanning, P. (2011). Thoughts and feelings: Taking control of your moods and your life. New Harbinger Publications.

PERSISTENCE

318 Roosevelt, T. (1910). The man in the arena. Speech given at the Sorbonne, Paris, 23.

319 Roosevelt, T. (1901). The strenuous life: Essays and addresses. Century.

320 When I discuss success, it's meant in the most fundamental sense. One could achieve their goals, great or small, in any area which they define as success. The idea is to show that there are some basic attitudes and methods which one can cultivate to determine what success means to them, and ultimately to believe it's possible to achieve it.

321 Knowles, E. (2009). Oxford dictionary of quotations (seventh edition). Oxford University Press. (Quote attributed to Coolidge at a memorial service in 1933.)

322 Mortimer, P. (2018). The dawn wall. J. Lowell (Ed.). Red Bull Media House.

323 Caldwell, T. (2017). The push: A climber's journey of endurance, risk, and going beyond limits. Penguin.

324 Goggins, D. Can't hurt me: Master your mind and Defy the odds - clean edition, 139-141. Lioncrest Publishing. Kindle edition.

325 Ibid

326 Tharp, T. (2008). The creative habit. Simon and Schuster.

METHODS OF CHANGE

327 Everson, C. A., Bergmann, B. M., & Rechtschaffen, A. (1989). Sleep deprivation in the rat: III. Total sleep deprivation. *Sleep, 12(1)*, 13-21.

328 Lange, T., Perras, B., Fehm, H. L., & Born, J. (2003). Sleep enhances the human antibody response to hepatitis A vaccination. *Psychosomatic Medicine, 65(5)*, 831-835.

329 Spiegel, K., Tasali, E., Penev, P., & Cauter, E. V. (2004). Brief communication: sleep curtailment in healthy young men is associated with decreased leptin levels, elevated ghrelin levels, and increased hunger and appetite. *Annals of Internal Medicine, 141(11)*, 846-850. And Knutson, K. L., Spiegel, K., Penev, P., & Van Cauter, E. (2007). The metabolic consequences of sleep deprivation. *Sleep Medicine Reviews, 11(3)*, 163-178.

330 Qureshi, A. I., Giles, W. H., Croft, J. B., & Bliwise, D. L. (1997). Habitual sleep patterns and risk for stroke and coronary heart disease: A 10-year follow-up from NHANES I. *Neurology, 48(4)*, 904-910. And Newman, A. B., Spiekerman, C. F., MD, P. E., Lefkowitz, D., Manolio, T., Reynolds, C. F., & Robbins, J. (2000). Daytime sleepiness predicts mortality and cardiovascular disease in older adults. *Journal of the American Geriatrics Society, 48(2)*, 115-123.

331 Baldwin Jr, D. C., & Daugherty, S. R. (2004). Sleep deprivation and fatigue in residency training: Results of a national survey of first- and second-year residents. *Sleep, 27*(2), 217-223. And Strine, T. W., & Chapman, D. P. (2005). Associations of frequent sleep insufficiency with health-related quality of life and health behaviors. *Sleep Medicine, 6*(1), 23-27. And: Pilcher, J. J., & Huffcutt, A. I. (1996). Effects of sleep deprivation on performance: A meta-analysis. *Sleep, 19*(4), 318-326.

332 Fredriksen, K., Rhodes, J., Reddy, R., & Way, N. (2004). Sleepless in Chicago: Tracking the effects of adolescent sleep loss during the middle school years. *Child Development, 75*(1), 84-95.

333 Belenky, G., Wesensten, N. J., Thorne, D. R., Thomas, M. L., Sing, H. C., Redmond, D. P., ... & Balkin, T. J. (2003). Patterns of performance degradation and restoration during sleep restriction and subsequent recovery: A sleep dose-response study. *Journal of Sleep Research, 12*(1), 1-12.

334 Jenco, M., & American Academy of Pediatrics. (2016). AAP endorses new recommendations on sleep times. AAP News.

335 U.S. Department of Health and Human Services. (2020, November 3). A good night's sleep. National Institute on Aging. Retrieved November 24, 2021, from https://www.nia.nih.gov/health/good-nights-sleep.

336 Zeevi, D., Korem, T., Zmora, N., Israeli, D., Rothschild, D., Weinberger, A., ... & Segal, E. (2015). Personalized nutrition by prediction of glycemic responses. *Cell, 163*(5), 1079-1094.

337 Sánchez-Villegas, A., Ruíz-Canela, M., Gea, A., Lahortiga, F., & Martínez-González, M. A. (2016). The association between the Mediterranean lifestyle and depression. *Clinical Psychological Science, 4*(6), 1085-1093.

338 Estruch, R., Ros, E., Salas-Salvadó, J., Covas, M. I., Corella, D., Arós, F., ... & Martínez-González, M. A. (2013). Primary prevention of cardiovascular disease with a Mediterranean diet. *New England Journal of Medicine, 368*(14), 1279-1290.

339 Schwingshackl, L., Hoffmann, G. (2014). Adherence to Mediterranean diet and risk of cancer: A systematic review and meta-analysis of observational studies. *International Journal of Cancer, 135*(8), 1884-1897.

340 Koloverou, E., Esposito, K., Giugliano, D., & Panagiotakos, D. (2014). The effect of Mediterranean diet on the development of type 2 diabetes mellitus: A meta-analysis of 10 prospective studies and 136,846

participants. *Metabolism: Clinical and Experimental, 63(7)*, 903-911. https://doi.org/10.1016/j.metabol.2014.04.010

341 Singh, B., Parsaik, A. K., Mielke, M. M., Erwin, P. J., Knopman, D. S., Petersen, R. C., et al. (2014). Association of Mediterranean diet with mild cognitive impairment and Alzheimer's disease: A systematic review and meta-analysis. *Journal of Alzheimer Disease, 39(2)*, 271-282.

342 Schuch, F. B., Vancampfort, D., Richards, J., Rosenbaum, S., Ward, P. B., & Stubbs, B. (2016). Exercise as a treatment for depression: A meta-analysis adjusting for publication bias. *Journal of Psychiatric Research, 77*, 42-51. And Craft, L. L., & Perna, F. M. (2004). The benefits of exercise for the clinically depressed. *Primary Care Companion to the Journal of Clinical Psychiatry, 6(3)*, 104.

343 Greist, J. H., Klein, M. H., Eischens, R. R., Faris, J., Gurman, A. S., & Morgan, W. P. (1979). Running as treatment for depression. *Comprehensive Psychiatry, 20(1)*, 41-54.

344 Pate, R. R., Pratt, M., Blair, S. N., Haskell, W. L., Macera, C. A., Bouchard, C., ... & Wilmore, J. H. (1995). Physical activity and public health: A recommendation from the Centers for Disease Control and Prevention and the American College of Sports Medicine. *Jama, 273(5)*, 402-407.

345 Cotman, C. W., Berchtold, N. C., & Christie, L. A. (2007). Exercise builds brain health: Key roles of growth factor cascades and inflammation. *Trends in Neurosciences, 30(9)*, 464-472. https://doi.org/10.1016/j.tins.2007.06.011.

346 Singh, N. A., Clements, K. M., & Fiatarone, M. A. (1997). A randomized controlled trial of progressive resistance training in depressed elders. *The Journals of Gerontology Series A: Biological Sciences and Medical Sciences, 52(1)*, M27-M35.

347 Franz, S. I., & Hamilton, G. V. (1905). The effects of exercise upon the retardation in conditions of depression. *American Journal of Psychiatry, 62(2)*, 239-256. And Berger, B. G., & Owen, D. R. (1998). Relation of low and moderate intensity exercise with acute mood change in college joggers. *Perceptual and Motor Skills, 87(2)*, 611-621. And DiLorenzo, T. M., Bargman, E. P., Stucky-Ropp, R., Brassington, G. S., Frensch, P. A., & LaFontaine, T. (1999). Long-term effects of aerobic exercise on psychological outcomes. *Preventive Medicine, 28(1)*, 75-85.

348 Babyak, M., Blumenthal, J. A., Herman, S., Khatri, P., Doraiswamy, M., Moore, K., ... & Krishnan, K. R. (2000). Exercise treatment for

major depression: Maintenance of therapeutic benefit at 10 months. *Psychosomatic Medicine, 62(5)*, 633-638. And Craft, L. L., & Perna, F. M. (2004). The benefits of exercise for the clinically depressed. *Primary Care Companion to the Journal of Clinical Psychiatry, 6(3)*, 104–111. https://doi.org/10.4088/pcc.v06n0301.

349 Piercy, K. L., Troiano, R. P., Ballard, R. M., Carlson, S. A., Fulton, J. E., Galuska, D. A., ... & Olson, R. D. (2018). The physical activity guidelines for Americans. *Jama, 320(19)*, 2020-2028. And Centers for Disease Control and Prevention. (2016). How much physical activity do adults need? Google Scholar.

350 Black, S. V., Cooper, R., Martin, K. R., Brage, S., Kuh, D., & Stafford, M. (2015). Physical activity and mental well-being in a cohort aged 60–64 years. *American Journal of Preventive Medicine, 49(2)*, 172-180.

351 Ilardi, S. S. (2009). The depression cure: The 6-step program to beat depression without drugs. Da Capo Lifelong Books.

352 Hari, Johann. Lost Connections, 221-222. Bloomsbury Publishing. Kindle Edition.

353 Scott, J. G., Cohen, D., Dicicco-Bloom, B., Miller, W. L., Stange, K. C., & Crabtree, B. F. (2008). Understanding healing relationships in primary care. *Annals of Family Medicine, 6(4)*, 315-322

354 Van der Kolk, B. The body keeps the score, 210. Penguin. Kindle Edition.

355 McDougle, L., Handy, F., Konrath, S., Walk, M. Health outcomes and volunteering: The moderating role of religiosity. *Soc Indic Res. 2014*, 117, 337-351. https://doi.org:10.1007/s11205-013-0336-5. And Piliavin, J.A. & Siegl, E. J. Health benefits of volunteering in the Wisconsin longitudinal study. *Health Soc Behav. 2007 Dec, 48(4)*, 450-64.

356 Claessens, B. C., van Eerde, W., Rutte, C. G., & Roe, R. A. (2007). A review of the time management literature. *Personnel Review, 36(1/2)*, 255-276.

357 Spidal, D. (2009). Time management. *Key Words, 17(1)*, 15-31.

358 Britton, B. K., and Tesser, A. (1991). Effects of time management practices on college grades. *Journal of Educational Psychology 83(3)*, 405-410.

359 Macan, T., Shahani, C., Dipboye, R., & Phillips, A. (1990). College students' time management: Correlations with academic performance and stress. *Journal of Educational Psychology, 82(4)*, 760–768. And Schuler, R. (1979, January 1). Managing stress means managing time.

360 Ibid

361 Nonis, S. A., Hudson, G. I., Logan, L. B., & W. Ford, C. W. (1998). Influence of perceived control over time on college students' stress and stress-related outcomes. *Research in Higher Education, 39*(5), 587-605. And Rocha-Singh, I. A. (1994). Perceived stress among graduate students: Development and validation of the graduate stress inventory. *Educational and Psychological Measurement, 54*(3), 714-727. https://doi.org/10.1177/0013164494054003018 Singularity University. (n.d.)

362 Razali, S. N. A. M., Rusiman, M. S., Gan, W. S., & Arbin, N. (2018, April). The impact of time management on students' academic achievement. *Journal of Physics: Conference Series 995*(1), 12042. IOP Publishing.

GENERATING SELF-AWARENESS

363 Plato (1996). The dialogues of Plato, volume 3: Ion, hippias minor, laches, protagoras.

364 Avidyā. (2009). A dictionary of Hinduism (first ed.). Oxford University Press.

365 Noakes, T. D., Gibson, A. S. C., & Lambert, E. V. (2005). From catastrophe to complexity: A novel model of integrative central neural regulation of effort and fatigue during exercise in humans: Summary and conclusions. *British Journal of Sports Medicine, 39*(2), 120-124. And Noakes T. D. (2012). Fatigue is a brain-derived emotion that regulates the exercise behavior to ensure the protection of whole body homeostasis. *Frontiers in Physiology, 3*, 82. https://doi.org/10.3389/fphys.2012.00082. And Noakes T. D. The central governor model of exercise regulation applied to the marathon. *Sports Med, 2007, 37*(4-5), 374-377.

366 Bacon, F., & Kennedy, J. F. (1996). Nam et ipsa scientia potestas est (Knowledge is power). In Problems of drug dependence: Proceedings of the… annual scientific meeting, the College on Problems of Drug Dependence, Inc (Vol. 57, p.6). US Department of Health and Human Services, Public Health Service, National Institutes of Health, National Institute on Drug Abuse.

367 Vaitl, D. (1996). Interoception. *Biological Psychology, 42*(1), 1-27. https://doi.org/10.1016/0301-0511(95)05144-9.

368 Cannon, W. B. (1927). The James-Lange theory of emotions: A critical examination and an alternative theory. *The American Journal of*

Psychology, 39(1/4), 106-124.

369 Cameron, O. G. (2001): Interoception: The inside story – A model for psychosomatic processes. *Psychosom Med 63,* 697–710. And Craig, A. D. (2003). Interoception: The sense of the physiological condition of the body. *Curr Opin Neurobiol 13,* 500-505. And Stern, E. R., Grimaldi, S. J., Muratore, A., Murrough, J., Leibu, E., Fleysher, L., ... & Burdick, K. E. (2017). Neural correlates of interoception: Effects of interoceptive focus and relationship to dimensional measures of body awareness. *Human Brain Mapping, 38*(12), 6068-6082. And Craig, A. D. (2002): How do you feel? Interoception: The sense of the physiological condition of the body. *Nat Rev Neurosci 3,* 655-666.

370 Pollatos, O., Kirsch, W., & Schandry, R. (2005). Brain structures involved in interoceptive awareness and cardioafferent signal processing: A dipole source localization study. *Human Brain Mapping, 26*(1), 54-64. https://doi.org/10.1002/hbm.20121.

371 McFarlane, A. C. (2010). The long-term costs of traumatic stress: Intertwined physical and psychological consequences, *World Psychiatry 9*(1), 3-10.

372 Paulus, M. P., & Stein, M. B. (2010). Interoception in anxiety and depression. *Brain Structure and Function, 214*(5), 451-463.

373 Buckner, R., Andrews-Hanna, J., & Schacter, D. (2008). The brain's default network: Anatomy, function, and relevance to disease. *Annals of the New York Academy of Sciences, 1124*(1), 1–38.

374 Limmer J, Kornhuber J, Martin A (2015): Panic and comorbid depression and their associations with stress reactivity, interoceptive awareness and interoceptive accuracy of various bioparameters. *J Affect Disord 185,* 170-179.

375 Parvizi, J., & Damasio, A. (2001). Consciousness and the brainstem. *Cognition, 79*(1-2), 135-160. And Damasio, A., & Meyer, K. (2009). Consciousness: An overview of the phenomenon and of its possible neural basis. The neurology of consciousness: Cognitive neuroscience and neuropathology, 3-14. And Laureys, S., Gosseries, O., & Tononi, G. (2016). The neurology of consciousness: Cognitive neuroscience and Neuropathology. Academic Press. And Damasio, A. R. (1999). The feeling of what happens: Body and emotion in the making of consciousness. Houghton Mifflin Harcourt.

376 Bremner, J. D., Narayan, M., Staib, L. H., Southwick, S. M., McGlashan,

T., & Charney, D. S. (1999). Neural correlates of memories of childhood sexual abuse in women with and without posttraumatic stress disorder. *American Journal of Psychiatry, 156*(11), 1787-1795. And Bremner, J. D., Staib, L. H., Kaloupek, D., Southwick, S. M., Soufer, R., & Charney, D. S. (1999). Neural correlates of exposure to traumatic pictures and sound in Vietnam combat veterans with and without posttraumatic stress disorder: A positron emission tomography study. *Biological Psychiatry, 45*(7), 806-816. And Lanius, R. A., Williamson, P. C., Densmore, M., Boksman, K., Gupta, M. A., Neufeld, R. W., ... & Menon, R. S. (2001). Neural correlates of traumatic memories in posttraumatic stress disorder: A functional MRI investigation. *American Journal of Psychiatry, 158*(11), 1920-1922.

377 R. L. Bluhm, et al. (2009) Alterations in default network connectivity in posttraumatic stress disorder related to early-life trauma. *Journal of Psychiatry & Neuroscience 34*(3), 187. And Daniels, J. K., et al. (2010) Switching between executive and default mode networks in posttraumatic stress disorder: Alterations in functional connectivity. *Journal of Psychiatry & Neuroscience 35*(4), 258.

378 D'Argembeau, A., et al. (2007) Distinct regions of the medial prefrontal cortex are associated with self-referential processing and perspective taking. *Journal of Cognitive Neuroscience 19*(6), 935-44. And Farb, N. A., et al. (2007) Attending to the present: Mindfulness meditation reveals distinct neural modes of self-reference. *Social Cognitive and Affective Neuroscience 2*(4), 313-22. And Hölzel, B. K., et al. (2008) Investigation of mindfulness meditation practitioners with voxel-based morphometry. *Social Cognitive and Affective Neuroscience 3*(1), 55-61.

379 Ibid.

380 McKay, M., Davis, M., & Fanning, P. (2011). Thoughts and feelings: Taking control of your moods and your life. New Harbinger Publications.

381 Roberts, J. R., Greenberg, M. I., Knaub, M. A., Kendrick, Z. V., & Baskin, S. I. (1979). Blood levels following intravenous and endotracheal epinephrine administration. *Journal of the American College of Emergency Physicians, 8*(2), 53-56.

382 McKay, M., Davis, M., & Fanning, P. (2011). Thoughts and feelings: Taking control of your moods and your life. New Harbinger Publications.

383 Hackman, A., Clark, D. M., Salkovskis, P. M., Wells, A., & Gelder, M. (1992, June). Making cognitive therapy for panic more efficient:

Preliminary results with a four session version of the treatment. In symposium presented at the Worm Congress of Cognitive Therapy, Toronto. And Brown, T. A., Hertz, R. M., & Barlow, D. H. (1992). New developments in cognitive-behavioral treatment of anxiety disorders. *American Psychiatric Press Review of Psychiatry*. And McKay, M., Davis, M., & Fanning, P. (2011). Thoughts and feelings: Taking control of your moods and your life. New Harbinger Publications.

384 Van der Kolk, B. A. (2015). The body keeps the score: Brain, mind, and body in the healing of trauma, 258. Penguin.

385 A. F. Arnsten. (1998). Enhanced: The biology of being frazzled. *Science 280(5370)*, 1711-12. And A. Arnsten. (2009) Stress signalling pathways that impair prefrontal cortex structure and function. Nature Reviews. *Neuroscience 10(6)*, 410-22.

386 LeDoux, J. E. (2000) Emotion circuits in the brain. *Annual Review of Neuroscience 23(1)*, 155–84. And Morgan, M. A., Romanski, L. A. & LeDoux J. E. (1993). Extinction of emotional learning: Contribution of medial prefrontal cortex. *Neuroscience Letters 163(1)*, 109-113. And Moscarello, J. M. & LeDoux, J. E. (2013) Active avoidance learning requires prefrontal suppression of amygdala-mediated defensive reactions. *Journal of Neuroscience 33(9)*, 3815–3823.

387 Porges, W. (2010). Stress and parasympathetic control. *Stress Science: Neuroendocrinology 306*. And Porges, S. W. (2009). Reciprocal influences between body and brain in the perception and expression of affect. In The healing power of emotion: Affective neuroscience, development & clinical practice, Norton series on interpersonal neurobiology. New York: W. W. Norton. And van der Kolk, B. A., et al. (June 2014). Yoga as an adjunctive treatment for PTSD. *Journal of Clinical Psychiatry 75(6)*, 559-65. And Fisher, S. F. (2014). Neurofeedback in the treatment of developmental trauma: Calming the fear-driven brain. New York: W. W. Norton & Company. And Brown, R. P. & Gerbarg, P. L. (2005). Sudarshan kriya yogic breathing in the treatment of stress, anxiety, and depression—part II: Clinical applications and guidelines. *Journal of Alternative & Complementary Medicine 11(4)*, 711-17. And Mandle, C. L., et al. (1996) The efficacy of relaxation response interventions with adult patients: A review of the literature. *Journal of Cardiovascular Nursing 10*, 4-26. And Nakao, M., et al. (2001) Anxiety is a good indicator for somatic symptom reduction through behavioral medicine intervention in a mind/body medicine clinic. *Psychotherapy and Psychosomatics 70*,

50-57. And Van der Kolk, B. A. (2015). The body keeps the score: Brain, mind, and body in the healing of trauma. Penguin Books.

388 Chaudoin, F. J. (2017). The psychological experience of advanced-level martial artists during board breaking training: A phenomenological study (Doctoral dissertation, Grand Canyon University).

389 Leikind, B. J., & McCarthy, W. J. (1988). Firewalking. *Experientia, 44*(4), 310-315. And Danforth, L. (1989). Firewalking and religious healing: The Anastenaria of Greece and the American firewalking movement. Princeton University Press.

390 Rutter, M. (2006). Implications of resilience concepts for scientific understanding. *Annals of the New York Academy of Sciences, 1094,* 1–12. https://doi.org/10.1196/annals.1376.002.

391 Smith, C. (1991). The self, appraisal and coping. In Handbook of social and clinical psychology: The health perspective, 116-137. New York, NY: Pergamon Press.

392 Nelson, D. L., & Simmons, B. L. (2003). Eustress: An elusive construct, an engaging pursuit. In Emotional and physiological processes and positive intervention strategies. Emerald Group Publishing Limited.

393 Frankenhauser, M. (1983). Dembroski, T. M., Schmidt, T. H., Blumchen, G. (Eds.). Biobehavioral bases of coronary heart disease, 91-105. New York: Plenum Press.

394 Crum, A. J., Salovey, P., & Achor, S. (2013). Rethinking stress: The role of mindsets in determining the stress response. *Journal of Personality and Social Psychology, 104*(4), 716.

METHODS OF SELF-UNDERSTANDING

395 Nyklíček, I., Vingerhoets, A., & Zeelenberg, M. (2011). Emotion regulation and well-Being (first ed.). New York: Springer. https://doi.org/10.1007/978-1-4419-6953-8. And Gross, J. (2014). Handbook of emotion regulation (second ed.). The Guilford Press.

396 Bandura, A. (1997). Self-efficacy: The exercise of control. W.H. Freeman and Company.

397 Ochsner, K., Ray, R., Cooper, J., Robertson, E., Chopra, S., Gabrieli, J., & Gross, J. (2004). For better or for worse: Neural systems supporting the cognitive down- and up-regulation of negative emotion. *NeuroImage, 23*(2), 483-499.

398 Beauregard, M. (2007). Mind does really matter: Evidence from neuroimaging studies of emotional self-regulation, psychotherapy, and placebo effect. *Progress in Neurobiology, 81(4)*, 218-236.

399 Lévesque, J., Eugene, F., Joanette, Y., Paquette, V., Mensour, B., Beaudoin, G., ... & Beauregard, M. (2003). Neural circuitry underlying voluntary suppression of sadness. *Biological psychiatry, 53(6)*, 502-510.

400 Lewis, B. (1994). Psychotherapy, neuroscience, and philosophy of mind. *American Journal of Psychotherapy, 48(1)*, 85-93.

401 Etkin, A., Pittenger, C., Polan, H. J., & Kandel, E. R. (2005). Toward a neurobiology of psychotherapy: Basic science and clinical applications. *The Journal of Neuropsychiatry and Clinical Neurosciences, 17(2)*, 145-158.

402 Kandel, E.R., 1998. A new intellectual framework for psychiatry. *Am. J. Psychiatry 155*, 457-469.

403 Cuijpers, P., Sijbrandij, M., Koole, S. L., Andersson, G., Beekman, A. T., & Reynolds III, C. F. (2014). Adding psychotherapy to antidepressant medication in depression and anxiety disorders: A meta-analysis. *Focus, 12(3)*, 347-358.

404 Flint, A. J. (2005). Generalised anxiety disorder in elderly patients. *Drugs & Aging, 22(2)*, 101-114. And Hunsley, J., Elliott, K., & Therrien, Z. (2014). The efficacy and effectiveness of psychological treatments for mood, anxiety, and related disorders. *Canadian Psychology = Psychologie Canadienne, 55(3)*, 161-176.

405 Vieta, E., & Colom, F. (2004). Psychological interventions in bipolar disorder: From wishful thinking to an evidence-based approach. *Acta Psychiatrica Scandinavica, 110*, 34-38.

406 Blagys, M. D., & Hilsenroth, M. J. (2002). Distinctive activities of cognitive-behavioral therapy: A review of the comparative psychotherapy process literature. *Clinical Psychology Review, 22*, 671-706. https://doi.org/10.1016/S0272-7358(01)00117-9. And Burum, B. A., & Goldfried, M. R. (2007). The centrality of emotion to psychological change. *Clinical Psychology: Science and Practice, 14*, 407-413.

407 Shedler, J. (2010). The efficacy of psychodynamic psychotherapy. *American Psychologist, 65(2)*, 98.

408 McKay, M., Davis, M., & Fanning, P. (2011). Thoughts and feelings: Taking control of your moods and your life. New Harbinger Publications.

409 Ellis, A. (1962). Reason and emotion in psychotherapy: A new and comprehensive method of treating human disturbances. Citadel Pr.

And Rector, N. A., & Beck, A. T. (2012). Cognitive behavioral therapy for schizophrenia: An empirical review Rector, N.A., &Beck, A. T.(2001). Reprinted from *The Journal of Nervous and Mental Disease*, 189, 278-287. *The Journal of Nervous and Mental Disease, 200(10)*, 832-839. https://doi.org/10.1097/NMD.0b013e31826dd9af.

410 Hofmann, S. G., Asnaani, A., Vonk, I. J., Sawyer, A. T., & Fang, A. (2012). The efficacy of cognitive behavioral therapy: A review of meta-analyses. *Cognitive Therapy and Research, 36(5)*, 427-440.

411 Corey, G., Bawa, U., & Nicholas, L. J. (2017). Theory and practice of counselling and psychotherapy. Cengage Learning.

412 Sussex Publishers. (n.d.). How to find the best therapist for you. *Psychology Today*. Retrieved September 22, 2021, from https://www.psychologytoday.com/us/blog/freudian-sip/201102/how-find-the-best-therapist-you.

413 Epple, D. M. (2007). Journal writing for life development. *Advances in Social Work, 8(2)*, 288-304.

414 Allison, N. (1999). The illustrated encyclopedia of body-mind disciplines. Taylor & Francis.

415 Frattaroli, J. (2006). Experimental disclosure and its moderators: A meta-analysis. *Psychological Bulletin, 132*, 823-865

416 Emmons, R. A. (1986). Personal strivings: An approach to personality and subjective well-being. *Journal of Personality and Social Psychology, 51*, 1058-1068.

417 Emmons, R. A., & King, L. A. (1988). Conflict among personal strivings: Immediate and long-term implications for psychological and physical well-being. *Journal of Personality and Social Psychology, 48*, 1040-1048.

418 Pham, L. B., & Taylor, S. E. (1999). From thought to action: Effects of process- versus outcome-based mental simulations on performance. *Personality and Social Psychology Bulletin, 25*, 250-260.

419 King, L. A. (2001). The health benefits of writing about life goals. *Personality and Social Psychology Bulletin, 27*, 798-807.

420 Pavlacic, J. M., Buchanan, E. M., Maxwell, N. P., Hopke, T. G., & Schulenberg, S. E. (2019). A meta-analysis of expressive writing on posttraumatic stress, posttraumatic growth, and quality of life. *Review of General Psychology, 23(2)*, 230-250.

421 Pennebaker, J. W. (2018). Expressive writing in psychological science. *Perspectives on Psychological Science, 13*(2), 226-229.

422 Pennebaker, J. W. (2004). Writing to heal: A guided journal for recovering from trauma & emotional upheaval. Oakland, CA: New Harbinger Publications.

423 Sussex Publishers. (n.d.). Expressive writing. *Psychology Today*. Retrieved October 16, 2021, from https://www.psychologytoday.com/us/blog/write-yourself-well/201208/expressive-writing.

424 McKee, M. G. (2008). Biofeedback: An overview in the context of heart-brain medicine. *Cleveland Clinic Journal of Medicine, 75*, S31-S34.

425 DeCharms, R. C., Maeda, F., Glover, G. H., Ludlow, D., Pauly, J. M., Soneji, D., … & Mackey, S. C. (2005). Control over brain activation and pain learned by using real-time functional MRI. *Proceedings of the National Academy of Sciences, 102*(51), 18626-18631.

426 McKee, M. G. (2008). Biofeedback: An overview in the context of heart-brain medicine. *Cleveland Clinic Journal of Medicine, 75*, S31-S34.

427 Goessl, V., Curtiss, J., & Hofmann, S. (2017). The effect of heart rate variability biofeedback training on stress and anxiety: A meta-analysis. *Psychological Medicine, 47*(15), 2578-2586.

428 Kleiger, R. E., Miller, J. P., Bigger Jr, J. T., & Moss, A. J. (1987). Decreased heart rate variability and its association with increased mortality after acute myocardial infarction. *The American Journal of Cardiology, 59*(4), 256-262.

429 Sack, M., Hopper, J. W., & Lamprecht, F. (2004). Low respiratory sinus arrhythmia and prolonged psychophysiological arousal in posttraumatic stress disorder: Heart rate dynamics and individual differences in arousal regulation. *Biological Psychiatry, 55*(3), 284-290.

430 Jönsson, P. (2007). Respiratory sinus arrhythmia as a function of state anxiety in healthy individuals. *International Journal of Psychophysiology, 63*(1), 48-54.

431 Nickel, P., & Nachreiner, F. (2003). Sensitivity and diagnosticity of the 0.1-Hz component of heart rate variability as an indicator of mental workload. *Human factors, 45*(4), 575-590.

432 Napadow, V., Dhond, R., Conti, G., Makris, N., Brown, E. N., & Barbieri, R. (2008). Brain correlates of autonomic modulation: Combining heart rate variability with fMRI. *NeuroImage, 42*(1), 169-177. https://doi.org/10.1016/j.neuroimage.2008.04.238.

433 Laborde, S., Mosley, E., & Thayer, J. F. (2017). Heart rate variability and cardiac vagal tone in psychophysiological research – Recommendations for experiment planning, data analysis, and data reporting. *Frontiers in Psychology, 8*, 213.

434 Thayer, J. F., & Lane, R. D. (2009). Claude Bernard and the heart–brain connection: Further elaboration of a model of neurovisceral integration. *Neuroscience & Biobehavioral Reviews, 33(2)*, 81-88.

435 Ramírez, E., Ortega, A. R., & Del Paso, G. A. R. (2015). Anxiety, attention, and decision making: The moderating role of heart rate variability. *International Journal of Psychophysiology, 98(3)*, 490-496.

436 Cuthbert, B., Kristeller, J., Simons, R., Hodes, R., & Lang, P. J. (1981). Strategies of arousal control: Biofeedback, meditation, and motivation. *Journal of Experimental Psychology: General, 110(4)*, 518.

THE MIDDLE PATH BETWEEN ACCEPTANCE AND CHANGE

437 Gill, B. & Lovell, J. (2019, January 02). What are the chances? The probability curve at NYSCI. Retrieved March 10, 2021, from https://nysci.org/what-are-the-chances-the-probability-curve-at-nysci/.

438 Hoover, W. G., & Hoover, C. G. (2012). Time reversibility, computer simulation, algorithms, chaos (Vol. 13). World Scientific. And Galton board. (n.d.). Retrieved March 10, 2021, from https://galtonboard.com/.

439 Niebuhr, R. (1943). The serenity prayer. Bulletin of the Federal Council of Churches.

Made in the USA
Middletown, DE
23 December 2021